Special Education Law Annual Review 2021

Special Education Law, Policy, and Practice

Series Editors: Mitchell L. Yell, PhD, University of South Carolina
David F. Bateman, PhD, Shippensburg University

The Special Education Law, Policy, and Practice series highlights current trends and legal issues in the education of students with disabilities. The books in this series link legal requirements with evidence-based instruction and highlight practical applications for working with students with disabilities. The titles in the Special Education Law, Policy, and Practices series are designed not only to be required textbooks for general education and special education preservice teacher education programs but also for practicing teachers, education administrators, principals, school counselors, school psychologists, parents, and others interested in improving the lives of students with disabilities. The Special Education Law, Policy, and Practice series is committed to research-based practices working to provide appropriate and meaningful educational programming for students with disabilities and their families.

Titles in Series

The Essentials of Special Education Law
by Andrew M. Markelz and David F. Bateman

Special Education Law Annual Review 2020
by David F. Bateman, Mitchell L. Yell, and Kevin P. Brady

Developing Educationally Meaningful and Legally Sound IEPs
by Mitchell L. Yell, David F. Bateman, and James G. Shriner

Sexuality Education for Students with Disabilities
by Thomas C. Gibbon, Elizabeth Harkins Monaco, and David F. Bateman

Creating Positive Elementary Classrooms: Preventing Behavior Challenges to Promote Learning
by Stephen W. Smith and Mitchell L. Yell

Service Animals in Schools: A Comprehensive Guide for Administrators, Teachers, Parents, and Students
by Anne O. Papalia, Kathy B. Ewoldt, and David F. Bateman

Guide to Evidence-Based Practices for Practitioners Working with Individuals with Autism Spectrum Disorder
by Laura C. Chezan, Katie Wolfe, and Erik Drasgow

Special Education Law Annual Review 2021
by David F. Bateman, Mitchell L. Yell, and Kevin P. Brady

Special Education Law Annual Review 2021

David F. Bateman
Shippensburg University

Mitchell L. Yell
University of South Carolina

Kevin P. Brady
University of Arkansas

ROWMAN & LITTLEFIELD
Lanham • Boulder • New York • London

Acquisitions Editor: Courtney Packard
Assistant Editor: Sarah Rinehart
Sales and Marketing Inquiries: textbooks@rowman.com

Credits and acknowledgments for material borrowed from other sources, and reproduced with permission, appear on the appropriate pages within the text.

Published by Rowman & Littlefield
An imprint of The Rowman & Littlefield Publishing Group, Inc.
4501 Forbes Boulevard, Suite 200, Lanham, Maryland 20706
www.rowman.com

86-90 Paul Street, London EC2A 4NE

Copyright © 2023 by The Rowman & Littlefield Publishing Group, Inc.

All rights reserved. No part of this book may be reproduced in any form or by any electronic or mechanical means, including information storage and retrieval systems, without written permission from the publisher, except by a reviewer who may quote passages in a review.

British Library Cataloguing in Publication Information Available

Library of Congress Cataloging-in-Publication Data Available

Disclaimer

The information in the *Special Education Law Annual* is not legal advice, nor should it replace legal advice. Information in the annual may be affected by state statutes, regulations, and local or district policies and practices. In incidences involving potentially legal situations, the services of a licensed attorney should be secured.

Brief Contents

Introduction   xiii

1 The US Department of Education, the IDEA, and Section 504   1

2 Policy Letters from the US Department of Education   3

3 A Primer on Dispute Resolution Under the IDEA and Section 504   101

4 Topics Covered by US Courts of Appeals in 2020   115

5 Case Summaries by Circuit   123

6 Case Studies   217

Glossary of Legal Terms   225
References   233
Index   235
About the Authors   249

Contents

Introduction xiii

1 The US Department of Education, the IDEA, and Section 504 1

2 Policy Letters from the US Department of Education 3
    2.1 Dear Colleague Letters 4
    2.2 Guidance from the Office of Special Education Programs (OSEP) 8

3 A Primer on Dispute Resolution Under the IDEA and Section 504 101
    3.1 Dispute Resolution 101
    3.2 Special Education Disputes in the Federal Court System 104
    3.3 Published and Unpublished Decisions 109
    3.4 Researching Cases Online 109

4 Topics Covered by US Courts of Appeals in 2021 115
    4.1 504 Implementation 115
    4.2 Attorney's Fees 115
    4.3 Cause of Action 115
    4.4 Charter Schools 115
    4.5 Child Find 116
    4.6 Coronavirus 116
    4.7 Corporal Punishment 116
    4.8 Deliberate Indifference 116
    4.9 Discrimination 116
    4.10 Eligibility 117
    4.11 Emotional Disturbance 117
    4.12 Evaluation 117
    4.13 Fourth Amendment Rights 117
    4.14 Free Appropriate Public Education 117

- 4.15 Frivolous Lawsuit   117
- 4.16 Exhaustion of Administrative Remedies   117
- 4.17 Harassment   118
- 4.18 Homebound   119
- 4.19 Identification   119
- 4.20 IEP   119
- 4.21 Independent Educational Evaluations   119
- 4.22 Initial IEP   119
- 4.23 IQ Testing   119
- 4.24 Judicial Review   119
- 4.25 Jurisdiction   119
- 4.26 Maintenance of Program   120
- 4.27 Masks   120
- 4.28 Mootness   120
- 4.29 Paraprofessional   120
- 4.30 Private School Reimbursement   120
- 4.31 Procedural Matters   120
- 4.32 Procedural Violations   120
- 4.33 Qualified Immunity   120
- 4.34 Referral   121
- 4.35 Relationship between Conduct and Disability   121
- 4.36 Retaliation   121
- 4.37 Safety   121
- 4.38 Settlement Agreements   121
- 4.39 Sexual Assault   121
- 4.40 Stay Put   121

5 Case Summaries by Circuit   123

- 5.1 Summary of a Ruling by the US Supreme Court   128
- 5.2 Summaries of Rulings from the US Court of Appeals for the Second Circuit   131
- 5.3 Summaries of Rulings from the US Court of Appeals for the Third Circuit   142
- 5.4 Summaries of Rulings from the US Court of Appeals for the Fourth Circuit   161
- 5.5 Summaries of Rulings from the US Court of Appeals for the Fifth Circuit   163

5.6 Summaries of Rulings from the US Court of Appeals for the Sixth Circuit   184

5.7 Summaries of Rulings from the US Court of Appeals for the Ninth Circuit   190

5.8 Summaries of Rulings from the US Court of Appeals for the Tenth Circuit   212

5.9 Summaries of Rulings from the US Court of Appeals for the Eleventh Circuit   214

6 Case Studies   217

6.1 How Much Supervision Is Enough?   217

6.2 Providing Services   219

6.3 How Much Progress Monitoring?   220

6.4 How Much Is a Request?   221

6.5 The IDEA's "Child Find" Provision: Whose Legal Responsibility Is It?   222

6.6 Is There a Preference for Mediation-Based Approaches to Special Education Disputes?   223

Glossary of Legal Terms   225
References   233
Index   235
About the Authors   249

Introduction

In this 2021 edition of the *Special Education Law Annual*, we include copies of all policy statements, Dear Colleague Letters, and frequently asked question (FAQ) documents from the US Department of Education related to the education of students with disabilities. We review rulings related to the IDEA and Section 504 from US circuit courts of appeals for 2021, presented by circuit. The list of cases was developed by analyzing all circuit cases in the LRP and Westlaw Databases for special education for the calendar year 2021. The summaries we present do not address all points covered in a case. If a case has been published, we reference the citation for the reader who would like to review the complete case. We also provide a primer on the IDEA dispute resolution process, a guide on researching cases online, and lists of websites for follow-up research related to online special education law. This annual edition is a comprehensive summary of 2021 appellate court cases in special education and comprises important information and principles for all those who work closely with students with disabilities in K–12 educational settings. It also includes one case from the US Supreme Court, not a special education one, but one with educational implications.

In the introduction to the 2020 edition, we addressed COVID-19 and how it had changed the way educators provide instruction and the way they interact with students. In that volume, there were *no* cases addressing COVID-19 in schools and the provision of services. The reason for this was that the process of litigation is slow. Whereas there are specific timelines for a due process hearing decision, there are fewer such timelines after a case leaves the due process hearing administrative process. Some cases take five to seven years to be eventually decided, and the needs of the student have likely changed, sometimes rather dramatically, during this time. A reason for the timelines in due process hearings is because students eligible for special educational and related services are in a crucial developmental period and the more quickly we can address their needs the sooner we can ensure we are providing appropriate services.

Readers may expect that this year's review would include a large number of cases addressing the effect of COVID-19 on the special education system; however, this is not the case. There was a drop-off in the numbers of special education cases at the circuit court level, and the scarcity of cases involving COVID-19 and special education is largely due to the speed of the legal system after a case leaves a due process hearing. For a case to reach a US circuit court of appeals, it usually goes through a due process hearing and then through appeals to a US district court, perhaps multiple appeals. The process may take several years. There may be cases involving the education that students with disabilities received during the

COVID-19 pandemic in the US circuit courts beginning now. The pace of appeals is often slow. Due process hearings at the first tier are supposed to be held with a decision reached within 45 days of the hearing request. No such speed exists once the hearing is appealed up the judicial system. We believe these pandemic cases will be coming—watch this space for next year's summary.

The right to a free appropriate public education (FAPE) has not changed. Public school districts are still required to provide FAPE even when students need to be quarantined, despite the problems inherent in getting to and from school and in the challenges of providing virtual learning experiences. The reader will note that the cases involving COVID-19 mostly involve the use of masks in schools. We may look to these cases for guidance. Hopefully any guidance these cases provide on COVID-19 will not be necessary in the future.

Many students have no doubt regressed and experienced learning loss to some degree during the closure of public schools during the pandemic; unfortunately, students with disabilities who have serious educational needs requiring intensive instruction have most likely regressed significantly and will have difficulty recouping these losses. In addition to these problems, students with poor or no internet access may not have been able to access the virtual instruction offered by their local school district. Moreover, school personnel may not have had information regarding their students' educational and functional progress over the past year. We believe summaries of cases involving such issues will be included in future editions of the *Special Education Law Annual*.

CHAPTER 1

The US Department of Education, the IDEA, and Section 504

The US Department of Education (ED) is composed of a number of offices, three of which are especially crucial to the education of children and youth with disabilities. One of these offices is the Office of Special Education and Rehabilitative Services (OSERS). The mission of OSERS is "to improve early childhood, educational, and employment outcomes and raise expectations for all people with disabilities, their families, their communities, and the nation" (OSERS, p. 1). The Office of Special Education Programs (OSEP) is located within OSERS. The OSEP is dedicated to improving results for infants, toddlers, children and youth with disabilities ages birth through 21 by providing leadership and financial support to assist states and local districts through the IDEA. Both OSERS and OSEP provide leadership, enforcement, and fiscal resources to assist states and local school districts to educate students with disabilities.

Another office within the US Department of Education is the Office for Civil Rights (OCR). "The mission of the Office for Civil Rights is to ensure equal access to education and to promote educational excellence throughout the nation through vigorous enforcement of civil rights" (OCR Website, p. 1). The OCR enforces several civil rights laws that prohibit discrimination against individuals with disabilities including Section 504 of the Rehabilitation Act, which prohibits discrimination against individuals with disabilities in entities receiving federal financial assistance, and Title II of the Americans with Disabilities Act, which prohibits discrimination against individuals with disabilities by public entities whether or not they receive federal funding.

All three of these offices develop, communicate, and disseminate federal policy interpretations through policy letters, guidance documents, question-and-answer documents, and memos that address special education and children and youth with disabilities. The letters issued by these offices may be in the form of answers to queries by individuals (e.g., Letter to ___) or open letters called Dear Colleague Letters. The purposes of these documents are to explain or interpret federal law and regulations. Although these guidance documents are nonbinding and do not have the force of law, they may be cited in hearings or court cases because the guidance has some legal authority. Moreover, it is important to pay attention to these guidance documents because they are helpful explanations of existing laws and regulations and provide information regarding how these administrative agencies will enforce the existing laws and regulations.

During 2020, OSERS, OSEP, and OCR issued several policy statements regarding children and youth with disabilities. Although any federal agency (e.g., US Department of Justice) may issue administrative guidance, we are most concerned with guidance from the US Department of Education, most specifically letters issued by OSERS, OSEP, and OCR. These guidance documents are very important to special education administrators, special education teachers, related service providers, and parents of children and youth with disabilities because they provide official guidance and clarification on the implementation of the IDEA, and the implementation of Section 504. The Department of Education maintains websites that collect the letters of guidance and other policy documents. These guidance documents from OSEP and OSERS can be found at https://www2.ed.gov/policy/speced/guide/idea/memosdcltrs/index.html. Guidance documents from OCR can be found in the OCR Reading Room at https://www2.ed.gov/about/offices/list/ocr/frontpage/faq/readingroom.html.

CHAPTER 2

Policy Letters from the US Department of Education

2.1 Dear Colleague Letters

    2.1.1 August 24, 2021 Special Education and Early Intervention Partners

2.2 Guidance from the Office of Special Education Programs (OSEP)

    2.2.1 May 12, 2021 OSEP Policy Letter, Letter to Tymeson

    2.2.2 July 1, 2021 Section 2014 of the American Rescue Plan Act of 2021 and the Individuals with Disabilities Education Act

    2.2.3 July 26, 2001 Long COVID under Section 504 and the IDEA: A Resource to Support Children, Students, Educators, Schools, Service Providers, and Families

    2.2.4 August 9, 2021 Questions and Answers on the National Instructional Materials Accessibility Standard (NIMAS)

    2.2.5 September 24, 2021 Return to School Roadmap under the IDEA, Letter to Frumkin

    2.2.6 September 30, 2021 Return to School Roadmap: Development and Implementation of Individualized Education Programs in the Least Restrictive Environment under the Individuals with Disabilities Education Act

    2.2.7 October 29, 2021 Return to School Roadmap: Child Find, Referral, and Eligibility under Part C of the Individuals with Disabilities Education Act (IDEA)

    2.2.8 October 29, 2021 Return to School Roadmap: Provision of Early Intervention Services for Infants and Toddlers with Disabilities and Their Families under Part C of the Individuals with Disabilities Education Act (IDEA)

2.1 Dear Colleague Letters
2.1.1

UNITED STATES DEPARTMENT OF EDUCATION

OFFICE OF SPECIAL EDUCATION AND REHABILITATIVE SERVICES

OSEP DCL 21-01

August 24, 2021

Dear Special Education and Early Intervention Partners:

The Office of Special Education and Rehabilitative Services (OSERS) in the US Department of Education (herein referred to as the Department) is committed to ensuring that infants and toddlers with disabilities and their families, and children with disabilities, have successful early intervention and educational experiences in the upcoming school year. Since March 2020, due to the COVID-19 pandemic, we have all been challenged to provide services and supports to children with disabilities in ways we could never anticipate. As a result, OSERS wants to emphasize the importance of infants and toddlers with disabilities and their families receiving equitable access to high-quality early intervention services and children with disabilities receiving special education and related services in accordance with the Individuals with Disabilities Education Act (IDEA).

Infants and toddlers with disabilities and their families and children with disabilities were disproportionately affected by the pandemic compared to their peers without disabilities.[1] Even with the support of the special education and related services required by their individualized education programs (IEPs), some children with disabilities experienced difficulty accessing the general education curriculum in ways that could allow them to make meaningful progress.

---

1. This has been well documented. See, for example, "Special education amid pandemic poses challenges for Metro Atlanta schools," https://www.ajc.com/news/atlanta-news/special-education-amid-pandemic-poses-challenges-for-metro-atlanta-schools/4CCHBX7ITBBPVF7PLGBEQXMWKE/

Parents, educators, and related services providers responded to the unprecedented challenge of the COVID-19 pandemic by finding new ways to collaborate so that the needs of children with disabilities could continue to be met. Despite these efforts, some children with disabilities were unable to progress toward achieving the functional and academic goals included in their IEPs. Similarly, some infants and toddlers with disabilities and their families were unable to achieve the expected outcomes described in their individualized family services plans (IFSPs).

Early on in the pandemic, OSERS issued Questions and Answers on Providing Services to Children with Disabilities during the Coronavirus Disease 2019 Outbreak (March 12, 2020), and a Supplemental Fact Sheet Addressing the Risk of COVID-19 in Preschool, Elementary, and Secondary Schools While Serving Children with Disabilities (March 21, 2020). OSERS also released a series of Questions and Answers documents from June 2020 through October 2020. In the Questions and Answers on IDEA Part B Service Provision (September 28, 2020), OSERS made clear that, for the 2020–2021 school year, no IDEA requirements were waived. OSERS further clarified that, no matter what primary instructional delivery approach was chosen for that year, state educational agencies (SEAs) and local educational agencies (LEAs) remained responsible for ensuring that a free appropriate public education (FAPE) was available to all children with disabilities and implementing Part B requirements. Similarly, OSERS released companion guidance regarding IDEA Part C provision of services (October 20, 2020) to clarify that IDEA Part C requirements remained in effect, notwithstanding the pandemic. Likewise, state lead agencies (LAs) for Part C and early intervention service (EIS) providers remained responsible for ensuring the provision of early intervention services to infants and toddlers with disabilities and their families and implementing Part C requirements.

Subsequently, OSERS has received multiple requests from a diverse group of stakeholders asking that the Department clarify expectations and requirements for implementing IDEA in light of the many challenges of the COVID-19 pandemic and as more schools and programs are returning to in-person services. These inquiries address a range of topics, such as meeting timelines, ensuring implementation of initial evaluation and reevaluation procedures, determining eligibility for special education and related services, and providing the full array of special education and related services that children with disabilities need to receive FAPE. Similarly, stakeholders have inquired about the implications of delayed evaluations and early intervention services to infants and toddlers with disabilities and their families served under IDEA Part C.

As a part of the Department's Return to School Roadmap, OSERS will release IDEA guidance documents in the coming weeks and months, which focus on school reopening efforts and are intended to support the full implementation of IDEA requirements by SEAs, LEAs, LAs, and EIS providers. The Return to School Roadmap IDEA guidance documents are also intended to provide useful information to parents of infants, toddlers, and children with disabilities. The documents will focus on those topics most closely related to ensuring that, regardless of the COVID-19 pandemic or the mode of instruction, children with disabilities receive FAPE, and that infants and toddlers with disabilities and their families receive early intervention services.

Moving Forward: School Year 2021–2022 and Beyond

With the availability of vaccinations for all adults and for a growing number of children, the influx of new federal funds, especially the Elementary and Secondary School Emergency Relief Fund made available by the American Rescue Plan Act of 2021 (ARP Act), and additional IDEA Part B and Part C funds made available under Section 2014 of the ARP Act, the Department expects that all LEAs will provide every student with the opportunity for full-time, in-person learning for the 2021–2022 school year. The Department recognizes that some parents may have specific health and safety concerns about sending their children back to in-person instruction because of the perceived health risk to the student's immediate family and to other household members—even as parents are also concerned about their child missing the instructional and social and emotional opportunities that come with in-person learning.[2] Therefore, reopening schools safely is of utmost importance. SEAs and LEAs should put in place layered prevention strategies including promoting vaccination and universal and correct mask wearing in schools.

The Centers for Disease Control and Prevention (CDC) recommends that everyone in K through 12 schools wear a mask indoors, including teachers, staff, students, and visitors, regardless of vaccination status. SEAs and LEAs may use ARP Act funds, as appropriate, to ensure the health and safety of all students and teachers as part of the reopening efforts. OSERS encourages families and educators to continue to review the Department's and CDC's websites for updated guidance on ensuring the health and safety of all students and educators.[3]

We recognize that SEAs, LEAs, LAs, and EIS providers have worked hard to meet children's needs and provide required services, given the unprecedented educational disruptions and other challenges resulting from the pandemic.[4] OSERS wants to reiterate and emphasize that, notwithstanding these challenges, infants and toddlers with disabilities and their families and children with disabilities retain their rights to receive

---

2. ED COVID-19 Handbook Volume 1: Strategies for Safely Reopening Elementary and Secondary Schools.
3. COVID-19 Resources for Schools, Students, and Families | U.S. Department of Education; https://www.cdc.gov/coronavirus/2019-ncov/community/schools-childcare/k-12-guidance.html.
4. States have reported that these difficulties include the following: challenges with providing the equipment and technology, including Wi-Fi access, needed for children to participate in virtual learning; having adequate personnel to provide early intervention, special education, and related services due to COVID-related illness and employees' concerns for their safety and the safety of their families; and taking the necessary health and safety precautions required for public facilities to reopen.

appropriate services under IDEA. This includes ensuring that IEPs are in effect for children with disabilities at the start of the upcoming school year, and all other rights of children with disabilities and their parents under IDEA Part B are protected. Similarly, IDEA Part C requires IFSPs to be implemented and that all other rights of parents and their infants and toddlers with disabilities must be protected.

With few exceptions,[5] IDEA does not provide waiver authority to the Department; thus, OSERS is unable to grant waivers under IDEA Parts B and C to SEAs or LAs as a result of the pandemic or to otherwise create safe harbors from potential or existing litigation by parents or others. SEAs and LAs continue to have a reasonable degree of flexibility in how, but not whether, they monitor their LEAs and EIS programs and providers, using multiple components of the state's general supervision system. The Department will monitor states' implementation under Parts B and C of the IDEA, which includes reviewing whether states used alternative methods of exercising their general supervisory, accountability, and oversight responsibilities.

Looking forward, we emphasize the importance of SEAs and LAs focusing their general supervisory responsibilities on providing technical assistance and support to LEAs and EIS providers to—(1) mitigate and address the impact of service disruptions on the progress of infants and toddlers with disabilities and their families and children with disabilities, with a particular emphasis on children who have been most impacted by the pandemic; and (2) ensure full implementation of IDEA during the 2021–2022 school year.

Thank you for your continued support and partnership in improving early intervention services for infants and toddlers with disabilities and their families and education access and opportunities for children with disabilities.

Sincerely, /s/

Katherine Neas
Acting Assistant Secretary, Office of Special Education
and Rehabilitative Services

David Cantrell, PhD, Acting Director, Office of Special
Education Programs

---

5. A notable exception is the authority to grant a waiver of the IDEA's maintenance of state financial support requirement under 34 C.F.R. § 300.163.

2.2 Guidance from the Office of Special Education Programs (OSEP)

2.2.1

UNITED STATES DEPARTMENT OF EDUCATION
OFFICE OF SPECIAL EDUCATION AND REHABILITATIVE SERVICES
OFFICE OF SPECIAL EDUCATION PROGRAMS DIRECTOR

May 12, 2021

OSEP Policy 21-01

Garth Tymeson, PhD
Center on Disability Health and Adapted Physical Activity
University of Wisconsin–La Crosse
Department of Exercise and Sport Science
1725 State Street
108 Mitchell Hall
La Crosse, Wisconsin 54601

Dear Dr. Tymeson:

This letter responds to your April 9, 2020, correspondence addressed to Laurie VanderPloeg, former director of the Office of Special Education Programs (OSEP) in the US Department of Education (herein referred to as the Department). In that letter, you asked that OSEP clarify requirements related to the provision of physical education, including adapted physical education (APE), to children with disabilities under the Individuals with Disabilities Education Act (IDEA). Specifically, you asked that OSEP clarify "issues including the substitution or replacement of required physical education services by related services such as physical or occupational therapy for children with disabilities in special education, ages 3–21, and the qualifications/licensure required to teach specially designed physical education included in the [individualized education program (IEP)] IEP." You shared a scenario of a child who had received APE at her elementary school but, when she was to transition to middle school, the local educational agency members of the IEP team proposed to replace the child's APE with physical therapy services due to the unavailability of a qualified APE teacher at the middle school. On January 26, 2021, Daniel Schreier, policy advisor to the acting OSEP director, and Lisa Pagano, OSEP policy specialist, spoke with you by telephone to gather additional information related to your request. We regret the delay in responding.

We note that section 607(d) of the IDEA prohibits the secretary of the Department from issuing policy letters or other statements that establish a rule that is required for compliance with, and eligibility under, IDEA without following the rulemaking requirements of section 553 of the Administrative Procedure Act. Therefore, based on the requirements of IDEA section 607(e), this response is provided as informal guidance and is not legally binding. It represents an interpretation by the Department of the requirements of IDEA in the context of the specific facts presented and does not establish a policy or rule that would apply in all circumstances. Other than statutory and regulatory requirements included in the document, the contents of this IDEA defines special education as "specially designed instruction, at no cost to parents, to meet the unique needs of a child with a disability, including (A) instruction conducted in the classroom, in the home, hospitals and institutions, and in other settings; and (B) instruction in physical education" (IDEA section 602(29)). The IDEA regulations define physical education to mean "[t]he development of (A) [p]hysical and motor fitness; (B) [f]undamental motor skills and patterns; and (C) [s]kills in aquatics, dance, and individual and group games and sports (including intramural and lifetime sports)" (34 C.F.R. § 300.39(b)(2)(i)). Physical education "[i]ncludes special physical education, adapted physical education, movement education, and motor development" (34 C.F.R. § 300.39(b)(2)(ii)).

Under 34 C.F.R. § 300.108(a), the state is required to ensure that public agencies in the state make physical education services, specially designed if necessary, available to every child with a disability receiving a free appropriate public education (FAPE), unless the public agency enrolls children without disabilities and does not provide physical education to children without disabilities in the same grades. Further, each child with a disability must be afforded the opportunity to participate in the regular physical education program available to nondisabled children unless (1) the child is enrolled full time in a separate facility; or (2) the child needs specially designed physical education, as prescribed in the child's IEP (34 C.F.R. § 300.108(b)). If specially designed physical education is prescribed in a child's IEP, the public agency responsible for the education of that child must provide the services directly or make arrangements for those services to be provided through other public or private programs (34 C.F.R. § 300.108(c)).

Since instruction in physical education is included in the definition of special education, the IEP team must determine the extent to which the child can access the regular physical education program available to nondisabled peers, in addition to the extent to which physical education is required as specially designed instruction to meet the child's unique needs. Therefore, even if a school does not provide physical education to children without disabilities in the same grades as children with disabilities, the school is not relieved of the duty to provide physical education to those students who have unique needs requiring physical education and have IEPs setting out physical education as part of that student's special education and related services. Thus, under IDEA Part B, "if physical education is specially designed to meet the unique needs of a child with a disability and is set out in that child's IEP, those services must be provided whether or not they are provided to other children in the agency" (U.S. Department of Education, Analysis of Comments and Changes to the final IDEA Part B regulations, 71 Fed. Reg. 46540, 46583 (August 14, 2006); see also 34 C.F.R. § 300.108(c)).

When the IEP team determines a child requires physical education as specially designed instruction to meet the unique needs of a child with a disability, the service is considered special education and not a related service. As with other services in the IEP, the IEP team determines the frequency, location, and duration of the service based on the needs of the child. See 34 C.F.R. § 300.320(a)(7). It would be inconsistent with IDEA for the IEP team to base its determination of services necessary to provide FAPE, including specially designed instruction in physical education, on the availability of qualified staff.

During the January 26, 2021, telephone discussion with OSEP staff, you asked that this response specifically address whether it would be appropriate for a physical therapist to develop and implement goals in a child's IEP that require specially designed instruction in physical education. You shared concerns that, in the absence of an APE teacher, IEP teams may be inclined to substitute physical therapy for the specially designed physical education that had been determined necessary for FAPE. While Part B of the IDEA does not mandate any particular personnel standards, each state's policies and procedures must provide for the establishment and maintenance of standards to ensure that personnel necessary to carry out the purposes of Part B are appropriately and adequately prepared and trained (34 C.F.R. § 300.156(a)). This includes ensuring that personnel have the content knowledge and skills to serve children with disabilities (*Id*). The Part B regulations at 34 C.F.R. § 300.156 address separately the requirements for related services personnel and paraprofessionals (34 C.F.R. § 300.156(b)) and the qualifications for special education teachers (34 C.F.R. § 300.156(c)). The determination of who is qualified to provide physical education as specially designed instruction, including APE, is dependent upon the state's policies and procedures.

Finally, you asked whether an IEP team meeting is required if a public agency proposes to remove APE included in a child's IEP and replace it with one-to-one physical therapy services. You inquired whether such a change would constitute a change in educational placement. Unless the parent and public agency agree to use the IEP amendment procedures in 34 C.F.R. § 300.324(a)(4) and (6), the public agency would need to convene the IEP team to discuss making the revisions to the child's IEP that you describe. A public agency must provide the parent with prior written notice, as required by 34 C.F.R. § 300.503, a reasonable time before proposing to initiate or change, or refusing to initiate or change, the identification, evaluation, educational placement, or provision of FAPE to the child.

Generally, OSEP does not opine on whether the scenarios set forth in policy inquiries constitute a change in a child's educational placement. Determinations about whether a revision to a child's program results in a change in placement are made based on the facts and circumstances of the specific child, examining a number of factors. To help guide that decision-making process, OSEP set out several factors to consider in its Letter to Fisher, 21 IDELR 992 (July 6, 1994):

In determining whether a "change in educational placement" has occurred, the public agency responsible for educating the child must determine whether the proposed change would substantially or materially alter the child's educational program. In making such a determination, the effect of the change in location on the following factors must be examined: whether the educational program set out in the child's IEP has been revised; whether the child will be able to be educated with nondisabled children to the same extent; whether the child will have the same opportunities to participate in nonacademic and extracurricular services; and whether the new placement option is the same option on the continuum of alternative placements.

We thank you for your continued commitment to ensuring children with disabilities have access to appropriate instruction to meet their unique physical education needs and trust that the information in this letter is responsive to your inquiry. If you have further questions, please contact Lisa Pagano at 202-245-7413 or by e-mail at Lisa.Pagano@ed.gov.

Sincerely, /s/

David Cantrell, PhD, Acting Director,
Office of Special Education Programs

2.2.2

OSEP Policy Support 21-02

US DEPARTMENT OF EDUCATION FACT SHEET

Section 2014 of the American Rescue Plan Act of 2021 and the Individuals with Disabilities Education Act

July 1, 2021

Part B and Part C of the Individuals with Disabilities Education Act (IDEA) authorize assistance to states to support the provision of special education and related services to children with disabilities and the provision and coordination of early intervention services for infants and toddlers with disabilities and their families, respectively. Section 2014(a) of the American Rescue Plan Act of 2021 (ARP) provided more than $3 billion in supplemental funding for Fiscal Year 2021 for the three IDEA formula grant programs described here:

- $2,580,000,000 for IDEA Part B Grants to States (Section 611)
- $200,000,000 for IDEA Part B Preschool Grants (Section 619)
- $250,000,000 for IDEA Part C Grants for Infants and Families

This document provides an overview of the major statutory and regulatory requirements for IDEA Part B and Part C. Supplemental funding made available by the ARP is subject to the same requirements as federal fiscal year (FFY) 2021 IDEA funding made available under Public Law 116-260 (Consolidated Appropriations Act of 2021).

Part B of the IDEA provides funds to eligible states and entities under the Grants to States program authorized by section 611 of IDEA for children with disabilities aged 3 through 21 and the Preschool Grants program authorized by section 619 of IDEA for children with disabilities aged 3 through 5. The IDEA Part B funds assist states, and through them, eligible local educational agencies (LEAs), in providing special education and related services to children with disabilities. Part B funds are awarded to each state educational agency (SEA) that has established its eligibility under section 612 of IDEA for IDEA Part B funds to assist in providing special education and related services to eligible children with disabilities.[6] States are required to distribute any IDEA section 611 and section 619 funds that the state does not reserve for state-level activities[7] to LEAs that have established their eligibility under section 613 of IDEA under a statutory formula and must be used only to pay the excess costs of providing special education and related services in accordance with Part B of IDEA.[8] All IDEA Part B ARP funds must be used consistently with the current IDEA Part B statutory and regulatory requirements.

Part C of the IDEA provides funds to each state lead agency designated by the governor to implement statewide systems of coordinated, comprehensive, multidisciplinary, interagency programs to make early intervention services available to infants and toddlers with disabilities and their families. All IDEA Part C ARP funds must be used consistently with the current IDEA Part C statutory and regulatory requirements. IDEA Part C ARP funds may be used for any allowable purpose under Part C of the IDEA, including the direct provision of early intervention services to infants and toddlers with disabilities and their families, and implementing a statewide, comprehensive, coordinated, multidisciplinary, interagency system to provide early intervention services.

Under Public Law 116-260 (Consolidated Appropriations Act of 2021), states may use IDEA Part C FFY 2021 and IDEA Part C ARP funds allotted under section 643(c) of the IDEA to make subgrants to LEAs, institutions of higher education, other public agencies, and private nonprofit organizations to carry out activities authorized by section 638 of the IDEA. States may also apply for state incentive grants (SIGs) to fund the Part C extension option under IDEA sections 635(c) and 643(e) and 34 C.F.R. §§ 303.211 and 303.734.

The additional IDEA Part B and Part C funds that section 2014 of the ARP made available for states, in addition to state IDEA Part B and Part C formula grant awards for federal fiscal year (FFY) 2021, are subject to all IDEA statutory requirements reflected in 20 U.S.C. 1401 *et seq.* and applicable regulatory requirements in 34 CFR Parts 300 and 303. These statutory and regulatory provisions apply to IDEA grant awards and include requirements and provisions under IDEA, the Education Department General Administrative Regulations (EDGAR), applicable provisions of the General Education Provisions Act (GEPA), and the Office of Management and Budget's (OMB) Uniform Administrative Requirements, Cost Principles, and Audit Requirements for Federal Awards (Uniform Guidance). State allocation summary tables for FFY 2021 IDEA Part B and Part C grant awards (including both the regular formula grant funds and the supplemental IDEA grant funds provided under section 2014 of the ARP) are available on the IDEA ARP page in the linked locations.

---

6. See also 34 C.F.R. § 300.100.
7. States are limited in the amount they may reserve for state-level activities by the formula in 34 C.F.R. § 300.704.
8. 34 C.F.R. §§ 300.705(a) and 300.815; see also 34 C.F.R. § 300.202(a)(2).

Table 2.1 describes major statutory and regulatory requirements of IDEA Parts B and C. These requirements apply equally to funds made available under the ARP and the Consolidated Appropriations Act of 2021. Table 2.1 is intended to highlight key topics with links to statutory and regulatory text but is not a comprehensive list of all requirements.

TABLE 2.1. Statutory and Regulatory Requirements of IDEA Parts B and C

Topic	IDEA Part B, Sections 611 and 619	IDEA Part C
Authorizing Statutes	Section 611 and section 619 of the IDEA (for the IDEA Part B FFY 2021 formula grant funds), and section 2014 of the ARP (for the supplemental IDEA section 611 and section 619 funds).	Section 643 of the IDEA (for the IDEA Part C FFY 2021 IDEA formula grant funds), and section 2014 of the ARP (for the supplemental IDEA Part C funds).
Amount of IDEA Regular FFY 2021 Funds (Not Including ARP)	$12,937,457,000 for IDEA section 611. $397,620,000 for IDEA section 619.	$477,000,000 for IDEA Part C.
Amount of IDEA Funds Awarded in ARP	$2,580,000,000 for IDEA section 611. $200,000,000 for IDEA section 619.	$250,000,000 for IDEA Part C.
Period of Funds Availability	Funds are available for obligation by SEAs and LEAs between July 1, 2021, and September 30, 2023, and must be liquidated by January 28, 2024.	Funds are available for obligation by Part C lead agencies between July 1, 2021, and September 30, 2023, and must be liquidated by January 28, 2024.
Reservation of IDEA Funds for State Administration and Other State-Level Activities	IDEA allows states to reserve funds for state-level activities (state administration and other state-level activities) for both sections 611 and 619; however, because the provisions governing the maximum amount of funds that may be reserved are slightly different for section 611 and section 619, the impact of the additional ARP funds is different. For section 611, the amounts that states may reserve for state administration and other state-level activities are set in accordance with section 611(e) of the IDEA. Under these provisions, the maximum amount that a state may reserve is subject to the rate of inflation and not the total amount of IDEA funds made available. As a result, the additional IDEA funds made available by ARP do not increase the amount that can be reserved for state administration and other state-level activities.	N/A

TABLE 2.1. (continued)

Topic	IDEA Part B, Sections 611 and 619	IDEA Part C
Reservation of IDEA Funds for State Administration and Other State-Level Activities (continued)	For section 619, the amounts that states may reserve for state administration and other state-level activities are set in accordance with section 619(d) of the IDEA. Under these provisions, the maximum amount that a state may reserve is determined by the lesser of (1) the increase in the state's allocation under the program, or (2) the rate of inflation. As a result of the additional ARP Act funding, there was a small increase in the amount that states may reserve compared to FFY 2020. Section 619 grants funds that the state does not reserve for state-level activities to LEAs in the state (including public charter schools that operate as LEAs) in the state that have established their eligibility under section 613 of the IDEA, in accordance with the formula in section 619(g)(1)(A) and (B).	
Cash Management	For the IDEA section 611 program, cash management principles apply, and IDEA funds are usually included in the treasury-state agreement (31 C.F.R. Part 205, Subpart A). IDEA subgrants are subject to the OMB Uniform Guidance payment requirements in 2 C.F.R § 200.305(b). For the IDEA section 619 program, cash management principles in 31 C.F.R. Part 205 Subpart B (rules applicable to federal assistance programs not included in a treasury-state agreement) apply.	Cash management principles in 31 C.F.R. Part 205 Subpart B (rules applicable to federal assistance programs not included in a treasury-state agreement) apply.
Uses of Funds	Funds may be used for all allowable purposes under Part B of IDEA and are subject to all requirements and provisions that apply to IDEA funds, including requirements and provisions under IDEA, EDGAR, and the OMB Uniform Guidance.	Funds may be used for all allowable purposes under Part C of IDEA and are subject to all requirements and provisions that apply to IDEA funds, including requirements under IDEA, EDGAR, and the OMB Uniform Guidance.

Prior Approvals (for Selected Items of Cost)	Under section 605 of the IDEA, if the secretary determines that a program authorized under IDEA Part B will be improved by permitting program funds to be used to acquire appropriate equipment, or to construct new facilities or alter existing facilities, the secretary is authorized to allow the use of those funds for those purposes. Note that SEAs will continue to have the authority, as the pass-through entity, to review and approve LEA requests to use IDEA Part B funds for the purchase of equipment, including the alteration of existing facilities (2 C.F.R. § 200.439(b) (1)–(3)). States may also wish to review the October 2019 Frequently Asked Questions (2019 FAQs) Prior Approval—OSEP and RSA Formula Grants, which provides prior approval flexibilities for certain equipment and participant support costs.	Under section 605 of the IDEA, if the secretary determines that a program authorized under IDEA Part C will be improved by permitting program funds to be used to acquire appropriate equipment, or to construct new facilities or alter existing facilities, the secretary is authorized to allow the use of those funds for those purposes. States may also wish to review the October 2019 Frequently Asked Questions (2019 FAQs) Prior Approval—OSEP and RSA Formula Grants, which provides prior approval flexibilities for certain equipment and participant support costs.
Maintenance of State Financial Support (MFS)/Maintenance of Effort (MOE) (State)	Under section 612(a)(18) of the IDEA, a state may not reduce the amount of state financial support for special education and related services for children with disabilities, or otherwise made available because of the excess costs of educating those children, below the amount of that support for the preceding fiscal year. Under section 612(a)(18)(C) of the IDEA, the Department is authorized to waive the MFS requirement for a state, for one fiscal year at a time, if the Department determines that doing so would be equitable due to an exceptional or uncontrollable circumstance, such as a natural disaster or a precipitous and unforeseen decline in the financial resources of the state.	Section 637(b)(5)(B) of the IDEA includes a supplement not supplant provision, implemented through the Part C regulations at 34 C.F.R. § 303.225. The IDEA Part C MOE provision in 34 C.F.R. § 303.225(b) requires each state to ensure that the total amount of state and local funds budgeted for expenditures in the current fiscal year for early intervention services for children eligible under this part and their families must be at least equal to the total amount of state and local funds actually expended for early intervention services for these children and their families in the most recent preceding fiscal year for which the information is available. States must meet this standard to be eligible for the receipt of Federal IDEA Part C funds.

(continued)

TABLE 2.1. (continued)

Topic	IDEA Part B, Sections 611 and 619	IDEA Part C
Part C MOE Allowances	N/A	Allowances to the requirements in 34 C.F.R. § 303.225(b) may be made for: (1) a decrease in the number of infants and toddlers who are eligible to receive early intervention services under this part; and (2) unusually large amounts of funds expended for such long-term purposes as the acquisition of equipment and the construction of facilities.
Maintenance of Effort (LEA)	Under section 613(a)(2)(A)(iii) of the IDEA, an LEA may not reduce the level of expenditures for the education of children with disabilities made by the LEA from local funds below the level of those expenditures for the preceding fiscal year.	N/A
LEA MOE Exceptions	Under section 613(a)(2)(B) of the IDEA and 34 C.F.R. § 300.204, there are five instances where an LEA may reduce the level of expenditures for the education of children with disabilities made by the LEA below the level of those expenditures for the preceding fiscal year (for the compliance standard), and below the level of those expenditures for the most recent fiscal year for which information is available (for the eligibility standard). They are the following: The voluntary departure, by retirement or otherwise, or departure for just cause, of special education or related services personnel (e.g., special education teachers, speech pathologists, paraprofessionals assigned to work with children with disabilities);	N/A

- A decrease in the enrollment of children with disabilities;
- The termination of the obligation of the agency, consistent with IDEA Part B, to provide a program of special education to a particular child with a disability that is an exceptionally costly program, as determined by the SEA, because the child (1) has left the jurisdiction of the agency, (2) has reached the age at which the obligation of the agency to provide FAPE to the child has terminated, or (2) no longer needs the program of special education;
- The termination of costly expenditures for long-term purchases, such as the acquisition of equipment or the construction of school facilities; and
- The assumption of cost by the high-cost fund operated by the SEA under 34 C.F.R. § 300.704(c).

Adjustment to Local Effort	Under section 613(a)(2)(C) of the IDEA, for any fiscal year that an LEA's IDEA allocation exceeds the amount the LEA received for the previous fiscal year, under certain circumstances, the LEA may reduce the level of local, or state and local, expenditures otherwise required to meet MOE by up to 50% of the amount of the excess, as long as the LEA uses the freed-up local funds for activities that could be supported under the ESEA. Note that an LEA may not take this reduction if the SEA determines that the LEA is unable to establish and maintain programs of free appropriate public education for eligible children with disabilities or the SEA has taken action against the LEA under section 616 of IDEA. Also, an LEA that is required to reserve the maximum 15% of its IDEA Part B allocation on comprehensive coordinated early intervention services (CCEIS) because the LEA is identified with significant disproportionality under 34 C.F.R. § 300.646 will not be able to take advantage of the MOE reduction in 34 C.F.R. § 300.205(a).

(continued)

TABLE 2.1. *(continued)*

Topic	IDEA Part B, Sections 611 and 619	IDEA Part C
Adjustment to Local Effort *(continued)*	In addition, under IDEA section 616(f), if in making its annual determinations, an SEA determines that an LEA is not meeting the requirements of Part B, including meeting targets in the state's performance plan, the SEA must prohibit that LEA from reducing its MOE under IDEA section 613(a)(2)(C) for any fiscal year. Therefore, an SEA must prohibit an LEA from taking advantage of the MOE reduction under IDEA section 613(a)(2)(C) if the LEA's determination is Needs Assistance, Needs Intervention, or Needs Substantial Intervention.	
Part C Option		Under the reservation for state incentive grants in section 643(e) of the IDEA, for any fiscal year for which the amount appropriated pursuant to the authorization of appropriations under section 644 of this title exceeds $460,000,000, the secretary shall reserve 15% of such appropriated amount to provide grants to states that are carrying out the policy described in section 635(c) of this title in order to facilitate the implementation of such policy.
Equitable Services Reservations	Under section 612(a)(10)(A)(i) of the IDEA, to the extent consistent with the number and location of children with disabilities in the state who are enrolled by their parents in private elementary schools and secondary schools in the school district served by an LEA, provision is made for the participation of those children in the program assisted or carried out under Part B by providing for such children special education and related services in accordance with equitable services requirements in IDEA (34 C.F.R. §§ 300.130-300.144).	N/A

Amounts to be expended for the provision of those services (including direct services to parentally placed private school children) by the LEA shall be equal to a proportionate amount of federal funds made available under Part B of the IDEA.
In calculating the proportionate share required under IDEA section 612(a)(10)(A)(i)(I), an LEA must first aggregate the FFY 2021 funds received under the section 611 (Grants to States) regular and ARP awards and apply the formula outlined in 34 C.F.R. § 300.133 for calculating the proportionate share to the aggregated amount. Similarly, for children aged 3–5, the proportionate share is based on the total FFY 2021 funds received under the section 619 (PreschoolGrants) regular and ARP awards.

Indirect Cost Rates

Indirect costs are restricted. Under 34 C.F.R. §§ 76.564 through 76.569 apply to agencies of state and local governments that are grantees under programs with a statutory requirement prohibiting the use of federal funds to supplant non-federal funds, and to their subgrantees under these programs.

Indirect cost rates are approved by the secretary pursuant to 34 C.F.R. § 76.561. Restricted indirect cost rates apply to the IDEA Part B regular formula grant funds and supplemental funds provided by the ARP. States should calculate their restricted indirect costs on the IDEA Part B ARP funds in the same way as they calculate indirect costs on their IDEA Part B regular formula grant award.

Indirect costs are restricted. Under 34 C.F.R. § 76.563 of EDGAR, 34 C.F.R. § 76.564 through 76.569 apply to agencies of state and local governments that are grantees under programs with a statutory requirement prohibiting the use of federal funds to supplant non-federal funds, and to their subgrantees under these programs. Under 34 C.F.R. § 303.225(c), states may not charge indirect costs to IDEA Part C FFY 2021 formula funds as well as ARP supplemental IDEA Part C funds unless they are charged on a restricted basis.

States should calculate their restricted indirect costs on the IDEA Part C ARP funds in the same way as they calculate indirect costs on their IDEA Part C regular formula grant award.

(continued)

TABLE 2.1. (continued)

Topic	IDEA Part B, Sections 611 and 619	IDEA Part C
CEIS	Section 613(f) of the IDEA and the regulations in 34 C.F.R. § 300.226 permit an LEA to use not more than 15% of the amount the LEA receives under Part B for any fiscal year (i.e., the aggregate of the LEA's section 611 and section 619 amounts for both the regular formula IDEA awards and the supplemental IDEA awards made available by the ARP), less any amount reduced by the LEA pursuant to 34 C.F.R. § 300.205, to develop and provide CEIS for students in kindergarten through grade 12 (with a particular emphasis on students in kindergarten through grade 3) who are currently not identified as needing special education or related services but who need additional academic and behavioral support to succeed in a general education environment.	
Comprehensive CEIS (CCEIS)	Under section 618(d)(2)(B) of the IDEA and the regulations in 34 C.F.R. § 300.646(d), the state or the secretary of the interior shall require any LEA identified under 34 C.F.R. § 300.646(a) and (b) to reserve the maximum amount of funds under section 613(f) of the IDEA (i.e., 15% of the amount the LEA receives under Part B for any fiscal year) to provide CCEIS to address factors contributing to the significant disproportionality. The 15% is calculated based on the aggregate of the LEA's section 611 and section 619 amounts for both the regular formula IDEA awards and the supplemental IDEA awards made available by the ARP.	

Reporting	All prime recipients of IDEA Part B funds must report subaward information as required by the Federal Funding Accountability and Transparency Act of 2006 (FFATA), as amended in 2008. First-tier subaward information must be reported by the end of the following month from when the award was made or obligated. FFATA guidance is found at https://www.fsrs.gov/. The supplemental IDEA awards made available by the ARP will be assigned separate Catalog of Federal Domestic Assistance (CFDA) numbers, allowing the funds to be tracked separately from the regular IDEA awards.	All prime recipients of IDEA Part C funds must report subaward information as required by the Federal Funding Accountability and Transparency Act of 2006 (FFATA), as amended in 2008. First-tier subaward information must be reported by the end of the following month from when the award was made or obligated. FFATA guidance is found at https://www.fsrs.gov/. The supplemental IDEA awards made available by the ARP will be assigned separate Catalog of Federal Domestic Assistance (CFDA) numbers, allowing the funds to be tracked separately from the regular IDEA awards.
Audit	Under 2 C.F.R. § 200.501(a), a non-federal entity that expends $750,000 or more during the non-federal entity's fiscal year in federal awards must have a single or program-specific audit conducted for that year in accordance with the Uniform Guidance provisions. Under 2 C.F.R. § 200.501(b), a non-federal entity that expends $750,000 or more during the non-federal entity's fiscal year in federal awards must have a single audit conducted in accordance with the scope of the audit requirements in § 200.514 except when it elects to have a program-specific audit conducted in accordance with 2 C.F.R. § 200.501(c).	Under 2 C.F.R. § 200.501(a), a non-federal entity that expends $750,000 or more during the non-federal entity's fiscal year in federal awards must have a single or program-specific audit conducted for that year in accordance with the Uniform Guidance provisions. Under 2 C.F.R. § 200.501(b), a non-federal entity that expends $750,000 or more during the non-federal entity's fiscal year in federal awards must have a single audit conducted in accordance with the scope of the audit requirements in § 200.514 except when it elects to have a program-specific audit conducted in accordance with 2 C.F.R. § 200.501(c).

2.2.3

UNITED STATES DEPARTMENT OF EDUCATION OFFICE FOR CIVIL RIGHTS

OFFICE OF SPECIAL EDUCATION AND REHABILITATIVE SERVICES

July 26, 2021

Long COVID under Section 504 and the IDEA: A Resource to Support Children, Students, Educators, Schools, Service Providers, and Families

Introduction

The COVID-19 pandemic has created significant challenges for schools in meeting the needs of all children and students in early childhood, elementary, secondary, and postsecondary education. These challenges will continue as schools and public agencies[9] seek to ensure support and equity for children and students experiencing the long-term adverse health effects of COVID-19, commonly referred to as long COVID.

This resource is issued jointly by the US Department of Education's Office for Civil Rights (OCR) and the Office of Special Education and Rehabilitative Services (OSERS) to provide information about long COVID as a disability and about schools'[10] and public agencies' responsibilities for the provision of services and reasonable modifications to

---

9. The information in this document under IDEA applies to public agencies, which includes state educational agencies (SEAs), local educational agencies (LEAs), educational service agencies (ESAs), nonprofit public charter schools that are not otherwise included as LEAs or ESAs and are not a school of an LEA or ESA, and any other political subdivisions of the state that are responsible for providing education to children with disabilities. IDEA also requires state lead agencies to provide early intervention services for infants and toddlers. This resource refers to all these entities as "public agencies."
10. The information in this document regarding Section 504 applies to all schools, which includes public schools and school districts, as well as private schools, public charter schools, and magnet schools, and postsecondary institutions that receive federal financial assistance from the department. Although some Section 504 regulatory requirements are different for public and private school recipients, both public and private schools that receive federal financial assistance from the US Department of Education must comply with Section 504. See 34 C.F.R. § 104.33 and 39. Section 504 falls under OCR's jurisdiction.

children and students for whom long COVID is a disability. The discussion here focuses on two federal laws: Section 504 of the Rehabilitation Act of 1973 (Section 504) and Parts B and C of the Individuals with Disabilities Education Act (IDEA).[11]

This resource has four sections:

1. Background Information on Section 504 and IDEA
2. What Is Long COVID, and What Is Its Impact on Children and Students?
3. Protections and Services under IDEA and Section 504 for Children and Students with Long COVID
4. What to Do If a Child or Student Is Experiencing Long COVID

Additional Resources from the Department of Education

The US Department of Education (herein referred to as the Department) is committed to providing resources to support schools and public agencies in reopening safely and in ways that support equity among all children and students. To date, the Department has released various important resources to assist schools and public agencies, including the *ED COVID-19 Handbook*, volumes 1, 2, and 3;[12] "Questions and Answers on Civil Rights and School Reopening in the COVID-19 Environment";[13] "Safer Schools and Campuses Best Practices Clearinghouse";[14] and this resource, which addresses the potential developmental and educational implications of long COVID for children and students[15] who have this condition.

---

11. Another federal disability civil rights law, the Americans with Disabilities Act (ADA), also applies to schools. Title II of the ADA prohibits disability discrimination by public entities, including public schools. Title III of the ADA prohibits disability discrimination by certain private entities, including certain private schools. OCR shares in the enforcement of Title II of the ADA with the US Department of Justice (DOJ); DOJ has enforcement authority for Title III of the ADA. This document focuses on Section 504 and the IDEA. More information about the ADA is available at www.ed.gov/ocr and www.ada.gov.
12. *ED COVID-19 Handbook*, vol. 1, *Strategies for Safely Reopening Elementary and Secondary Schools*, US Department of Education, 2021, https://www2.ed.gov/documents/coronavirus/reopening.pdf; vol. 2, *Roadmap to Reopening Safely and Meeting All Students' Needs*, https://www2.ed.gov/documents/coronavirus/reopening-2.pdf; and vol. 3, *Strategies for Safe Operation and Addressing the Impact of COVID-19 on Higher Education Students, Faculty, and Staff*, https://www2.ed.gov/documents/coronavirus/reopening-3.pdf..
13 "Questions and Answers on Civil Rights and School Reopening in the COVID-19 Environment," US Department of Education, May 2021, https://www2.ed.gov/about/offices/list/ocr/docs/qa-reopening-202105.pdf.
14. Safer Schools and Campuses Best Practices Clearinghouse, https://bestpracticesclearinghouse.ed.gov/.
15. For purposes of this document, "students with disabilities" generally refers to the definition of disability found in the Rehabilitation Act of 1973 at 29 U.S.C. § 705(9)(B), (20)(B); see also the department's Section 504 regulation at 34 C.F.R. § 104.3(j). "Child or children with disabilities" generally refers to the definitions of child with a disability or infant or toddler with a disability in Parts B and C of the IDEA. See 34 C.F.R. § 300.8 (Part B) and 34 C.F.R. § 303.21 (Part C). The terms and definitions are not mutually exclusive, however. All children with disabilities who are eligible for special education

Please note: Other than statutory and regulatory requirements included in the document, the contents of this guidance do not have the force and effect of law and are not meant to bind the public. This document is intended only to provide clarity to the public regarding existing requirements under the law or agency policies. The Department has determined that this document provides significant guidance under the Office of Management and Budget's Final Bulletin for Agency Good Guidance Practices, 72 Fed. Reg. 3432 (January 25, 2007).

Background Information on Section 504 and IDEA

Section 504 prohibits disability discrimination and ensures that students with disabilities have equal access to educational opportunities. In the education context, this law applies to schools that receive federal financial assistance from the Department and is enforced by the Department's OCR.

IDEA Part B ensures that a free appropriate public education (FAPE) is available to all children with disabilities residing in the state between the ages of 3 through 21 years, with a few specific exceptions, and including children with disabilities who have been suspended or expelled from school.[16] Under Part C of the IDEA, infants and toddlers (birth through age 2 years) with disabilities and their families are eligible to receive early intervention services.[17] OSERS's Office of Special Education Programs (OSEP) administers the IDEA, including the Federal Special Education Grants to States under Part B and Special Education Grants for Infants and Toddlers under Part C.

What Is Long COVID, and What Is Its Impact on Children and Students?

The US Centers for Disease Control and Prevention (CDC) has identified long COVID as another term for post-COVID conditions.[18] According to the CDC, **post-COVID conditions** "are a wide range of new, returning,

---

and related services under IDEA are protected by Section 504 (but the inverse is not true; not all students protected by Section 504 are IDEA eligible). See "Parent and Educator Resource Guide to Section 504 in Public Elementary and Secondary Schools," US Department of Education, Office for Civil Rights, December 2016, https://www2.ed.gov/about/offices/list/ocr/docs/504-resource-guide-201612.pdf.

16. 8 34 C.F.R. § 300.102(a).
17. Appropriate early intervention services are available to all infants and toddlers with disabilities in the state and their families, including Indian infants and toddlers with disabilities and their families residing on a reservation geographically located in the state, infants and toddlers with disabilities who are homeless children and their families, and infants and toddlers with disabilities who are wards of the state.
18. The Centers for Disease Control and Prevention also recognizes other post-COVID conditions, a series of illnesses resulting in debilitating conditions, that can be similar to long COVID. This guidance may also be applicable to other post-COVID conditions. For example, the CDC has identified a post-COVID condition called "Multisystem inflammatory syndrome in children (MIS-C)." MIS-C is a condition where different parts of a child's body can become inflamed, including the heart, lungs, kidneys, brain, skin, eyes, or gastrointestinal organs. Children with MIS-C may have a fever and various symptoms, including abdominal (gut) pain, vomiting, diarrhea, neck pain, rash, bloodshot eyes, or feeling extra tired. Currently, it is unknown how long multiorgan effects might last and whether the effects could lead to chronic health conditions. MIS-C, mental health conditions, and future conditions not yet identified as a result of contracting COVID may

or ongoing health problems people can experience more than four weeks after first being infected with the virus that causes COVID-19. Even people who did not have symptoms when they were infected can have post-COVID conditions."[19]

Preliminary studies show that children and students of all ages may experience long COVID, which can produce a combination of symptoms, including the following:[20]

- Tiredness or fatigue
- Difficulty thinking or concentrating (sometimes referred to as "brain fog")
- Headache
- Changes in smell or taste
- Dizziness on standing (lightheadedness)
- Fast-beating or pounding heart (also known as heart palpitations)
- Symptoms that get worse after physical or mental activities
- Chest or stomach pain
- Difficulty breathing or shortness of breath
- Cough
- Joint or muscle pain
- Mood changes
- Fever
- Pins-and-needles feeling
- Diarrhea
- Sleep problems
- Changes in period cycles
- Multiorgan effects or autoimmune conditions
- Rash

As the Departments of Justice and Health and Human Services explain, long COVID can be a disability under the Americans with Disabilities Act and Section 504 of the Rehabilitation Act of 1973.[21]

Protections and Services under IDEA and Section 504 for Children and Students with Long COVID

A child or student experiencing long COVID or other conditions that have arisen as a result of COVID-19 may be eligible for special education and

---

adversely impact a student's educational performance or other major life activity, and if they do, the same process described in this document applies to those students.
19. "Long COVID or Post-COVID Conditions," CDC, last updated June 17, 2022, https://www.cdc.gov/coronavirus/2019-ncov/long-term-effects/index.html?CDC_AA_refVal=https%3A%2F%2Fwww.cdc.gov%2Fcoronavirus%2F2019-ncov%2Flong-term-effects.html.
20. See "Long COVID or Post-COVID Conditions," CDC, updated May 5, 2022, https://www.cdc.gov/coronavirus/2019-ncov/long-term-effects.html.
21. For more information concerning long COVID as a disability, see "Guidance on 'Long COVID' as a Disability under the ADA, Section 504, and Section 1557," Department of Justice and Department of Health and Human Services, last reviewed July 26, 2021, https://www.hhs.gov/civil-rights/for-providers/civil-rights-covid19/guidance-long-covid-disability/index.html.

related services under IDEA and/or may be entitled to protections and services under Section 504. Some children and students who were already identified as having a disability under IDEA and/or Section 504 and who have contracted COVID-19 may experience new or worsened symptoms related to their preexisting disability, to COVID-19, or to both. If these symptoms persist in the form of long COVID, these children or students may need new or different related aids and services, specialized instruction, or reasonable modifications. Other children or students may be found eligible for services under IDEA and/or Section 504 for the first time because of the adverse impact of long COVID on the child's educational achievement and functioning (IDEA) or if long COVID substantially limits one or more of the student's major life activities (Section 504).

A. Eligibility under IDEA: To be eligible for special education and related services under Part B, the child must be evaluated and determined to be a child who has a disability and who requires specialized services as defined under IDEA.[22] For example, under the IDEA Part B regulations, a child may be eligible for special education and related services based on having an "other health impairment" if the child has limited strength, vitality, or alertness due to a chronic or acute health problem that adversely affects the child's educational performance.[23] To be eligible for early intervention services under IDEA Part C, an infant or toddler must receive a comprehensive, multidisciplinary evaluation and meet the state's eligibility criteria.[24] For example, infants with severe post-COVID conditions could, based on evaluation data, have developmental delays that make them eligible for early intervention services.

B. Eligibility under Section 504: Under Section 504, a person has a disability if they: (1) have a physical or mental impairment that substantially limits a major life activity; (2) have a record of such an impairment; or (3) are regarded as having such an impairment.[25] Major life activities include, for example, breathing and concentrating as well as major bodily functions such as functions of the immune system.[26] A student does not need to be substantially limited in their learning to be eligible for protection and services under Section 504. If a student's long COVID substantially limits one or more major life

---

22. 34 C.F.R. §§ 300.301-300.306.
23. IDEA does not require children to be identified with a particular disability category for purposes of the delivery of special education and related services, since a child's entitlement under IDEA is to FAPE and not to a particular disability label. See "Assistance to States for the Education of Children with Disabilities and Preschool Grants for Children with Disabilities"; Final Rule, 71 Fed. Reg. 46540, 46737 (August 14, 2006).
24. 34 C.F.R. §§ 303.303-303.322.
25. 29 U.S.C. § 705(9)(B), (20)(B).
26. For more examples of major life activities and bodily functions, see "Parent and Educator Resource Guide to Section 504 in Public Elementary and Secondary Schools (Resource Guide)," US Department of Education, December 2016, https://www2.ed.gov/about/offices/list/ocr/docs/504-resource-guide-201612.pdf.

activities, the student would have a disability under Section 504.[27] This analysis applies to all students, whether in preschool, elementary or secondary school, or a postsecondary setting.

What to Do If a Child or Student Is Experiencing Long COVID

Early Childhood, Elementary, and Secondary Children and Students

Long COVID impacts children and students in a variety of ways, and therefore, the determination of whether a child or student is eligible for IDEA and/or Section 504 services must be made on an individual basis following existing procedures in those laws and their implementing regulations.

A. Child Find and Evaluation Procedures under IDEA Part C. Child Find is a requirement that states have a system in place to identify, locate, and evaluate all infants and toddlers with disabilities who may be eligible for early intervention services as early as possible. A child suspected of having a disability should be referred as soon as possible—but in no case more than seven days—after the child has been identified.[28] With parental[29] consent, a timely, comprehensive, multidisciplinary evaluation must be completed, and if the child is determined eligible, a child and family assessment must be conducted to determine the appropriate early intervention services and supports for the child and family. The initial evaluation and the initial assessments of the child and family and the initial individualized family service plan (IFSP) meeting must be completed within 45 days from the date the lead agency or early intervention service (EIS) provider receives the referral of the child. The lead agency or EIS provider must ensure that once the IFSP is developed and the parent consents to services, the IFSP is implemented as soon as possible.

B. Child Find and Initial Evaluation Procedures under IDEA Part B. Similarly, Child Find for IDEA Part B requires public agencies to implement policies and procedures ensuring that all children with disabilities who need special education and related services are identified, located, and evaluated, regardless of the severity of the disability. This includes, for example, children who may have been identified as a child with a disability under the IDEA category of "other health impairment" as a result of contracting COVID-19 (e.g., long COVID or multisystem inflammatory syndrome in children, known as MIS-C).[30] Child Find activities typically involve a screening process to determine whether the child should be referred for a full evaluation to determine eligibility for special education and related services. If the public agency suspects the child may have

---

27. In addition, if a person with long COVID has a record of such impairment or is regarded as having such an impairment, the person would meet the definition of disability under Section 504.
28. 34 C.F.R. § 303.303.
29. In this document, "parent" refers to both parents and guardians.
30. 34 C.F.R. § 300.111.

a disability under IDEA, it must seek the parent's consent to conduct an initial evaluation. That <u>evaluation must be consistent with IDEA's requirements</u> and conducted within 60 days of receiving parental consent or within the state-established timeline. At the completion of the evaluation, a group of qualified professionals and the child's parent determine whether the child is a child with a disability as defined in IDEA and, if yes, identify the educational needs of the child.

C. Evaluation Procedures under Section 504. Under Section 504, schools must conduct an evaluation in a timely manner of any student who needs or is believed to need special education or related services because of a disability.[31] The evaluation of a student must be individualized and not make any conclusions based on the child's diagnosis alone.

Once the evaluations are completed, a group of people knowledgeable about the child and the child's evaluation data and placement options (for example, the child's parents, school nurses, teachers, counselors, psychologists, school administrators, social workers, doctors, etc.) reviews the evaluation results.[32] Then the group determines the child's placement based on whether the student has a disability and what, if any, supports are needed. For example, a student who has had COVID-19 and who continues to have difficulty concentrating may require an evaluation to determine if the student has a disability and needs special education or related services such as additional time to finish classwork and tests. For students who already receive services under Section 504, schools must provide reevaluations periodically and prior to a significant change in placement.[33]

D. Eligibility and Implementation under IDEA and Section 504. If the child is eligible for services under Part C of IDEA, an IFSP will be developed by the IFSP team, which includes the infant's or toddler's parent. For example, an IFSP team may determine that a toddler with developmental delays as a result of the effects of long COVID may require early intervention services and occupational therapy to address fine and visual motor skills. The IFSP could also include parent services or family-centered interventions to foster social-emotional well-being as the toddler recovers from long COVID. Likewise, a child determined eligible for services under Part B will have an individualized education program (IEP) developed by the IEP team, which includes the child's parent.[34] For example, an IEP team may determine that a child whose disability meets the definition of "other health impairment" under IDEA and who is experiencing difficulty concentrating and anxiety symptoms related to long COVID may need to receive special education and related services and supplementary aids and services to improve academic engagement during instructional periods,

---

31. 34 C.F.R. § 104.35.
32. 34 C.F.R. § 104.35(c).
33. 34 C.F.R. § 104.35(d). A reevaluation procedure consistent with the IDEA is one means of meeting this Section 504 requirement.
34. Parentally placed private school children with disabilities may receive special education and related services through a services plan. See 34 C.F.R. §§ 300.130-300.144.

counseling services to address anxiety, and a plan for positive behavioral interventions and supports to promote on-task behavior and adaptive responses to stress triggers.

If a student is eligible for services or reasonable modifications under Section 504, schools often record those services and modifications in a document called a Section 504 plan.[35] Under Section 504, for example, a group of knowledgeable people may determine that a student requires a reasonable modification to the attendance policy to receive excused absences for long COVID-related illness or medical appointments beyond the initial period of illness.

Postsecondary Education Students. Colleges and universities also have obligations under Section 504 and must provide students with disabilities an opportunity to participate that is equal to that of students without disabilities.[36] This obligation extends to students whose long COVID substantially limits a major life activity.

Postsecondary education students who are experiencing long COVID may have a disability; if so, they may require academic adjustments and/or reasonable modifications.[37] For example, a student with asthma may experience increased difficulty breathing and new difficulty with walking as a result of long COVID. That student may need a reasonable modification to register early for a class schedule that minimizes the distance between classes.

In the postsecondary setting, Section 504 does not require colleges or universities to identify students with disabilities. Students who require academic adjustments or reasonable modifications may request them; typically, students work with a postsecondary institution's disability services office to identify appropriate modifications.

> *Students with disabilities—including those whose long COVID is a disability—have a right to be free from discrimination in school. Federal disability laws, such as Section 504, guarantee equal opportunity to learn for students with disabilities. OCR is committed to enforcing Section 504 and ensuring that all students with disabilities have the supports and services needed to fulfill the law's commitment.*—Suzanne B. Goldberg, Acting Assistant Secretary for the Office for Civil Rights

> *Long COVID is an emerging issue that may affect many children (and educators) across the country. Early intervention and local educational agencies need to ensure that children who are living with impaired development or health due to long COVID that is a disability are identified*

---

35. For more information about identification, evaluation, placement, and other Section 504 procedures, refer to the "Parent and Educator Resource Guide to Section 504," US Department of Education, Office for Civil Rights, December 2016, https://www2.ed.gov/about/offices/list/ocr/docs/504-resource-guide-201612.pdf.
36. For more information about identification, evaluation, placement, and other Section 504 procedures, refer to the "Parent and Educator Resource Guide to Section 504," https://www2.ed.gov/about/offices/list/ocr/docs/504-resource-guide- 201612.pdf.
37. 34 C.F.R. § 104.44.

and are provided the appropriate services and supports covered under IDEA.—Katherine Neas, Acting Assistant Secretary for the Office of Special Education and Rehabilitative Services

E. Language Assistance. On request, this publication is available in alternate formats, such as Braille or large print. For more information, please contact the Department's Alternate Format Center at 202-260-0818 or alternateformatcenter@ed.gov. If you have difficulty understanding English and need more information about interpretation or translation services, please call 1-800-USA-LEARN (1-800-872-5327) (TTY: 1-800-877-8339), e-mail us at Ed.Language.Assistance@ed.gov, or write to US Department of Education, Information Resource Center, 400 Maryland Avenue SW, Washington, DC 20202.

F. About the Department of Education's Office of Special Education and Rehabilitative Services (OSERS) and Office for Civil Rights (OCR). OSERS's mission is to improve early childhood, educational, and employment outcomes and raise expectations for all people with disabilities, their families, their communities, and the nation. In implementing this mission, OSERS supports programs that help educate children and youth with disabilities and provides for the rehabilitation of youth and adults with disabilities. OSERS provides a wide array of supports to parents and individuals, school districts, and states in two main areas—special education and vocational rehabilitation—through its two main components: OSEP and Rehabilitation Services Administration. For more information, visit the Department's Office of Special Education and Rehabilitative Services website (https://www2.ed.gov/osers).

OCR's mission is to ensure equal access to education and to promote educational excellence through vigorous enforcement of civil rights in our nation's schools. An important OCR responsibility is resolving complaints of discrimination, which can be filed by anyone who believes that an education institution that receives federal financial assistance[38] has discriminated against someone on the basis of race, color, national origin, sex, disability, or age. For more information, visit the department's Office for Civil Rights website (https://www2.ed.gov/ocr). There, a complaint of discrimination can also be filed (https://www2.ed.gov/about/offices/list/ocr/complaintintro.html).

---

38. Under Title II of the Americans with Disabilities Act (Title II), which prohibits disability discrimination by public entities, including public schools, OCR has jurisdiction regardless of whether the entity receives federal financial assistance.

2.2.4

OSEP QA 21-04

UNITED STATES DEPARTMENT OF EDUCATION
OFFICE OF SPECIAL EDUCATION AND REHABILITATIVE SERVICES
OFFICE OF SPECIAL EDUCATION PROGRAMS

August 9, 2021

QUESTIONS AND ANSWERS ON THE NATIONAL INSTRUCTIONAL MATERIALS ACCESSIBILITY STANDARD (NIMAS)

Introduction

The 2004 Individuals with Disabilities Education Act (IDEA) established the National Instructional Materials Accessibility Standard (NIMAS) and the National Instructional Materials Access Center (NIMAC) to assist states[39] in meeting the needs of students with disabilities in elementary and secondary schools who require accessible formats for instructional materials.

Regulations for Part B of the IDEA 2004 were published in the *Federal Register* on August 14, 2006, and became effective on October 13, 2006. The NIMAC began its work on December 3, 2006, and has been in continuous operation since that time.[40] While parts B and D of the IDEA outline the duties and responsibilities of the NIMAC and provide the key definitions framing its operations, the process for providing NIMAS-sourced materials to eligible students is also impacted by section 121 of the Copyright Act (also known as the "Chafee Amendment") and the 1931 Act to Provide Books for the Adult Blind.

The Office of Special Education and Rehabilitative Services (OSERS) in the US Department of Education (herein referred to as the Department)

---

39. The NIMAC assists all state educational agencies that receive funding under IDEA, including in states, territories, freely associated states, the District of Columbia, and the Department of Defense Education Activity.
40. The NIMAC is a national file repository for NIMAS files received from publishers (https://www.nimac.us).

issued a Q&A document in August 2010 to provide states, state educational agencies (SEAs), local educational agencies (LEAs), and other interested parties with information to facilitate implementation of the NIMAS and coordination with the NIMAC. OSERS updated this document to reflect changes in the NIMAS resulting from the 2020 Notice of Interpretation (NOI)[41] and the Marrakesh Treaty Implementation Act (MTIA).[42] This Q&A document supersedes the previous document and will be updated with new questions and answers as important issues arise or to amend existing questions and answers, as needed.

Other than statutory and regulatory requirements included in the document, the contents of this guidance do not have the force and effect of law and are not meant to bind the public. This document is intended only to provide clarity to the public regarding existing requirements under the law or agency policies. In addition, it does not create or confer any rights for or on any person.

The questions and answers in this document are not intended to be a replacement for careful study of the IDEA and its implementing regulations. The IDEA, its implementing regulations, and other important documents related to the IDEA and the regulations are found on the Department of Education's IDEA website.

If you are interested in commenting on this guidance, please e-mail your comments to OSERSguidancecomments@ed.gov and include NIMAS in the subject of your e-mail, or write us at the following address:

Larry Wexler
US Department of Education Potomac Center Plaza
550 12th Street SW, Room 5147
Washington, DC 20202

---

41. On May 26, 2020, the Department issued a final NOI to clarify that digital instructional materials that can conform to the NIMAS standard may be accepted by the NIMAC repository; such materials are included under the definition of "printed instructional materials" referenced in the IDEA 2004.
42. In 2018, Congress passed the MTIA, which amends section 121 of the Copyright Act. In the Further Consolidated Appropriations Act, 2020, Congress amended the 1931 Act to Provide Books for the Adult Blind to incorporate definitions found in the MTIA. As a result of changes made to these two laws, the Department provided clarification regarding eligibility criteria for receiving NIMAS-sourced materials and the types of formats that may be developed from NIMAS files.

Contents

Question 1: What is the definition of NIMAS?

Question 2: What is the definition of "accessible format"?

Question 3: What is the NIMAC, and what does it mean to coordinate with the NIMAC?

Question 4: Which students are eligible to receive accessible formats produced from NIMAS files from the NIMAC?

Question 5: May an accessible format produced from a NIMAS file for an eligible student also be used by other students who may benefit from its use?

Question 6: Who has responsibility for determining if particular students are eligible to receive accessible materials produced from NIMAS files obtained from the NIMAC?

Question 7: Can programs that serve 3- to 5-year-old children pursuant to section 619 of Part B of the IDEA use NIMAS-sourced accessible formats on behalf of eligible students?

Question 8: Are NIMAS files suitable for distribution directly to students for use in the classroom?

Question 9: For what types of instructional materials must NIMAS files be submitted to the NIMAC?

Question 10: Instructional materials such as textbooks are typically acquired through textbook purchasing offices at the SEA or LEA level. Are these offices required to comply with NIMAS requirements in their purchase of textbooks and other instructional materials?

Question 11: What is the turnaround time from the NIMAC to the students receiving accessible materials?

Question 12: What are the costs associated with converting NIMAS into the accessible format needed by the student?

Question 13: Does the NIMAC receive file sets for standardized assessments?

Question 14: Under what circumstances will foreign language textbooks be available in NIMAS and through the NIMAC?

Question 15: Can the NIMAC accept the files of books that are written for general use (i.e., trade books), such as novels, given that the IDEA only authorizes access to materials written and published primarily for use in elementary school and secondary school?

36 Chapter 2

Question 16: Do SEAs and LEAs have to request permission to use the image content in NIMAS files?

Question 17: If I am a publisher seeking resources to work with the NIMAC and produce NIMAS files, where can I find guidance?

Question 18: How can I locate information on how my state is working with NIMAC to serve students eligible to receive materials in accessible formats?

Question 1: What is the definition of NIMAS?

NIMAS is the National Instructional Materials Accessibility Standard (for further background on NIMAS, please see the introduction at the beginning of this Q&A). NIMAS is the standard, established by the secretary of education, in the preparation of electronic files suitable and used solely for efficient conversion into accessible formats.

Question 2: What is the definition of "accessible format"?

"Accessible format" means a copy of a work in an alternative manner or form that gives eligible students access to the work, including to permit the person to have access as feasibly and comfortably as a person without visual impairment or other print disability. The accessible format copy must respect the integrity of the original work, taking due consideration of the changes needed to make the work accessible in the alternative format and of the accessibility needs of the eligible student (17 U.S.C. § 121(d)(1)). Accessible formats produced from NIMAS may include Braille, large print, digital audio, and a range of accessible digital text formats.[43]

Question 3: What is the NIMAC, and what does it mean to coordinate with the NIMAC?

The NIMAC is the National Instructional Materials Access Center (for further background on the NIMAC, please see the introduction at the beginning of this Q&A). Coordinating with the NIMAC means that the SEA has signed a coordination agreement with the NIMAC, or an LEA has a coordination plan on file with its SEA. SEAs and LEAs agree to direct publishers to provide NIMAS files to the NIMAC as a part of their adoption contracts or purchase agreements when acquiring student instructional materials. SEAs also agree to designate authorized users who will have access to the NIMAC repository on behalf of students in their state. These authorized users can search the NIMAC repository and directly download the NIMAS files they need or assign these files within the system to registered accessible media producers, to convert into accessible formats for use by eligible students in elementary and secondary schools.

Question 4: Which students are eligible to receive accessible formats produced from NIMAS files from the NIMAC?

Under the copyright law, "'Eligible person means an individual who, regardless of any other disability—(A) is blind; (B) has a visual

---

43. "Accessible formats" recently replaced the term "specialized formats," which is the term currently used in the IDEA. The term "specialized formats" is defined in the IDEA at 20 U.S.C. § 1412(a)(23)(E)(iii) (and the IDEA's definition cross-references the Copyright Act). The IDEA Part B regulations at 34 C.F.R. § 300.172(e)(1)(iv) also incorporate this IDEA statutory definition. As a result of changes made to the Copyright Act, 17 U.S.C. § 121, the term "specialized formats" has also been removed from the IDEA and its regulations and replaced with the term "accessible format."

impairment or perceptual or reading disability that cannot be improved to give visual function substantially equivalent to that of a person who has no such impairment or disability and so is unable to read printed works to substantially the same degree as a person without an impairment or disability; or (C) is otherwise unable, through physical disability, to hold or manipulate a book or to focus or move the eyes to the extent that would be normally acceptable for reading" (17 U.S.C. § 121(d)(3)).[44]

Only eligible students in elementary schools and secondary schools, under section 674(e)(2) and (3) of the IDEA, may receive accessible formats produced from NIMAS files from the NIMAC. In addition to being eligible under copyright law, students must be identified as eligible and served under the IDEA in order to receive NIMAS-sourced accessible formats. Students whose parents elect for them not to have an individualized education program are not served under IDEA, and thus are not eligible to receive accessible formats produced from NIMAS files.

Question 5: May an accessible format produced from a NIMAS file for an eligible student also be used by other students who may benefit from its use?

No. SEAs and LEAs may not share accessible formats with students who are not eligible for NIMAS under the IDEA. SEAs are required to ensure that children with disabilities who need instructional materials in accessible formats but are not eligible to receive educational materials produced in accessible formats from NIMAS files obtained from the NIMAC receive those instructional materials in a timely manner (34 CFR § 300.172(a)). In order to comply with this requirement, SEAs and LEAs must obtain the materials from other sources.

If SEAs or LEAs provide students with accessible educational materials from other non-NIMAS sources, IDEA restrictions specific to NIMAC and NIMAS do not apply.

Question 6: Who has responsibility for determining if particular students are eligible to receive accessible materials produced from NIMAS files obtained from the NIMAC?

SEAs and LEAs are responsible for providing a free appropriate public education to all children with disabilities and for ensuring that children who need instructional materials in accessible formats are provided these materials in a timely manner; therefore, LEAs have the responsibility, including the assumption of any associated costs, to determine eligibility (34 CFR § 300.101, 300.172(b)(4), and 300.201; 20 U.S.C. §

---

44. The term "blind persons or other persons with print disabilities" has been removed from the Copyright Act and replaced with the term "eligible person." The IDEA defines the term "blind or other persons with print disabilities" in 20 U.S.C. § 1412(a)(23)(E)(i). The IDEA Part B regulation at 34 C.F.R. § 300.172(e)(1)(i) incorporates the IDEA statutory definition.

1412(a)(1)(A)).[45] The NIMAC itself is not involved in determining eligibility for individual students.

Question 7: Can programs that serve 3- to 5-year-old children pursuant to section 619 of Part B of the IDEA use NIMAS-sourced accessible formats on behalf of eligible students?

If a state includes 3- to 5-year-olds in preschool programs as part of its definition of elementary schools, then these students, if they are eligible persons under copyright law and are served under IDEA, can receive materials produced in accessible formats from NIMAS files received from the NIMAC. Likewise, if the SEA or LEA considers preschool to be included under elementary education, the SEA or LEA must include NIMAS language in its adoption contracts for instructional materials for preschool students, so that files will be available in the NIMAC for these materials for use in the production of accessible formats on behalf of these students.

Question 8: Are NIMAS files suitable for distribution directly to students for use in the classroom?

No, NIMAS file sets are source files and are designed to be converted into accessible formats by accessible media producers, using specialized software for this purpose, before distribution to students. NIMAS files are used in the production of a range of accessible formats, including Braille, large print, digital audio, and a variety of accessible digital text formats, including DAISY and EPUB. When an accessible format is provided for use by the student, it is important to ensure that the material is made available for use only by qualifying students.

Question 9: For what types of instructional materials must NIMAS files be submitted to the NIMAC?

The IDEA does not impose any blanket requirement for publishers to submit instructional materials to the NIMAC. SEAs and LEAs determine which materials will be submitted to the NIMAC by including language requiring NIMAS in their adoption contracts and purchase agreements when acquiring new instructional materials, including when acquiring materials for preschool students where the SEA or LEA considers preschool students to be included under elementary education (see question 7).

---

45. The Library of Congress's updated regulations for certifying eligible students state that eligibility must be certified by one of the following: doctor of medicine, doctor of osteopathy, ophthalmologist, optometrist, psychologist, registered nurse, therapist, and professional staff of hospitals, institutions, and public or welfare agencies (such as an educator, a social worker, case worker, counselor, rehabilitation teacher, certified reading specialist, school psychologist, superintendent, or librarian). For the purposes of distributing materials produced from NIMAS files, LEAs and accessible media producers develop processes to ensure that these materials are only distributed to eligible students. See "Loans of Library Materials for Blind and Other Print-Disabled Persons," *Federal Register*, February 8, 2021, https://www.federalregister.gov/documents/2021/02/12/2021-02837/loans-of-library-materials-for-blind-and-other-print-disabled-persons.

The IDEA defines materials appropriate for the NIMAC as "printed textbooks and related printed core materials that are written and published primarily for use in elementary school and secondary school instruction and are required by a state educational agency or local educational agency for use by students in the classroom."

The NOI clarified this definition to include digital instructional materials when those materials can be provided to the NIMAC in valid NIMAS format.[46]

Question 10: Instructional materials such as textbooks are typically acquired through textbook purchasing offices at the SEA or LEA level. Are these offices required to comply with NIMAS requirements in their purchase of textbooks and other instructional materials?

Yes. If an SEA chooses to coordinate with the NIMAC, the SEA must, as part of any instructional materials adoption process, procurement contract, or other practice or instrument used for purchase of student instructional materials, enter into a written contract[47] with the publisher of the instructional materials to (1) require the publisher to prepare and, on or before delivery of the instructional materials, provide to the NIMAC electronic files containing the contents of the instructional materials using the NIMAS; or (2) purchase instructional materials from the publisher that are produced in or may be rendered in accessible formats (see 34 C.F.R. §§ 300.172(c) and 300.210(a)). The SEA must ensure that all public agencies take all reasonable steps to provide instructional materials in accessible formats to children with disabilities who need those instructional materials at the same time as other children who receive instructional materials (34 C.F.R. § 300.172(b)(4)). Therefore, SEAs should inform all relevant offices and parties within the state, including LEAs, of their obligation to meet the requirements for access to instructional materials. For example, SEAs and LEAs should communicate these requirements to textbook adoption committees, as well as procurement and contracting offices. When an SEA or LEA considers preschool students to be included under elementary education, relevant offices and parties should be aware of the need for NIMAS requirements in the procurement of instructional materials for preschool students (see question 7).

---

46. The NOI states that "given the purpose of NIMAC, the trend toward digital instructional materials and resources, and the silence of the statute on the acceptance of digital files, the Department interprets the phrase 'printed textbooks and related printed core materials' referred to in the definition of 'print instructional materials' in section 674(e)(3)(C) of the IDEA (20 U.S.C. § 1474(e)(3)(C)) to include digital instructional materials that comply with NIMAS, because that is the primary medium through which many textbooks and core materials are now produced. The Department considers digital materials submitted to NIMAC to be in digital print format, which falls under the larger category of 'print' and is consistent with the statutory language of section 674(e)(3)(C) of the IDEA (20 U.S.C. § 1474(e)(3)(C))." Given this interpretation, the term "print instructional materials" will now include digital instructional materials that conform to the NIMAS format.
47. The AEM Center provides sample language for use in written contracts with publishers.

Question 11: What is the turnaround time from the NIMAC to the students receiving accessible materials?

After the NIMAC receives NIMAS file sets from the publisher, the file sets undergo a metadata and quality review process before acceptance into the repository. If the publisher does not need to make any corrections before the NIMAC can accept the files, they typically will be available almost immediately for accessible media producers (AMPs) to download and convert into accessible formats. The time between the downloading of a file from the NIMAC to the delivery of accessibly formatted material to a student depends on the type of accessible format being produced and the timeline of the AMPs.

Question 12: What are the costs associated with converting NIMAS into the accessible format needed by the student?

There is no cost to use the NIMAC or to obtain files through the NIMAC; however, the cost to the SEA or LEA for having an accessible format produced will vary depending on the required format and the organization producing the format. Some NIMAS-sourced accessible formats are available at no cost to the SEA or LEA, while production of other formats or by other organizations may involve a cost.[48]

Question 13: Does the NIMAC receive file sets for standardized assessments?

No. Standardized assessments do not fall within the definition of print instructional materials as that term is defined in section 674(e)(3)(C) of the IDEA. Ensuring that accessible formats are provided for standardized assessments must be achieved through other means.

Question 14: Under what circumstances will foreign language textbooks be available in NIMAS and through the NIMAC?

The IDEA specifies that NIMAS applies to "print instructional materials," which is defined in section 674(e)(3)(C) of the IDEA as printed textbooks and related printed core materials that are written and published primarily for use in elementary school and secondary school instruction and are required by an SEA or LEA for use by students in the classroom. Thus, all foreign language textbooks that fall within the definition of "print instructional materials" are subject to the NIMAS. This applies both to textbooks for foreign language classes and textbooks translated into a foreign language for use by students with limited English proficiency.

Question 15: Can the NIMAC accept the files of books that are written for general use (i.e., trade books), such as novels, given that the IDEA only authorizes access to materials written and published primarily for use in elementary school and secondary school?

---

48. Costs incurred to acquire or produce accessible materials necessary to provide students with free and appropriate public education are allowable expenditures of IDEA Part B funds (34 CFR § 300.704(b)(4)(x)).

Yes. Consistent with the IDEA, the NIMAC may accept trade book files from publishers, when they are bundled by the publisher as a supplement alongside other instructional materials for use in the classroom, as required by the SEA- or LEA-approved curriculum. This means that publishers must provide a textbook or supplementary guide that identifies how each trade book in the bundle is tied into the curriculum required by an SEA or LEA for use by students in the classroom. This must be done by substantially linking each trade book to analysis, questions, study guides, or other curriculum materials contained in the textbook or supplementary guide.

Question 16: Do SEAs and LEAs have to request permission to use the image content in NIMAS files?

No. NIMAS file sets include some specifications for graphics. Separate permissions are not necessary if the publisher submits NIMAS files to the NIMAC for eligible students. These uses are authorized under section 674(e) of the IDEA, which is consistent with the Chafee Amendment to the Copyright Act (17 U.S.C. § 121).[49]

Question 17: If I am a publisher seeking resources to work with the NIMAC and produce NIMAS files, where can I find guidance?

Resources for publishers and conversion vendors can be found on the NIMAC website (https://www.nimac.us/publishers-conversion-houses/) and also on the National Accessible Educational Materials (AEM) Center website (https://aem.cast.org/get-started/by-role#publisher). NIMAS exemplars can be found at https://aem.cast.org/nimas-nimac/nimas-exemplars; and additional resources can be found at https://aem.cast.org/get-started/resources/2020/creating-nimas-files.

Question 18: How can I locate information on how my state is working with NIMAC to serve students eligible to receive materials in accessible formats?

For information on how your state is working with the NIMAC, the best contact will be your NIMAC state coordinator. Contact information for all NIMAC state coordinators, as well as for additional key staff involved in state AEM systems, can be found on the National AEM Center website: https://aem.cast.org/nimas-nimac/nimac-state-coordinators. The NIMAC will assist schools or teachers in locating accessible formats needed by eligible students or will contact NIMAC authorized users or other providers in their state. Please reach out at 1-877-526-4622 or nimac@aph.org.

---

49. Portions of mathematics, science, geography, and other textbooks that do not use literary Braille are often not fully accessible using NIMAS alone. To the extent that the NIMAS files do not cover the graphs, pictures, and other visual elements in the textbooks, AMPs may have to use alternative measures to produce a completely accessible version of a textbook. This responsibility should be addressed in the agreement between the SEA or LEA and the AMP.

2.2.5

UNITED STATES DEPARTMENT OF EDUCATION
OFFICE OF SPECIAL EDUCATION AND REHABILITATIVE SERVICES
THE ASSISTANT SECRETARY
RETURN TO SCHOOL ROADMAP UNDER THE IDEA

September 24, 2021

RE: Docket Number ED-2021-OSERS-0117

Dear Mr. Daniel Frumkin,

Thank you for contacting the US Department of Education (herein referred to as the Department). This letter is in response to your petition for rulemaking dated July 26, 2021, in which you request that the Department amend the Individuals with Disabilities Education Act (IDEA) regulations at 34 C.F.R. § 300.323(d)(2) to establish a timeline for providing access to a child's individualized education program (IEP) to teachers and service providers. Your petition was forwarded to the Department's Office of Special Education and Rehabilitative Services (OSERS). In accordance with 5 U.S.C. § 555(e), OSERS has carefully considered the information in your petition and respectfully denies your request for rulemaking on this matter for the reasons detailed below.

You petitioned the Department to revise the regulation in 34 C.F.R. § 300.323(d)(2) to include the **bold and underlined** language below:

(d) Accessibility of child's IEP to teachers and others. Each public agency must ensure that—
   (1) **Before the beginning of each school year,** each teacher and provider described in paragraph (d)(1) of this section is informed of—
      (i) His or her specific responsibilities related to implementing the child's IEP; and
      (ii) The specific accommodations, modifications, and supports that must be provided for the child in accordance with the IEP.

You state that this change will "remove ambiguity regarding when teachers and providers must be notified of IEP responsibilities, accommodations, modifications, and supports in accordance with the IEP before the first day of school."

OSERS declines to amend the regulation as requested for several reasons. The IDEA statute and regulations are clear that every child's IEP must be in effect at the beginning of each school year (IDEA section 614(d)(2)(A) and 34 C.F.R. § 300.323(a)). The statute and regulations also make clear that an IEP team meeting may be convened at any time throughout the year, as warranted, pursuant to IDEA section 614(d)(4)(A) and 34 C.F.R. § 300.324(b), or by using the amendment process provided under IDEA section 614(d)(3)(D) and 34 C.F.R. § 300.324(a)(4).[50] This could occur before or after the school year begins. After the development of, or revisions to, the IEP, the public agency must provide access to the IEP to the teachers and providers who are responsible for implementing the IEP as set forth at 34 C.F.R. § 300.323(d). For example, if an IEP is revised in December, teachers and service providers, including those responsible for IEP implementation during the remainder of the school year, must be made aware of changes to that child's IEP within a reasonable amount of time. In such instances, it would be unreasonable and inconsistent with the purposes of IDEA to delay taking those steps until "before the beginning" of the following school year. As discussed below, IDEA provides sufficient protections and flexibility to account for the variety of time frames during which an IEP may be developed or updated.

There is an inherent expectation that before a child's IEP that is "in effect" can be implemented, all those responsible for implementing any part of it will be aware of the IEP content and their specific responsibilities related to implementing the IEP, including the provision of any specific accommodations, modifications, and supports, prior to the required implementation date. When an explicit timeline is not specified in the IDEA or its implementing regulations, the Department interprets that the requirement will be met within a reasonable period of time. The Department has not defined "a reasonable period of time" but has explained with respect to implementation of services in a child's IEP that "with very limited exceptions, IEPs for most children with disabilities should be implemented without undue delay following the IEP meetings" and that "[t]here may be exceptions in certain situations. It may be appropriate to have a short delay (e.g., (1) when the IEP meetings occur at the end of the school year or during the summer, and the IEP team determines that the child does not need special education and related services until the next school year begins); or (2) when there are circumstances that require a short delay

---

50. Although the public agency is responsible for determining when to conduct an IEP team meeting, the parents of a child with a disability have the right to request an IEP meeting at any time. For example, if the parents believe that the child is not progressing satisfactorily, the parents, as a member of the IEP team, can request an IEP team meeting at any time during the year. See appendix A to the 1999 final IDEA Part B regulations, 64 Fed. Reg. 12406, 12476 (March 12, 1999).

in the provision of services (e.g., finding a qualified service provider, or making transportation arrangements for the child)." The Department has further noted that a pattern of practice within a given state of not making services available within a reasonable period of time (e.g., within a week or two following IEP meetings) could raise a question as to whether the state is in compliance, unless one of these exceptions applies. See 64 Fed. Reg. at 12579.

Finally, IDEA and the IDEA Part B regulations provide for the basic floor of protections, but certain aspects of implementation are better addressed by state and local education authorities. We believe that there is nothing in IDEA that would prevent a state from establishing a reasonable timeline in its rules implementing this IDEA requirement.

Accordingly, OSERS concludes that it would not be appropriate for the Department to undertake such rulemaking on this specific matter as you have requested.

We regret to read that your son experienced delays in receiving the services required by his IEP. As we previously advised in a July 13, 2021, e-mail, under IDEA, a parent can pursue several dispute resolution options, if they disagree with a school's actions. A parent has a right to request mediation to resolve disputes using the IDEA's mediation process under 34 C.F.R. § 300.506.

Also, a parent has the right to file a state complaint or a due process complaint to request a due process hearing (34 C.F.R. §§ 300.151 through 300.153 and 300.507). For more information about how these procedures are implemented in the State of Maryland, or to file a state complaint, you may contact the Maryland State Department of Education (MSDE), Division of Early Intervention and Special Education Services. Contact information for MSDE is provided below for your convenience:

Marcella E. Franczkowski, M.S. Assistant State Superintendent
Division of Early Intervention and Special Education Services
200 W. Baltimore St.
Baltimore, Maryland 21201
Phone: 410-767-0238
E-mail: marcella.franczkowski@maryland.gov

You may also wish to visit MSDE's Family Support and Dispute Resolution Branch's web page (https://marylandpublicschools.org/programs/Pages/Special-Education/FSDR/index.aspx), which includes web links to the state's model forms for state complaints and requests for mediation and/or due process.

Please note that Section 607(d) of the IDEA prohibits the secretary of the Department from issuing policy letters or other statements that establish a rule that is required for compliance with, and eligibility under, IDEA without following the rulemaking requirements of Section 553 of the Administrative Procedure Act. Therefore, based on the requirements of IDEA Section 607(e), this response is provided as informal guidance and is not legally binding. It represents an interpretation by the Department of the requirements of IDEA in the context of the specific facts presented and does not establish a policy or rule that would apply in all circumstances.

Thank you for your petition. We share your dedication to the education of children with disabilities and appreciate your communication with the Department.

Sincerely, /s/

Katherine Neas
Acting Assistant Secretary

2.2.6

UNITED STATES DEPARTMENT OF EDUCATION

OFFICE OF SPECIAL EDUCATION AND REHABILITATIVE SERVICES

OSEP QA 21-06

RETURN TO SCHOOL ROADMAP: DEVELOPMENT AND IMPLEMENTATION OF INDIVIDUALIZED EDUCATION PROGRAMS IN THE LEAST RESTRICTIVE ENVIRONMENT UNDER THE INDIVIDUALS WITH DISABILITIES EDUCATION ACT

September 30, 2021

The Office of Special Education and Rehabilitative Services (OSERS) in the US Department of Education (herein referred to as the Department) has received requests from a diverse group of stakeholders asking that the Department issue new guidance interpreting requirements of the Individuals with Disabilities Education Act (IDEA) in light of the many challenges of the COVID-19 pandemic and as more schools and programs are returning to in-person services. Topics include meeting timelines, ensuring implementation of initial evaluation and reevaluation procedures, determining eligibility for special education and related services, and providing the full array of special education and related services that children with disabilities need in order to receive a free appropriate public education (FAPE).[51] In addition, stakeholders have inquired about the implications of delayed evaluations and early intervention services to infants and toddlers with disabilities and their families served under IDEA Part C.[52] The purpose of

---

51. Free appropriate public education (or FAPE) means special education and related services that (1) are provided at public expense, under public supervision, and without charge; (2) meet the standards of the state educational agency (SEA), including the requirements of IDEA; (3) include an appropriate preschool, elementary school, or secondary school education in the state involved; and (4) are provided in conformity with an individualized education program that meets the requirements of 34 C.F.R. §§ 300.320 through 300.324. 34 C.F.R. § 300.17.
52. Additional guidance, including requirements of Part C of IDEA, will be forthcoming.

the Return to School Roadmap IDEA guidance documents,[53] which focus on school reopening efforts, is to support the full implementation of IDEA requirements. The documents also serve to clarify that, regardless of the COVID-19 pandemic, or the mode of instruction, children with disabilities are entitled to FAPE, and infants and toddlers with disabilities and their families to appropriate IDEA Part C services.

The Department recognizes that some parents may have specific health and safety concerns about sending their children back to in-person instruction because of the health risk to the student, the student's immediate family, and to other household members—even as parents are also concerned about their child missing the instructional and social and emotional opportunities that come with in-person learning.[54] Therefore, reopening schools safely is of utmost importance. State educational agencies (SEAs) and local educational agencies (LEAs)[55] should put in place layered prevention strategies, including promoting vaccination and universal and correct mask wearing in schools. The Centers for Disease Control and Prevention (CDC) recommends that everyone in K through 12 schools wear a mask indoors, including teachers, staff, students, and visitors, regardless of vaccination status.[56]

---

53. Other than statutory and regulatory requirements included in this Q&A document, the contents of this guidance do not have the force and effect of law and are not meant to bind the public. This document is intended only to provide clarity to the public regarding existing requirements under the law or agency policies. The questions and answers in this document are not intended to be a replacement for careful study of IDEA and its implementing regulations. The IDEA, its implementing regulations, and other important documents related to IDEA and the regulations are found at https://sites.ed.gov/idea/.
54. ED COVID-19 Handbook Volume 1: Strategies for Safely Reopening Elementary and Secondary Schools.
55. To increase readability, the Department has used the term "LEA" in place of "public agency." "Public agency" is defined in 34 C.F.R. § 300.33 to include the SEA, LEAs, educational services agencies (ESAs), nonprofit public charter schools that are not otherwise included as LEAs or ESAs and are not a school of an LEA or ESA, and any other political subdivisions of the state that are responsible for providing education to children with disabilities.
56. To increase readability, the Department has used the term "LEA" in place of "public agency." Public agency is defined in 34 C.F.R. § 300.33 to include the SEA, LEAs, educational services agencies (ESAs), nonprofit public charter schools that are not otherwise included as LEAs or ESAs and are not a school of an LEA or ESA, and any other political subdivisions of the state that are responsible for providing education to children with disabilities.

Contents

Introduction

A. Ensuring IEPs Are in Effect at the Start of the School Year
B. Convening the IEP Team
C. Consideration of Special Factors
    a. Considering the Assistive Technology Needs of a Child with a Disability
    b. Addressing the Social, Emotional, Behavioral, and Mental Health Needs of Children with Disabilities
    c. Addressing the School-Related Health Needs of Children with Disabilities with Underlying Medical Conditions
D. Determining Appropriate Measurable Annual Goals and Considering the Child's Need for Compensatory Services
E. Making Extended School Year (ESY) Services Determinations
F. Considering Secondary Transition Services
G. Making Educational Placement Decisions
H. Resolving Disagreements Regarding a Child's Educational Program

Introduction

The Department is committed to ensuring that children with disabilities receive the services and supports they are entitled to under IDEA so that they have successful educational experiences. For more than a year, educators across the country have provided services and supports to children with disabilities in ways never anticipated prior to the COVID-19 pandemic. The Department recognizes that SEAs and LEAs have worked hard to meet children's needs and provide required services, given the unprecedented educational disruptions and other challenges resulting from the pandemic.[57] Even with these efforts, some children with disabilities were unable to receive appropriate services to address their needs so that they could make progress toward achieving the functional and academic goals included in their individualized education programs (IEPs).

Therefore, the Department repeats and emphasizes that, notwithstanding the challenges associated with the COVID-19 pandemic, families and children retained their rights to receive appropriate services under IDEA (34 C.F.R. § 300.101). In this document, the Department highlights certain IDEA requirements related to the development and implementation of IEPs and other information that SEAs, LEAs, regular and special education teachers, related services providers, and parents should consider.

Parents who would like to request additional support in understanding IDEA's requirements may wish to contact their local regional parent training and information centers (PTIs) for direct assistance and referrals to other organizations and to gain skills to effectively participate in the education and development of their children. There are more than 100 PTIs and community parent resource centers in the United States and Territories that provide training, resources, and support on a wide variety of topics. Parents can locate the appropriate PTI for their area at https://www.parentcenterhub.org/find-your-center/.[58]

Although it is beyond the scope of this document, recipients of federal financial assistance from the Department (e.g., public agencies receiving IDEA funding) are reminded of their obligation to comply with

---

57. States have reported that these difficulties include challenges with providing the equipment and technology, including Wi-Fi access, needed for children to participate in virtual learning; having adequate personnel to provide early intervention, special education, and related services due to COVID-related illness and employees' concerns for their safety and the safety of their families; and taking the necessary health and safety precautions required for public facilities to reopen.
58. This document contains examples of resources that are provided for the user's convenience. The inclusion of these resources is not intended to reflect their importance, nor is it intended to endorse any views expressed, or products or services offered, by these entities. These resources may include materials that contain the views and recommendations of various subject-matter experts as well as hypertext links, contact addresses, and websites to information created and maintained by other public and private organizations. The opinions expressed in any of these materials do not necessarily reflect the positions or policies of the Department. The Department does not control or guarantee the accuracy, relevance, timeliness, or completeness of any outside information included in the materials that may be provided by these resources.

Section 504,⁵⁹ which prohibits discrimination on the basis of disability.⁶⁰ For example, in providing any aid, benefit, or service, a recipient may not, directly or through contractual, licensing, or other arrangements, deny a student with a disability an equal opportunity to participate in or benefit from the aid, benefit, or service (34 C.F.R. § 104.4(b)(1)). This is especially relevant where states or school districts, as a result of the pandemic, make available to all students additional educational programming or services, and choices for instructional delivery or program participation.

A. Ensuring IEPS Are in Effect at the Start of the School Year

The cornerstone of IDEA is the entitlement of each eligible child with a disability to FAPE that emphasizes special education and related services designed to meet the child's unique needs and that prepares the child for further education, employment, and independent living. Under IDEA, the vehicle for providing FAPE is through an appropriately developed IEP based on the individual needs of the child. An IEP must include a child's present levels of academic achievement and functional performance, and the impact of a child's disability on their involvement and progress in the general education curriculum. IEP goals must be aligned with grade-level content standards for all children with disabilities.⁶¹ The child's IEP must be developed, reviewed, and revised in accordance with the requirements outlined in IDEA in 34 C.F.R. §§ 300.320 through 300.328.

No matter what primary instructional delivery approach⁶² is used, SEAs and LEAs remain responsible for ensuring that FAPE is available to all children with disabilities. Therefore, before, during, and after the COVID-19 pandemic, the LEA must ensure that each child with a disability has access to educational opportunities, including all special education and related services, necessary to receive FAPE.

---

59. Children with disabilities also have rights under two civil rights laws that prohibit discrimination on the basis of disability—Section 504 of the Rehabilitation Act of 1973, 29 U.S.C. § 794; 34 C.F.R. Part 104 (Section 504) and Title II of the Americans with Disabilities Act 42 U.S.C. §§ 12131–12134; 28 C.F.R. Part 35 (Title II). Section 504 prohibits disability discrimination by recipients of federal financial assistance, such as SEAs and LEAs. Title II prohibits discrimination by public entities, including SEAs and LEAs, regardless of receipt of federal financial assistance. The Office for Civil Rights (OCR) in the US Department of Education enforces Section 504 in public elementary and secondary schools. Also, in this context, OCR shares in the enforcement of Title II with the US Department of Justice (DOJ). The DOJ is responsible for interpreting and providing technical assistance about the requirements of Title II. More information about these laws is available at: www.ed.gov/ocr and www.ada.gov.
60. See "Questions and Answers on Civil Rights and School Reopening in the COVID-19 Environment," US Department of Education, Office for Civil Rights, May 13, 2021, https://www2.ed.gov/about/offices/list/ocr/docs/qa-reopening-202105.pdf.
61. States are permitted to define alternate academic achievement standards for children with the most significant cognitive disabilities, provided those standards are aligned with the state's academic content standards, promote access to the general curriculum, and reflect professional judgment of the highest achievement standards possible, in accordance with 34 C.F.R. § 200.1(d) (34 C.F.R. § 300.160(c)(2)(i)).
62. As used in this document, "service delivery approach," "instructional delivery approach," and "instructional methodology" include the provision of services to a child with a disability in person, virtually, or a hybrid of in-person and virtual instruction.

Question A-1: Must an LEA ensure each child with a disability has an IEP in effect at the start of each school year?

Answer: Yes. Under 34 C.F.R. § 300.323(a), at the beginning of each school year, each LEA must have an IEP in effect for each child with a disability within its jurisdiction. To ensure that an appropriate IEP is in place, the LEA may need to convene a meeting of the child's IEP team prior to the start of the school year to determine whether any revisions to the IEP are needed (34 C.F.R. § 300.324(b)(1)). A parent may request, and an LEA may propose to conduct, IEP team meetings at any time during the year. For example, if the LEA conducts the IEP team meeting prior to the beginning of a school year, it must ensure that the child's IEP contains the necessary special education and related services and supplementary aids and services to ensure that the IEP can be appropriately implemented once the school year begins.

Question A-2: Are LEAs required to convene an IEP team meeting prior to the beginning of the school year to review the IEP of every child with a disability in its jurisdiction?

Answer: Generally, no. Under 34 C.F.R. § 300.324(b), each LEA must ensure that the IEP team reviews the child's IEP periodically, but not less than annually, to determine whether the annual goals for the child are being achieved; and revises the IEP, as appropriate, to address any lack of expected progress toward the annual goals and in the general education curriculum, if appropriate; the results of any reevaluation; information about the child provided to, or by the parents; the child's anticipated needs; or other matters. Therefore, if the child's IEP has been reviewed at least annually and neither the LEA nor the parent believes it is necessary to review those decisions prior to the start of the school year, the LEA would not need to convene another IEP team meeting prior to the start of the school year.

It will be important, however, for LEAs and parents to consider whether there are circumstances, such as an IEP that was developed that includes special education and related services to be delivered solely through virtual instruction, that cannot be modified to reflect in-person services for the upcoming school year. In these circumstances, the IEP team would need to convene as soon as possible to determine what revisions to the child's IEP are necessary to ensure FAPE.[63]

Question A-3: When reviewing and revising a child's IEP, can the IEP team also discuss how special education and related services could be provided if circumstances require a change in the service delivery approach, such as from in-person instruction to virtual learning or hybrid instruction?

---

63. Implementation of IDEA Part B Provision of Services in the Current COVID-19 Environment (September 28, 2020).

Answer: Yes. To help ensure the continued provision of FAPE, IEP teams can identify how the special education and related services included in a child's IEP can be provided if circumstances require a change from in-person learning. A proactive method that an IEP team may implement as a strategy for preparedness in the event of future long-term school closures is developing a contingency plan.[64] As part of a child's annual IEP team meeting, developing a contingency plan would address the provision of service delivery to account for virtual learning or hybrid instruction. It would also include a description of a child's specific services, frequency, type, and duration. Developing a contingency plan before circumstances require a change in the service-delivery approach also gives the child's service providers and the child's parents an opportunity to reach agreement as to what circumstances would trigger the use of the child's contingency plan and the contingency services that would be provided. As schools navigate virtual learning, a hybrid service delivery approach, or full reopening for in-person learning, they should prioritize equity, exercise flexibility, think creatively, collaborate with parents to respond to children's emerging needs, and must comply with applicable civil rights laws.[65] See also Q1 in Implementation of IDEA Part B Provision of Services in the Current COVID-19 Environment (September 28, 2020).

Question A-4: How can LEAs ensure that children who have moved between jurisdictions in the same state during the school year continue to receive FAPE?

Answer: If a child with a disability who had an IEP in effect transfers to a new LEA in the same state and enrolls in a new school within the new LEA in the same school year, the new LEA, in consultation with the parents, must provide FAPE to the child. This includes providing services comparable to those described in the child's IEP from the previous LEA, until the new LEA either (1) adopts the child's IEP from the previous LEA; or (2) develops, adopts, and implements a new IEP that meets the applicable requirements in 34 C.F.R. §§ 300.320 through 300.324. Thus, the new LEA must provide FAPE to the child with a disability when the child enrolls in the new LEA's school within the same school year and may not deny special education and related services to the child.

The new LEA in which the child enrolls must take reasonable steps to promptly obtain the child's records, including the IEP and supporting documents and any other records relating to the provision of special education or related services to the child, from the previous LEA in which the child was enrolled, pursuant to 34 C.F.R. § 99.31(a)(2); and the previous LEA in which the child was enrolled must take reasonable steps to promptly respond to the request from the new LEA (34 C.F.R. § 300.323(g)).

---

64. See also Question A-4 in Questions and Answers on Providing Services to Children with Disabilities During an H1N1 Outbreak (December 2009).
65. See the discussion on pages 3–4, including footnote 9, about Section 504 and Title II.

Question A-5: What is the LEA's obligation if a child with a disability moves into its jurisdiction from an LEA that is located outside of the state within the same school year?

Answer: In this circumstance, the new LEA (in consultation with the parents) must provide the child with FAPE (including services comparable to those described in the child's IEP from the previous LEA) until the new LEA (1) conducts an evaluation pursuant to 34 C.F.R. §§ 300.304 through 300.306 (if determined to be necessary by the new LEA); and (2) develops, adopts, and implements a new IEP, if appropriate, that meets the applicable requirements in 34 C.F.R. §§ 300.320 through 300.324. Thus, the new LEA must provide FAPE to the child with a disability when the child enrolls in the new LEA's school in the new state within the same school year and may not deny special education and related services to the child pending the development of a new IEP.

The new LEA in which the child enrolls must take reasonable steps to promptly obtain the child's records, including the IEP and supporting documents and any other records relating to the provision of special education or related services to the child, from the previous LEA in which the child was enrolled, pursuant to 34 C.F.R. § 99.31(a)(2); and the previous LEA in which the child was enrolled must take reasonable steps to promptly respond to the request from the LEA (34 C.F.R. § 300.323(g)). See also Question A-2, Questions and Answers on Individualized Education Programs (IEPs), Evaluations, and Reevaluations (September 2011).

Question A-6: What is the LEA's obligation if a child with a disability moves into its jurisdiction from another LEA between school years (i.e., during the summer break)?

Answer: IDEA and its implementing regulations require that, at the beginning of each school year, each LEA must have an IEP in effect for each child with a disability (34 C.F.R. § 300.323). Therefore, LEAs must ensure that an IEP is in effect at the beginning of the school year for children with disabilities who move into, and enroll in, a new LEA during the summer. How an LEA meets this requirement is a matter to be decided by each individual new LEA. The new LEA could decide to adopt and implement the IEP developed for the child by the previous LEA, unless the new LEA decides that an evaluation is needed.

Otherwise, the newly designated IEP team for the child in the new LEA could develop, adopt, and implement a new IEP for the child that meets the applicable requirements in 34 C.F.R. §§ 300.320 through 300.324. "Analysis of Comments and Changes" accompanying the final 2006 IDEA Part B regulations, 71 Fed. Reg. 46540, 46682 (August 14, 2006).

If the parent requests that the new LEA convene the IEP team prior to the start of the school year and the LEA refuses to do so, the LEA must provide written notice to the parent of the refusal. The prior written notice must include, among other content, an explanation of why the LEA determined that conducting the meeting prior to the beginning of the school year is not necessary to ensure the provision of appropriate services to the child (34 C.F.R. § 300.503). See also "Analysis of Comments and Changes" accompanying the final 1999 IDEA Part B regulations. 64 Fed. Reg. 12406, 12476-12477 (March 12, 1999).

B. Convening the IEP Team

IEP teams[66] are required to meet periodically, but at least annually, to review and revise, as appropriate, a child's IEP, and address the results of any reevaluation or any other data that describes the child's needs. The Department understands that, during the COVID-19 pandemic, it is often difficult for IEP teams to find effective ways to meet and obtain the information necessary to develop IEPs that fully addressed the unique needs of each child with a disability. Although in-person attendance at IEP team meetings may be preferable, IDEA provides flexibility for participation using alternate methods, as well as permitting some members of the IEP team to be excused under certain circumstances. Further, a parent and the LEA may agree to amend a child's IEP without convening the full IEP team, but not as a substitute for the annual review.

Question B-1: Does IDEA require a child's IEP team to meet more than one time each year?

Answer: It will depend on the child-specific circumstances and whether the parent and LEA agree to change the IEP without a meeting. Under 34 C.F.R. § 300.324(a)(5), to the extent possible, the LEA must encourage the consolidation of reevaluation meetings and other IEP team meetings for the child. This, however, should not be read to discourage an IEP team from reconvening, if appropriate. An LEA must initiate and conduct meetings periodically, but at least once every 12 months, to review a child's IEP, in order to determine whether the annual goals for the child are being achieved, and to revise the IEP, as appropriate.[67] Although the LEA is responsible for determining when it is necessary to conduct an IEP team meeting, the parents of a child with a disability have the right to request an IEP team meeting at any time. If the LEA refuses the parent's request to reconvene the IEP team, it must provide written notice to the parents of the refusal, including an explanation of why the LEA has determined that conducting the meeting is not necessary to ensure the provision of FAPE to the child (34 C.F.R. § 300.503). If a child's teacher feels that the child's IEP or educational placement is not appropriate for the child, the teacher should follow the LEA's procedures with respect to (1) calling or meeting

---

66. The requirements for participants at IEP team meetings are found in 34 C.F.R. § 300.321.
67. In accordance with 34 C.F.R. § 300.324(b), the IEP team must meet periodically to review and revise the child's IEP, as appropriate, to address any lack of expected progress toward the annual goals described in § 300.320(a)(2), and in the general education curriculum, if appropriate; the results of any reevaluation conducted under § 300.303; information about the child provided to, or by, the parents; the child's anticipated needs; or other matters.

with the parents; or (2) requesting that the LEA hold another IEP team meeting to review the child's IEP.

IDEA also allows the parent of a child with a disability and the LEA to agree *not* to convene an IEP team meeting for the purpose of making changes to the IEP after the annual IEP team meeting for a school year, and instead develop a written document to amend or modify the child's current IEP (34 C.F.R. § 300.324(a)(4)). It is important to note that an amendment to an IEP *cannot* take the place of an annual IEP team meeting. For more information about the IEP amendment process, see Q3 of Implementation of IDEA Part B Provision of Services in the Current COVID-19 Environment (September 28, 2020), and Questions C-8 through C-10 in Questions and Answers on Individualized Education Programs (IEPs), Evaluations, and Reevaluations (September 2011).

Question B-2: Are all IEP team members required to attend all IEP team meetings in their entirety?

Answer: No. The IEP team members referenced in 34 C.F.R. § 300.321(a) are generally required to participate in meetings to develop, review, and revise a child's IEP. The IEP team includes, among other participants, the parents of the child; not less than one regular education teacher of the child (if the child is, or may be, participating in the regular education environment); and not less than one special education teacher of the child or, where appropriate, not less than one special education provider of the child. Under 34 C.F.R. § 300.321(e), however, it is permissible for certain members to be excused from attending the IEP team meeting, in whole or in part, if the parent of a child with a disability and the LEA agrees, in writing, that the attendance of the member is not necessary because the member's area of the curriculum or related services is not being modified or discussed in the meeting. If the IEP team meeting involves a modification to or discussion of the member's area of the curriculum or related services, the member may be excused from attending an IEP team meeting, in whole or in part, if the parent, in writing, and the LEA consent to the excusal; and the member submits, in writing to the parent and the IEP team, input into the development of the IEP prior to the meeting. There is nothing in IDEA or its implementing regulations that would limit the number of IEP team members who may be excused from attending an IEP team meeting, so long as the LEA meets the requirements of 34 C.F.R. § 300.321(e) that govern when IEP team members can be excused from attending IEP team meetings in whole or in part. See "Analysis of Comments and Changes" accompanying the final IDEA Part B regulations. 71 Fed. Reg. 46650, 46675 (August 14, 2006).

For more information about the excusal of IEP team members from IEP team meetings, see Q2 of Implementation of IDEA Part B Provision of Services in the Current COVID-19 Environment (September 28, 2020), and questions C-1 through C-5 in Questions and Answers on Individualized Education Programs, Evaluations, and Reevaluations (September 2011).

Question B-3: May LEAs continue to hold IEP team meetings virtually after school buildings reopen for in-person instruction, or must these meetings be conducted face to face?

Answer: LEAs may continue to hold IEP team meetings virtually after school buildings reopen if the parent agrees to a virtual meeting or if continued COVID-19 prevention practices necessitate it. Parents and schools are encouraged to work collaboratively, to find solutions to meeting IEP team requirements. LEAs must take steps to ensure that one or both parents attend, or are afforded the opportunity to participate in, an IEP team meeting by notifying them of the meeting early enough to ensure that they can attend and by scheduling the meeting at a mutually agreed upon time and place. Moreover, the parents and the LEA can agree to participate in IEP team meetings through alternate means such as telephone conference calls or video conferences for any reason (34 C.F.R. § 300.328). Therefore, LEAs may continue to convene IEP team meetings virtually, as appropriate.

Question B-4: Is it permissible for the LEA to hold an IEP team meeting without the child's parent?

Answer: In most cases, no. IDEA and its implementing regulations require that IEP team meetings be scheduled at a mutually agreed on time and place (34 C.F.R. § 300.322(a)(2)). IDEA does not address the specific times when LEAs can schedule IEP team meetings. LEAs should be flexible in scheduling IEP team meetings to accommodate reasonable requests from parents. Where LEAs and parents cannot schedule meetings to accommodate their respective scheduling needs, LEAs must take other steps to ensure parent participation, consistent with 34 C.F.R. § 300.322(c). These steps could include individual or conference telephone calls or video conferencing, consistent with 34 C.F.R. § 300.328 (see question B-3 above, regarding alternative means of participating in IEP meetings).

IDEA does permit an IEP team meeting to be conducted without a parent in attendance if the LEA is unable to convince the parents that they should attend. In this case, the LEA must keep a record of its attempts to arrange a mutually agreed on time and place (34 C.F.R. § 300.322(d)). This practice is permissible only if the LEA is unable to convince the parents that they should attend an IEP team meeting for their child regardless of the LEA's efforts to schedule the meeting at a mutually convenient time and place.

C. Consideration of Special Factors

When developing, reviewing, or revising a child's IEP, the IEP team must consider a variety of special factors, including, but not limited to, the communication needs of the child and whether the child needs assistive technology devices and services (34 C.F.R. § 300.324(a)(2)(iv) and (v)). For a child with behaviors that interfere with the child's learning or that of others, the IEP team must consider the use of positive behavioral interventions and supports, and other strategies, to address that behavior (34 C.F.R. § 300.324(a)(2)(i)). In addition to the required factors that must be considered under 34 C.F.R. § 300.324(a)(2), as a result of the COVID-19 pandemic, many children have experienced increased stress, anxiety, depression, fear, and physical isolation.

Some children have contracted COVID-19 and experience post-COVID conditions.[68] Some were displaced from their homes when a parent lost employment and even lost family members and friends to COVID-19. These circumstances can impact a child's ability to engage in their education, develop and reestablish social connections with peers and school personnel, and adapt to the structure of in-person learning. IEP teams should carefully discuss these difficult issues with a child's parents, when appropriate, gather updated information as necessary, and address any new or changed needs to ensure FAPE to the child.

Considering the Assistive Technology Needs of a Child with a Disability

When developing, reviewing, or revising a child's IEP, the IEP team must consider whether the child needs assistive technology devices and services (34 C.F.R. § 300.324(a)(2)(v)). As a result of the COVID-19 pandemic, some children with disabilities and their families may have, for the first time, used assistive technology devices and services as part of the child's access to FAPE. Challenges with ensuring equitable access to technology and Wi-Fi connectivity during this time may have affected whether and how the child received appropriate services to support skill development and progress toward attaining the child's IEP annual goals.

Question C-1: For LEAs that provided laptops or other technology devices or services to some or all children to facilitate virtual instruction, must they continue to provide such devices or services for a child with a disability who is returning to school for in-person instruction?

Answer: It will depend on the child's needs. As noted above, each child's IEP team must consider whether the child needs assistive technology devices and services as part of the determination of special education, related services, and supplementary aids and services that are needed to enable the child to receive FAPE (34 C.F.R. § 300.324(a)(2)(v)). For some children with disabilities, the continued provision of these devices or services will be appropriate to ensure the provision of FAPE.

Under IDEA, an assistive technology device means any item, piece of equipment, or product system, whether acquired commercially off the shelf, modified, or customized, that is used to increase, maintain, or improve the functional capabilities of a child with a disability (34 C.F.R. § 300.5). In this circumstance, the IEP team should review the child's use of the laptop computer or other such device that was provided for virtual instruction, along with information provided by the parent and others,

---

68. See Long COVID under Section 504 and the IDEA: A Resource to Support Children, Students, Educators, Schools, Service Providers, and Families (July 2021).

including the child, as appropriate. If the IEP team determines that the laptop or other technology device is an assistive technology device that the child requires in order to receive FAPE, the LEA must provide the necessary assistive technology device. The IEP team has discretion in determining the type of assistive technology that the child needs in order to receive meaningful educational benefit. In addition, the IEP team may consider the need for other devices that were not previously provided, if they are needed to ensure FAPE.

The IEP team also must consider whether the child requires assistive technology services as defined under 34 C.F.R. § 300.6. Generally, the assistive technology service directly assists a child with a disability in the selection, acquisition, or use of an assistive technology device.

This could include evaluating the child's needs, including a functional evaluation of the child in the child's customary environment; purchasing, leasing, or otherwise providing the necessary assistive technology device(s); selecting, designing, fitting, customizing, adapting, applying, maintaining, repairing, or replacing assistive technology devices; and coordinating and using other therapies, interventions, or services with assistive technology devices, such as those associated with existing education and rehabilitation plans and programs. One component of assistive technology services is training or technical assistance for a child with a disability or, if appropriate, that child's family. The IEP team could also consider whether parent counseling and training should be provided as a related service under IDEA to help the child's parent acquire the necessary skills that will allow them to support the implementation of the IEP, including the assistive technology device (34 C.F.R. § 300.34(c)(8)).

Question C-2: What steps can SEA and LEA leaders take to ensure equitable access to assistive technology devices, services, and connectivity to Wi-Fi to support the learning of children with disabilities?

Answer: Circumstances related to the COVID-19 pandemic exacerbated existing difficulties with equitable access to technology and digital learning for all learners. Barriers to access include factors such as the price of procuring services and devices privately (e.g., home internet service and mobile data); lack of broadband access in rural areas; and lack of parent understanding and familiarity with use of technology, including assistive technology to support their child's learning.

With the recent influx of federal funds, particularly those under the American Rescue Plan Act of 2021 (ARP Act), Congress specifically authorizes SEAs and LEAs to purchase educational technology (including hardware, software, and connectivity) for children who are served by the LEA that aids in regular and substantive educational interaction between children and their classroom instructors, including low-income children and children with disabilities, which may include assistive technology or adaptive equipment (Section 2001(e)(2)(K) of the ARP Act). See also Question C-19 of the Department's Frequently Asked Questions on the Elementary and Secondary School Emergency Relief (ESSER) Programs and Governor's Emergency Education Relief (GEER) Programs (May 2021 FAQ). Additionally, under Section 2014(a) of the ARP Act, Congress provided supplemental IDEA Part B and Part C funds for Fiscal Year 2021 to states and LEAs. These funds may also be used to address technology needs of children with disabilities.[69]

Addressing the Social, Emotional, Behavioral, and Mental Health Needs of Children with Disabilities

Many children have been exposed to trauma, disruptions in learning, physical isolation, and disengagement from school and peers, negatively affecting their mental health. Children learn, take academic risks, and achieve at higher levels in safe and supportive learning environments and in the care of responsive adults they can trust. The ongoing impact of the COVID-19 pandemic, however, has contributed to child experiences that are far from universal—with underserved children experiencing a disproportionate burden of the pandemic. As a result, many children might require additional support and interventions to take risks in their learning to achieve at higher levels.

A child whose behavior impedes their learning may need new or increased services and supports for the child to receive FAPE. These increased services and supports may include new or adjusted specially designed instruction, academic supports, positive behavioral interventions, and other supports such as counseling, psychological services, school health services, and social work services.

IEP teams are encouraged to review the pre-pandemic services required to provide FAPE to the child and determine if the child did or did not receive them during the school closure and other disruptions in service. IEP teams are also encouraged to make general observations about the child's attendance, engagement, attention, behavior, progress, and home experience during the COVID-19 pandemic.

Question C-3: When should social, emotional, behavioral, or mental health supports be included in a child's IEP?

Answer: As with other special education and related services, the IEP team makes the determination of whether, and if so which, social, emotional, behavioral, or mental health supports specific to conditions arising from COVID-19 or other situations should be included in a child's IEP. The child's need for such services may be detected during an initial evaluation or reevaluation process through the use of technically sound assessment instruments to assess the relative contribution of cognitive and behavioral factors toward educational performance (and other information provided by the child, parents, caregivers, educators, and related service providers, e.g., observations, informal assessment) (34 C.F.R. § 300.304(b)(3)). For a child already eligible under IDEA, these concerns can be addressed by

---

69. See IDEA American Rescue Plan Funds.

reconvening the IEP team to determine whether the current IEP requires revision to include specific social, emotional, behavioral, or mental health supports to ensure FAPE to the child. As part of their programs of FAPE, mental health–related services, such as counseling services, psychological services, and social work services in schools, could be included in a child's IEP, as appropriate.[70] See the response to question C-5, below, for additional examples. Schools should avoid routinely using discipline to address a child's behaviors that may arise when students return to school and consider developing or revising, or ensuring the provision of, positive behavioral interventions and supports and other strategies, as appropriate.[71]

Question C-4: Who can provide social, emotional, behavioral, or mental health supports to a child when the services are included in the child's IEP?

Answer: IDEA requires states and LEAs to ensure that all personnel necessary to carry out the purposes of Part B of IDEA are appropriately and adequately prepared and trained to provide the necessary support (34 C.F.R. §§ 300.156(a) and 300.207). Related services, which include social, emotional, behavioral, and mental health supports, must be carried out by a qualified professional who holds state-approved or state-recognized certification, licensing, registration, or other comparable requirements that apply to the professional discipline in which those personnel are providing special education or related services (34 C.F.R. § 300.156(b)(2)(i)). This responsibility includes ensuring that teachers and other school personnel have the training and experience necessary to provide required social, emotional, behavioral, and mental health supports to children with disabilities that meet the state's standards.[72] Paraprofessionals and assistants who are appropriately trained and supervised, in accordance with state law, regulation, or written policy, can assist in the provision of special education and related services to children with disabilities (34 C.F.R. § 300.156(b)(2)(iii)).

Question C-5: What are some examples of social, emotional, behavioral, and mental health supports related to the COVID-19 pandemic that could be included in a child's IEP?

Answer: The IEP team may address the child's social, emotional, behavioral, or mental health needs through special education and related services, supplementary aids and services provided to the child, and/or program modifications or supports for school personnel.

Special education and related services are provided to assist the child to make appropriate progress toward attaining the annual goals specified in the IEP and to be involved in and make progress in the general education curriculum, and to participate in extracurricular and other nonacademic

---

70. See also ED COVID-19 Handbook Roadmap to Reopening Safely and Meeting All Students' Needs (April 2021).
71. See Center on Positive Behavioral Interventions and Supports.
72. Ibid.

activities (34 C.F.R. § 300.320(a)(4)(i) and (ii)). These services and supports may include counseling services for mental health needs (e.g., anxiety, depression, etc.), social skill instruction, explicit reinforcement of positive behavior, and explicit instruction in stress, anxiety, and depression management.

Supplementary aids and services are defined to include aids, services, and other supports that are provided in regular education classes, other education- related settings, and in extracurricular and nonacademic settings to enable children with disabilities to be educated with nondisabled children to the maximum extent appropriate in accordance with 34 C.F.R. §§ 300.114 through 300.116. Supplementary aids and services may include consultation with a professional with expertise in behavioral interventions to create a positive behavioral support plan, access to counselors, and access to targeted strategies supported by peer-reviewed research to support social, emotional, behavioral, or mental health needs (e.g., anxiety scaling, mindfulness exercises).

Program modifications or supports for school personnel provided on behalf of the child may also be necessary to support the child's involvement and progress in the general education curriculum, appropriate advancement toward attaining the annual goals specified in the IEP, and participation in extracurricular and other nonacademic activities (34 C.F.R. §§ 300.320(a)(4)(i)–(ii) and 300.324(a)(3)(ii)). Usually, a modification means a change in what is being taught to or expected from the student.[73] Program modifications could include adapting a homework assignment or adjusting a reading passage to reflect the child's reading comprehension level, while supports for school personnel may include training on additional positive behavioral supports and universal design for learning and access to consultation with related service providers and others with specialized expertise.

Question C-6: What steps should the IEP team take when considering behavioral supports for children with disabilities as they return to in-person instruction?

Answer: Children who return to school, including those with disabilities and those who demonstrate challenges that were not evident before the school closure, may have new disability-related needs, regression of skills or a lack of expected progress toward attaining the child's annual IEP goals, or social, emotional, behavioral, or mental health needs due to the impact of the COVID-19 pandemic. If new or different social, emotional, behavioral, or mental health needs arise after a child has been determined to be eligible for special education and related services and an IEP has been developed, the IEP team must reconvene to consider these needs, including whether there is a need for additional related services and

---

73. See "Supports, Modifications, and Accommodations for Students," Center for Parent Information and Resources, March 2020, https://www.parentcenterhub.org/accommodations/.

positive behavioral interventions and supports to ensure the child's access to FAPE. In the alternative, the parent and the LEA may agree in writing to amend the IEP to address the child's needs through the addition of such interventions and supports (34 C.F.R. § 300.324(a)(2) and (a)(4)(i)). The LEA also may conduct or update a functional behavioral assessment (FBA). Although IDEA and its implementing regulations do not prescribe the components of an FBA, an FBA is generally understood as the process to identify the function or purpose behind a child's behavior. Typically, the process involves looking closely at a wide range of child-specific factors (e.g., social, affective, environmental). Knowing why a child behaves is directly helpful to the IEP team in developing a behavioral intervention plan that will reduce or eliminate the behavior.[74] The process generally involves qualified school personnel and the child's parent, and/or the IEP team (including the child's parent), systematically analyzing a wide range of child-specific factors. The results of the FBA generally are used to guide the development of a behavioral intervention plan to reinforce positive behaviors and prevent behavior that interferes with the child's learning and that of others. Resources are available to provide training for school personnel to conduct systematic FBAs and behavioral intervention plans[75] and ensure FAPE by providing appropriate behavioral supports to children with disabilities.[76] School personnel and IEP teams are encouraged to use evidence-based decision-making to select, implement, and closely monitor the effectiveness of behavioral and academic intervention.[77]

Addressing the School-Related Health Needs of Children with Disabilities with Underlying Medical Conditions

Some children with disabilities have underlying medical conditions, such as genetic, neurologic, or metabolic conditions, or congenital heart disease, that place them at increased risk of severe illness if they contract COVID-19.[78] Parents have raised questions about whether and how IEP teams should consider school-related health or medical information for children with disabilities. This is especially the case in states or local jurisdictions that have enacted state or local laws, rules, regulations, or policies that are inconsistent with CDC's COVID-19 prevention and risk reduction strategies. Therefore, in the questions and answers that follow, the Department reaffirms IDEA's requirements that IEP teams are responsible for identifying the services, supports, and program modifications that are necessary to

---

74. See "Supports, Modifications, and Accommodations for Students," Center for Parent Information and Resources, March 2020, https://www.parentcenterhub.org/accommodations/.
75. For more information, see Iris Center FBA Module, Autism Focused Intervention and Resource Modules FBA.
76. Ibid.
77. Torres, C., Farley, C. A., & Cook, B. G. (2014). A special educator's guide to successfully implementing evidence-based practices. *Teaching Exceptional Children, 47*(2), 85–93.
78. See "People with Certain Medical Conditions," CDC, updated May 2, 2022, https://www.cdc.gov/coronavirus/2019-ncov/need-extra-precautions/people-with-medical-conditions.html#ChildrenAndTeens.</fn>

provide a child with a disability FAPE in the least restrictive environment (LRE). Likewise, the group of knowledgeable persons making the placement decision is responsible for proposing an appropriate educational placement in the LRE that meets the child's school-related health needs.

Question C-7: Who should be included on a child's IEP team when a child with a disability has at least one underlying medical condition that puts them at increased risk of severe illness if they contract COVID-19?

Answer: In such situations, the IEP team should include a team member who knows about the health needs of the child, including whether COVID-19 prevention and risk reduction strategies may be needed. As with other children with disabilities, the IEP is developed at a meeting of the IEP team, which includes the child's parents and relevant school officials, including related service providers and, whenever appropriate, the child (34 C.F.R. § 300.321(a)). The IEP team could include, at the discretion of the parent or the LEA, individuals such as school health service staff, school nurses, and the child's health care professional, as appropriate, if the party inviting them determines that they have knowledge or special expertise regarding the child. See 34 C.F.R. § 300.321(a)(6) and (c). Such individuals can also be part of the group of knowledgeable persons making decisions about the child's educational placement.[79]

Question C-8: Are the child's IEP team and the group of knowledgeable persons making educational placement decisions responsible for addressing the school-related health needs of a child with a disability in the context of COVID-19?

Answer: Yes. As set out by the US Supreme Court in *Irving Independent School District v. Tatro*, 468 U.S. 883 (1984), eligible children with disabilities who need school-related health services are entitled to them as part of FAPE. Accordingly, LEAs must address the school-related health needs of eligible children with disabilities who are at increased risk of severe illness from COVID-19 infection.

Current evidence suggests that children with medical complexity; genetic, neurologic, or metabolic conditions; or congenital heart disease can be at increased risk for severe illness from COVID-19. Similar to adults, children with obesity, diabetes, asthma or chronic lung disease, sickle cell disease, or immunosuppression can also be at increased risk for severe illness from COVID-19.[80] If a parent or other member of the

---

79. Under 34 C.F.R. § 300.116(a), in determining the educational placement of a child with a disability, including a preschool child with a disability, each LEA must ensure that the placement decision is made by a group of persons that includes the parents and other persons knowledgeable about the child, the meaning of the evaluation data, and the placement options, and is made in conformity with the "least restrictive environment" provisions, including 34 C.F.R. §§ 300.114 through 300.118.
80. See CDC, "People with Certain Medical Conditions," https://www.cdc.gov/coronavirus/2019-ncov/need-extra-precautions/people-with-medical-conditions.html#ChildrenAndTeens.

IEP team believes that COVID-19 prevention strategies are necessary for the provision of FAPE to the child, the IEP team must consider whether and to what extent such measures are necessary, based on child-specific information, which may include medical or health records, diagnostic or other evaluative data, or information documented by medical or health professionals.[81] If the IEP team determines that COVID-19 prevention and risk reduction measures are necessary in order for a child with a disability to receive FAPE—where the prevention measures constitute special education, related services, supplementary aids and services,[82] or program modifications and supports for school personnel—the team must include these in the child's IEP consistent with 34 C.F.R. § 300.320(a)(4).

For example, the provision of FAPE in the LRE for some children with disabilities may require that the IEP address, and educational placement include, appropriate preventative and risk-reducing strategies, such as wearing masks or other personal protective equipment, and sanitizing; or, when necessary, avoiding shared use of personal and educational items, such as markers, rulers, and classroom materials. See 34 C.F.R. § 300.116(d). As with eligible children with disabilities who have severe food allergies, health plans may be included as part of the child's IEP to ensure that the health and safety of the child in the school environment is properly addressed. When health plans are included in the child's IEP, it is especially important that the IEP be accessible to each regular education teacher, special education teacher, related services provider, and any other service provider who is responsible for its implementation, consistent with IDEA requirements. Further, LEA staff responsible for implementing the IEP must be informed of the specific accommodations, modifications, and supports to be provided for the child in accordance with the child's IEP (34 C.F.R. § 300.323(d)).

State or local laws, rules, regulations, or policies relating to IDEA and its regulations must allow IEP teams and the group of knowledgeable persons making educational placement decisions to make individualized determinations under IDEA by ensuring that each eligible child with a disability has available FAPE in the LRE. Therefore, state or local laws, rules, regulations, or policies that have the effect of improperly limiting the ability of the IEP team to address the school-related health needs of a child with a disability, or the ability of the group of knowledgeable persons to propose an appropriate placement in the least restrictive environment for children with disabilities who have school-related health needs, would be a violation of IDEA. See IDEA Section 608(a)(1), 613(a)(1), 34 C.F.R. §§ 300.199, and 300.201.

---

81. See pp. 2 and 4 of OSERS's Dear Colleague Letter on Children in Nursing Homes, April 26, 2016.
82. Supplementary aids and services mean aids, services, and other supports that are provided in regular education classrooms, other education-related settings, and in extracurricular and nonacademic settings to enable children with disabilities to be educated with nondisabled children to the maximum extent appropriate in accordance with §§ 300.114 through 300.116 (34 § C.F.R. 300.42).

Question C-9: What steps could a parent of a child with a disability take if the IEP team, or if the group of knowledgeable persons making a placement decision, is unable or unwilling to address the health and safety of their child due to state or local prohibitions on the use of masks, personal protective equipment, or other COVID-19 prevention and risk reduction measures?

Answer: Consistent with 34 C.F.R. § 300.503, before an LEA proposes or refuses to initiate or change the identification, evaluation, or educational placement of the child or the provision of FAPE, the LEA must provide the child's parents with prior written notice, which includes an explanation of why the LEA is proposing or refusing to take the action. If the IEP team or group of knowledgeable persons making a placement decision is unable or unwilling to address the school-related health needs of an eligible child with a disability who is at increased risk of severe illness from COVID-19, the parent may utilize IDEA's dispute resolution procedures and mechanisms as discussed in question H-1 below.

Question C-10: Could a state or local law, regulation, rule, or policy that prohibits or limits COVID-19 prevention and risk reduction strategies in the regular education classroom or other settings where the child with a disability could interact with nondisabled peers be inconsistent with IDEA's requirement to ensure a continuum of educational placements related to placement in the LRE in 34 C.F.R. § 300.115?

Answer: Yes. Congress specifically enacted IDEA in part to rectify the exclusion of children with disabilities from public school classrooms. See section 601(c)(2) of IDEA (P.L. 108-446).

Under 34 C.F.R. § 300.115, LEAs must make available a continuum of alternative placements to meet the needs of children with disabilities consistent with their IEPs. The continuum must include instruction in regular classes, special classes, special schools, home instruction, and instruction in hospitals and institutions. Likewise, the regulation requires that the continuum include supplementary services (e.g., school-related health services) provided in conjunction with the regular class placement. As noted earlier, state or local laws, regulations, rules, or policies related to IDEA must conform to its purposes. Therefore, they may not result in the exclusion of, or prevention of, an eligible child with a disability from being educated in the regular classroom with appropriate supplementary services and with their nondisabled peers when such educational placement is appropriate to that child's individual needs. State or local laws, regulations, rules, or policies that prevent or improperly limit the IEP team or the group of knowledgeable persons that decide a child's educational placement from making individualized decisions under IDEA or that effectively prohibit the provision of needed supplementary aids and services generally would not conform to the purposes of IDEA. That is, IEP teams and the group deciding the educational placement must be able to appropriately address the in-person school-related health needs of a child with a disability with underlying medical conditions, including using COVID-19 prevention and risk reduction strategies. Otherwise, the child's parent is left with two equally unacceptable choices. The first, an in-person educational placement that puts their child at increased risk of severe illness, and the second, the exclusion of their child from school. In such scenarios, some children with disabilities for whom an in-person regular classroom setting with appropriate supplementary services is appropriate to their needs would be effectively precluded from receiving FAPE in their LRE.

Question C-11: In what ways can the Department ensure that children with disabilities who require school-related health services receive them in the LRE?

Answer: Under its monitoring authority, the Department intends to review publicly available information and stakeholder input, including concerns shared by parents and other stakeholders, and based on this may conduct additional monitoring to determine whether specific states are complying with IDEA in addressing the school-related health care needs of children with disabilities during the COVID-19 pandemic. The Department will provide technical assistance where needed. In situations where the Department finds noncompliance and voluntary compliance cannot be readily achieved, the Department will consider all its enforcement options, including a referral to the US Department of Justice. See, for example, IDEA Section 616(e) and 34 C.F.R. § 300.604.

D. Determining Appropriate Measurable Annual Goals and Considering the Child's Need for Compensatory Services

Each child's IEP must include a statement of measurable annual goals, including academic and functional goals designed to (1) meet the child's needs that result from the child's disability to enable the child to be involved in and make progress in the general education curriculum; and (2) meet each of the child's other educational needs that result from the child's disability. For children with disabilities who take alternate assessments aligned to alternate academic achievement standards, the IEP must also include a description of benchmarks or short-term objectives.

During the COVID-19 pandemic, some LEAs report having difficulty consistently providing the services determined necessary to meet the child's needs and address each of the goals in a child's IEP. As a result, some children may not have received appropriate services to allow them to make progress anticipated in their IEP goals. It will be critically important for IEP teams to make individualized decisions about each child's present levels of academic achievement and functional performance and determine whether, and to what extent, compensatory services may be necessary to mitigate the impact of the COVID-19 pandemic on the child's receipt of appropriate services.

Overall, the Department encourages IEP teams to focus on the individual needs of the child, whether the child received appropriate services, and how additional services may support the child to make progress in light of the child's unique circumstances. This includes ensuring that the instructional methodology for delivery (e.g., in-person, virtual, hybrid), timing, frequency, service setting, and location of such services, including any necessary transportation services, appropriately support the child with a disability under Part B of IDEA in achieving the functional and academic goals set out in the child's IEP.

Question D-1: How should an IEP team address the adverse impact of educational disruptions caused by the COVID-19 pandemic when developing, reviewing, or revising a child's IEP for the 2021–2022 school year?

Answer: With so many children receiving special education and related services through a variety of modalities during the 2020–2021 school year, it is critically important that the IEP team also consider any adverse impacts of the COVID-19 pandemic on each child with a disability. This includes a discussion of whether the child may have new or different needs than had been determined prior to the pandemic. Other considerations could include, but are not limited to, revising the IEP to address (1) lost skills or a lack of expected progress toward attaining the child's annual IEP goals and in the general curriculum at the end of the 2020–2021 school year; (2) updated data (e.g., information gathered from formal and informal assessments, parent input) that reflect the child's present levels of academic achievement and functional performance following the extended time without face-to-face, in-person special education and related services; (3) all areas of need, whether or not commonly related to the child's disability category, or if the child may require different or other services to address new areas of need (e.g., behavioral, social, emotional, and mental health needs, needs that arose during the pandemic); and (4) implementing COVID-19 prevention measures such as wearing a face covering/mask or practicing social distancing to provide a safe and healthy school environment and safe participation in the community.

Question D-2: May an IEP team revise the measurable annual IEP goals to reflect a decline in the child's knowledge and skills resulting from the disruption in instruction as a result of the COVID-19 pandemic?

Answer: Yes. When developing, reviewing, and revising the child's IEP, the IEP team, which includes the child's parents, must give "careful consideration of the child's present levels of achievement, disability, and potential for growth" (*Endrew F. v. Douglas County School District Re-1*, 137 S. Ct. 988, 999 (2017) (citing 20 U.S.C. 1414(d)(1)(A)(i)(I)–(IV) and (d)(3)(A)(i)–(iv)). See also Questions and Answers on U. S. Supreme Court Case Decision Endrew F. v. Douglas County School District Re-1 (December 7, 2017). The essential function of an IEP is to provide meaningful opportunities for appropriate academic and functional progress, and to enable the child to make progress appropriate in light of the child's circumstances. Each child's IEP must include, among other information, an accurate statement of the child's present levels of academic achievement and functional performance and measurable annual goals, including academic and functional goals. The IEP team's effectiveness in gathering and interpreting this information will ensure that, in establishing IEP goals, the IEP team has appropriately determined the individualized needs of the child and that it can develop measurable IEP goals that provide the child with the opportunity to meet challenging objectives.

Question D-3: What are compensatory services?

Answer: Under IDEA, courts have recognized compensatory services as an equitable remedy to prospectively address the past failure or inability of the LEA to provide appropriate services, including those that were identified on the child's IEP.[83] That is, courts have ordered such services to address the child's needs after a failure or inability to provide FAPE over a given period of time.[84] Likewise, the state complaint procedures provide for compensatory services as an available remedy when the SEA has found a failure or inability to provide appropriate services under IDEA in order to address the needs of the child (34 C.F.R. § 300.151(b)(1)).

Question D-4: Who should make the determination as to whether and to what extent compensatory services are needed?

Answer: Neither IDEA nor its implementing regulations expressly address who must make the determination of whether—and if so, what—compensatory services are necessary. The Department notes, however, that case law or other judicially established criteria (e.g., consent decrees) may be applicable. Therefore, LEAs may need to consult with their attorneys and should be transparent about the relevant legal standards that IEP teams must use to determine a child's need for, and the extent of, compensatory services (for guidance on how to use relevant data about a child to inform these decisions, see question D-5 that follows). It is the Department's position that, generally, many of the same types of individualized and child-centered deliberations that are appropriate for an IEP team meeting discussing the child's IEP, would be appropriate when considering the need for, and extent of, compensatory services. The Department also encourages IEP teams to consider input from, or encourage participation by, previous teachers and service providers, as appropriate, so that the other IEP team members can benefit from their knowledge of the child's skills and progress levels before the onset of, or during, the pandemic. Further, IEP teams should consider how any additional services determined necessary can be delivered in a manner that does not diminish the child's opportunities to interact with nondisabled peers to the maximum extent appropriate, and to participate in extracurricular and other nonacademic activities.

---

83. See, for example, *Reid ex rel. Reid v. District of Columbia*, 401 F.3d 516, 522 (D.C. Cir. 2005) (holding that compensatory services to remedy a previous denial of FAPE may be an appropriate equitable award).
84. See, for example, *G ex rel. RG v. Fort Bragg Dependent Schools*, 343 F.3d 295, 309 (4th Cir. 2003).

Question D-5: How can the IEP team use available data about the child to inform decisions about compensatory services?

Answer: In the absence of controlling federal or state law, including case law, or specific SEA or LEA guidance, IEP teams could consider the following factors, among others[85]: (1) the child's present levels of academic achievement and functional performance; (2) the child's previous rate of progress toward IEP goals; and (3) documented frequency and duration of special education and related services provided to the child prior to the service disruptions caused by the COVID-19 pandemic.

The child's present levels of academic achievement and functional performance can include concerns raised by parents, the child, and outside service providers, as well as reviewing present levels of performance in light of the anticipated levels of performance without service disruption due to the COVID-19 pandemic.[86]

Previous rates of progress may be determined by considering if the child's progress toward IEP goals has slowed or decreased and projecting if the child's current rate of progress will allow the child to attain their goals.

Frequency and duration of special education and related services may be determined by reviewing the previously agreed upon IEP compared with the actual services provided while the IEP was in effect.

These considerations could guide IEP team decisions on whether, how, and when the child will access individualized compensatory services, including the time, location, and format of the services needed to achieve the appropriate level of progress. Further, the IEP team could determine the appropriate timeline for the child to achieve the expected progress toward IEP goals addressed through the provision of compensatory services.

Question D-6: What are some situations in which it may be necessary to provide compensatory services to a child with a disability?

Answer: A child's IEP team may determine that compensatory services are necessary to mitigate the impact of disruptions and delays in providing appropriate services to the child. Some examples of situations that might require consideration of whether, and what, compensatory services are necessary include the following: (1) if the initial evaluation, eligibility determination, and identification, development, and implementation of the IEP for an eligible child were delayed; (2) if the special education and related services that were provided during the pandemic through virtual, hybrid, or in-person instruction were not appropriate to meet the child's needs; (3) if some or all of the child's IEP could not be implemented

---

85. Adapted from Washington's Roadmap to Special Education Recovery Services: 2021 & Beyond.
86. Goran, L., Harkins Monaco, E. A., Yell, M. L., Shriner, J., & Bateman, D. (2020). Pursuing academic and functional advancement: Goals, services, and measuring progress. *Teaching Exceptional Children, 52*(5), 333–343.

using the methods of service delivery available during the pandemic (for example, if the physical therapy and behavioral intervention strategies included in the child's IEP could not be provided through virtual means); and (4) if meaningful services to facilitate the transition from secondary school to activities such as postsecondary education, vocational education, integrated employment (including supported employment), continuing and adult education, adult services, independent living, or community participation were not provided due to the pandemic. These examples are not meant to be exhaustive and are provided to illustrate various situations that could require consideration of whether, and to what extent, compensatory services are needed to address the child's needs and mitigate the adverse impact of the COVID-19 pandemic.

Question D-7: Must states ensure that compensatory services are available for all IDEA-eligible children who need them because they did not receive appropriate services under Part B of IDEA due to pandemic-related closures and other service disruptions?

Answer: Generally, yes. States must ensure FAPE is available to all children residing in the state between the ages of 3 and 21,[87] inclusive, including children with disabilities who have been suspended or expelled from school (34 C.F.R. § 300.101).

The Department's long-standing position has been that IEP teams are the appropriate vehicle for addressing the need for, and extent of, compensatory services to address the child's needs based on any failure or inability to provide appropriate services due to circumstances such as teacher strikes, natural disasters, and pandemics.[88] The Department believes that IEP teams are already empowered under IDEA to make individualized determinations regarding the special education and related services that a child needs.[89] The consideration of compensatory services is just one subset of the IEP team's responsibility to address the child's needs and would arise, for example, due to the impact of the pandemic.[90] A determination of compensatory services by the child's IEP team is an appropriate

---

87. Based on state law governing the education of all children, some states do not provide public education to children through age 21. IDEA does not require the provision of FAPE to children with disabilities aged 3, 4, 5, 18, 19, 20, or 21 to the extent those ages are outside the public education age limit under state law or practice, or the order of any court. See 34 C.F.R. § 300.102(a)(1).
88. See, for example, OSEP's Letter to Pergament (December 20, 2013); Questions and Answers on Providing Services to Children with Disabilities during an H1N1 Outbreak (December 2009); Non-Regulatory Guidance on Flexibility and Waivers for Grantees and Program Participants Impacted by Federally Declared Disasters (September 2017).
89. See Questions and Answers on IDEA Part B Dispute Resolution Procedures, Question B-8 (July 23, 2013).
90. See Questions and Answers on Providing Services to Children with Disabilities during the Coronavirus Disease 2019 Outbreak: "If a child does not receive services during a closure, a child's IEP team (or appropriate personnel under Section 504) must make an individualized determination whether and to what extent compensatory services may be needed, consistent with applicable requirements, including to make up for any skills that may have been lost" (Question A-3, March 12, 2020).

proactive mitigating measure intended to address the needs of the child due to the LEA's failure or inability to provide appropriate services.

If challenged, such determinations may receive deference from a court if arrived at consistent with IDEA requirements and based on the expertise of, and the exercise of judgment by, school authorities.[91]

Question D-8: Does the SEA have a role in ensuring that compensatory services needs are considered and addressed?

Answer: Yes. Although decisions about compensatory services generally should be made by each child's IEP team, the SEA, through its general supervisory responsibilities, must ensure that its LEAs take appropriate action to mitigate the adverse impact of any failure to provide appropriate services, such as lost skills and lack of progress, for children with disabilities (34 C.F.R. §§ 300.149 and 300.600). To ensure appropriate individualized determinations of the need for, and extent of, compensatory services are made, SEAs can provide guidance to support LEAs and IEP teams in determining the frequency, location, and duration of services that may be appropriate to address the unique needs of each child with a disability. Likewise, if there is applicable case law or a consent decree that impacts how compensatory services are identified and determined, the SEA can ensure that IEP teams are appropriately aware of those requirements. Any such guidance could assist LEAs and IEP teams to identify the types of information they may need to assess the impact of service disruptions on individual children and should emphasize the IEP team's responsibility to make individualized determinations based on the individual facts and circumstances for each child.

Question D-9: Some states are using terms such as "recovery services" or "COVID mitigation services." Are these terms synonymous with compensatory services as defined by the Department?

Answer: It will depend on how these terms are defined, determined, and implemented. The Department acknowledges that some states are using the terms "recovery services" or "COVID-19 mitigation services" as a broad category of educational and support services intended to mitigate or address the negative impact of pandemic-related limitations. Some states are offering these services to all children (i.e., not based on individualized determinations), while others focus primarily on children with disabilities or at-risk children with other specific needs. For states and LEAs that do not utilize a process identified under IDEA for making individualized determinations about these services based on each child's unique needs and circumstances, such services likely would not be considered compensatory services.

---

91. See _Endrew F. v. Douglas County School District Re-1_, 137 S. Ct. 988 (2017).

Policy Letters from the US Department of Education **73**

Question D-10: Can compensatory services be provided to children who have graduated with a regular high school diploma or exceeded the age of eligibility for IDEA services?

Answer: Yes. Because the purpose of compensatory services is to remedy a failure to provide FAPE in order to address the needs of the child, for children who are beyond the period of eligibility for IDEA services, compensatory services could take the form of an additional period of eligibility. In fact, some federal courts have expressly addressed this issue. See generally, *Bd. of Educ. of Oak Park & River Forest High Sch. Dist. 200 v. Ill. State Bd. of Educ.*, 79 F.3d 654, 660 (7th Cir. 1996) (noting "[c]ompensatory education is a benefit that can extend beyond the age of 21 [the terminating FAPE age in Illinois]"); *Murphy v. Timberlane Reg'l Sch. Dist.*, 22 F.3d 1186 (lst Cir. 1994) (affirming an award of two years of compensatory education to a former student after the student had reached the [otherwise terminating-FAPE] age of 21 given the finding that FAPE had been denied to the student), cert. denied, 115 S.Ct. 484 (1994); *Pihl v. Mass. Dep't of Educ.*, 9 F.3d 184 (1st Cir. 1993) (noting that, if the former student "can prove that the school district denied him his right to an appropriate education under the IDEA during the challenged period, he could claim relief in the form of compensatory education, notwithstanding the fact that he is now twenty-seven years old"); and *Lester H. v. Gilhool*, 916 F.2d 865 (3d Cir. 1990), cert. denied, 499 U.S. 923 (1991) (finding that the student was entitled to 30 months of compensatory education because of the district's failure to provide an appropriate educational placement for that period of time). See also *School Comm. of Town of Burlington v. Dep't of Educ. of Mass.*, 471 U.S. 359, 369–70, 105 S.Ct. 1996, 2002–03 (1985).

Question D-11: What funds can be used to pay for compensatory services?

Answer: IDEA Part B funds (both the regular IDEA Part B funds and the additional IDEA Part B funds appropriated under section 2014 of the ARP Act), as well as funds provided to states and LEAs through the ESSER Fund and the GEER Fund, may be used for compensatory services. See question C-5 of the Frequently Asked Questions on the Elementary and Secondary School Emergency Relief (ESSER) Programs and Governor's Emergency Education Relief (GEER) Programs (May 2021 FAQ). If, however, an LEA uses ESSER, GEER, or IDEA Part B funds (either the regular IDEA Part B funds or the additional IDEA Part B funds appropriated under section 2014 of the ARP Act) to replace state and/or local funding for the education of children with disabilities, this may result in a failure of the LEA to meet the budget and/or expenditure requirements for LEA maintenance of effort (MOE) under IDEA Part B. See question E-12 of the May 2021 ESSER GEER FAQs. In addition, if an LEA elects to use state and/or local funds for compensatory services, the LEA should consider the impact this may have on the LEA's required level of effort to meet the MOE requirement under IDEA Part B in future years. See 34 C.F.R. §

300.203; and Q2 of the Question and Answer Document on Flexibility on IDEA Part B Fiscal Requirements (June 26, 2020).

E. Making Extended School Year (ESY) Services Determinations

A child's entitlement to ESY services needed for FAPE continues to apply even if schools do not provide other educational services during school breaks. It is important to remember that IEP team determinations regarding ESY services are prospective and not intended to make up for past denials of FAPE. The specific analysis and standards that an IEP team may use to determine whether a child requires ESY services in order to receive FAPE are left to states to determine. The determination, however, must be based on the individual needs of the child, and not on the category of the child's disability. See question 4 in Implementation of IDEA Part B Provision of Services in the Current COVID-19 Environment *(September 28, 2020).*

Question E-1: If an LEA provides additional services for all students during the summer to address lost instruction due to the pandemic, do IEP teams need to consider ESY services?

Answer: Yes. ESY services are defined as special education and related services that are (1) provided to a child with a disability beyond the normal school year of the LEA; (2) provided in accordance with the child's IEP; (3) provided at no cost to the parents of the child; and (4) meet the standards of the SEA. Each LEA must ensure that ESY services are available as necessary to provide FAPE to a child with a disability (34 C.F.R. § 300.106). Individualized determinations about the need of each child with a disability for ESY services are made through the IEP process and must be made annually. The IEP team could determine that a child's ESY service needs could be met through participation, with appropriate supports, in some or all of the additional services the LEA provides to all students.

Typically, ESY services are provided during the summer months. There is nothing, however, that limits the ability of an LEA to provide ESY services to a child with a disability during times other than the summer, such as during school breaks or vacations, where appropriate to the child's needs and consistent with applicable standards.

Question E-2: Could a child be eligible for both ESY and compensatory services?

Answer: Yes. These services have different standards and purposes and are not mutually exclusive. ESY services are (1) provided to a child with a disability beyond the normal school year of the LEA; (2) provided in accordance with the child's IEP; (3) provided at no cost to the parents of the child; and (4) meet the standards of the SEA (34 C.F.R. § 300.106).

Compensatory services are additional special education and related services to address the needs of the child that are intended to remedy a failure or inability to provide appropriate services. These would generally be additional services to those that the child would be receiving during the child's school attendance (including ESY services) or as an additional period of eligibility for IDEA services. See question D-10 above. Therefore, a child who requires ESY services could also receive compensatory services.

F. Considering Secondary Transition Services

Due to the circumstances of the COVID-19 pandemic, some children with disabilities did not receive appropriate or meaningful services to facilitate transition from secondary school to activities such as postsecondary education, vocational education, integrated employment (including supported employment), continuing and adult education, adult services, independent living, or community participation. As students return to school for the 2021–2022 school year and states and LEAs consider options for delivering quality transition services, they must ensure that children with disabilities receive the appropriate services, supports, and opportunities to achieve their desired post-school education and career goals. In the provision of services to children with disabilities remotely, in-person, or through a hybrid option, SEAs, LEAs, and IEP teams remain responsible for ensuring that all children with disabilities receive transition services necessary for FAPE in accordance with 34 C.F.R. § 300.320(b). The Department recognizes that some children with disabilities, including children of color and those living in less-resourced or rural communities, face greater and more complex challenges during the COVID-19 pandemic. Providing the necessary services and supports so that these children can transition to the next step in their lives will benefit them, their families, and the communities in which they live and work.

Question F-1: What should IEP teams consider for a child with a disability whose transition services or pre-employment transition services may have been disrupted by the COVID-19 pandemic?

Answer: Following the return to school and reconvening the IEP team meeting, the IEP team must consider whether the child's transition needs have changed, taking into account the child's strengths, preferences, and interests; and develop measurable goals that are focused on the child's life after high school, specifying the transition services needed to help the child reach those goals. The IEP team should discuss transition services and pre-employment transition services in light of the child's unique circumstances and experiences during the pandemic. IEP teams should address any need for compensatory services related to school closure or an inability to fully implement a child's transition plan. If the child is not making expected progress toward their annual transition goals in order to meet their post-school goals, the IEP team should revise, as appropriate, the IEP to address the lack of progress.

Pre-employment transition services are available only to "students with disabilities," as defined in Section 7(37) of the Rehabilitation Act of 1973, as amended (Rehabilitation Act), and 34 C.F.R. § 361.5(c)(51).[92] So long as a student who was slated to graduate from secondary school at the end of the 2019–2020 or 2020–2021 school year continues to participate in an educational program, including postsecondary education or another recognized educational program, that student would be able to continue receiving pre-employment transition services. Under the unprecedented circumstances caused by the COVID-19 pandemic, many students with disabilities, including those who were slated to graduate at the end of the 2019–2020 or 2020–2021 school year, were participating in a variety of recognized educational programs, such as remote learning and homeschooling. Participation in any of these educational programs would qualify for the receipt of pre-employment transition services. A graduating student with a disability who took summer school classes would still be participating in an educational program. As such, the student would be able to receive any pre-employment transition services provided while participating in summer school classes, through virtual and other remote strategies or in-person pre-employment transition services, to the extent available. The same would be true for a graduating student with a disability who enrolled in a postsecondary education program that started in the fall or later as part of a "gap-year" program. For more information, see question 14 of the Rehabilitation Services Administration's (RSA) Questions and Answers (October 16, 2020).

Question F-2: May pre-employment transition services be repeated for a student with a disability in the event the provision of those services was interrupted?

Answer: Vocational rehabilitation (VR) agencies must continue to make good faith and reasonable efforts to provide pre-employment transition services to each student with a disability based on the student's needs, and consistent with the health, safety, and welfare of both individuals with disabilities and those providing services. This means that a VR agency may need to repeat the provision of pre-employment transition services to a student with a disability in the event the provision of those services was interrupted, if doing so is necessary to meet the needs of the student. This would be true whether the interruption is due to the COVID-19

---

92. "Student with a disability" in the Rehabilitation Act means, in general, an individual with a disability in a secondary, postsecondary, or other recognized education program who—
    (A)(1) Is not younger than the earliest age for the provision of transition services under Section 614(d)(1)(A)(i)(VIII) of the Individuals with Disabilities Education Act (20 U.S.C. 1414(d)(1)(A)(i)(VIII)); or (2) If the state involved elects to use a lower minimum age for receipt of pre-employment transition services under this act, is not younger than that minimum age; and
    (B)(1) Is not older than 21 years of age; or (2) If the state law for the state provides for a higher maximum age for receipt of services under the Individuals with Disabilities Education Act (20 U.S.C. 1400 et seq.), is not older than that maximum age; and
    (C)(1) Is eligible for, and receiving, special education or related services under Part B of the Individuals with Disabilities Education Act (20 U.S.C. 1411 et seq.); or (2) Is a student who is an individual with a disability, for purposes of Section 504.

pandemic, a student's illness, or another reason. Pursuant to Section 113(a) of the Rehabilitation Act and 34 C.F.R. § 361.48(a), VR agencies, in coordination with LEAs, must provide, or arrange for the provision of, pre-employment transition services to all students with disabilities in need of such services. Neither the Rehabilitation Act nor its implementing regulations impose any limitations on the number or frequency of these services; however, the VR agency should make the determination to repeat services that have been disrupted on a case-by-case basis, considering the resources of the VR agency allocated for this purpose and the reasonable expenditure of funds. See question 7 of RSA's Questions and Answers (May 14, 2020).

G. Making Educational Placement Decisions

After the child's IEP has been developed, the placement in which the IEP will be implemented is determined. The LEA must ensure that the placement decision for each child is made by a group of persons, including the parents, who are knowledgeable about the child, the meaning of the evaluation data, and the placement options; and that placement is decided in conformity with the least restrictive environment (LRE) provisions in 34 C.F.R. §§ 300.114 through 300.118. The child's placement must be based on the child's IEP and determined at least annually (34 C.F.R. § 300.116(b)(1) and (2)).

Each LEA must ensure that (i) to the maximum extent appropriate, children with disabilities, including children in public or private institutions or other care facilities, are educated with children who are non-disabled; and (ii) Special classes, separate schooling, or other removal of children with disabilities from the regular educational environment occurs only if the nature or severity of the disability is such that education in regular classes with the use of supplementary aids and services cannot be achieved satisfactorily (34 C.F.R. § 300.114(a)(2)). The LEA responsible for providing FAPE to a child with a disability must make available the full continuum of alternative placements, including instruction in regular classes, including accelerated classes, special classes, special schools, home instruction, and instruction in hospitals and institutions, to meet the needs of all children with disabilities for special education and related services (34 C.F.R. § 300.115). In selecting the LRE, consideration also must be given to any potential harmful effect on the child or on the quality of services that the child needs (34 C.F.R. § 300.116(d)). As a result of disruptions arising from the COVID-19 pandemic and many children receiving instruction through hybrid or virtual approaches, LEAs and parents will likely need to review the appropriateness of the child's current educational placement for the 2021–2022 school year.

Question G-1: What is the state's obligation to ensure that its LEAs meet IDEA's LRE requirements?

Answer: IDEA requires that SEAs have in effect policies and procedures to ensure that LEAs in the state meet the LRE requirements (34 C.F.R. §

300.114(a)(1)). To the maximum extent appropriate, children with disabilities, including children in public or private institutions or other care facilities, are to be educated with children who are nondisabled; and special classes, separate schooling, or other removal of children with disabilities from the regular educational environment occurs only if the nature or severity of the disability is such that education in regular classes with the use of supplementary aids and services cannot be achieved satisfactorily (34 C.F.R. § 300.114(a)(2)). SEAs are required to

1. carry out activities to ensure that teachers and administrators in all LEAs are fully informed about their responsibilities for implementing the LRE requirements cited above;
2. provide technical assistance and training necessary to assist LEAs in meeting the LRE requirements; and
3. monitor LEAs for their compliance with the LRE requirements (34 C.F.R. §§ 300.119–300.120).

As a result of the changes in instructional delivery approaches for children with disabilities caused by the COVID-19 pandemic and the potential impact on ensuring LRE, the Department recommends that SEAs review their existing policies, technical assistance activities, and procedures for monitoring their LEAs' compliance with IDEA's LRE requirements to ensure they are sufficient in scope and include information on instructional delivery approaches that were not typically contemplated prior to the COVID-19 pandemic and the potential impact on providing FAPE in the LRE.

Question G-2: Under IDEA, is an LEA obligated to provide special education and related services through virtual instruction upon the parent's request?

Answer: It will depend on whether virtual instruction, in-person attendance, or a hybrid approach are available to all students. These decisions are made by state and local education leaders.[93] If virtual instruction is available to all students in an LEA, the LEA must ensure that a child with a disability whose needs can be met through virtual learning has an IEP implemented that provides all the services and supports necessary for the child to receive FAPE through such service delivery. IDEA also includes "home instruction" in the continuum of alternative placements an LEA must make available to ensure FAPE is available to children with disabilities (34 C.F.R. § 300.115(b)). Home instruction also could be delivered through a virtual, in-person, or hybrid approach. For more information about online instruction for children with disabilities, see OSERS' Dear Colleague Letter on Virtual Schools (August 5, 2016).

---

93. State and local leaders must make these decisions consistent with Section 504 and Title II. See the discussion in the response to question A-3 above.

Question G-3: How does the Department view virtual instruction under the IDEA's continuum of educational placements for children with disabilities?

Answer: Congress has previously expressed concerns about children with disabilities being excluded entirely from the public school system and about not being able to participate in the general curriculum with their nondisabled peers. See Section 601(b)(4) of the Education for All Handicapped Children Act of 1975 (P.L. 94-142); Section 601(c)(2) of IDEA (P.L. 108-446). IDEA has continually reflected a strong preference for educating children with disabilities in regular classes with appropriate aids and supports. See Section 601(c)(5) of IDEA (P.L. 108-446). Specifically, 34 C.F.R. § 300.114 provides that states must have in effect policies and procedures ensuring that LEAs meet the LRE requirements of IDEA by ensuring, to the maximum extent appropriate, children with disabilities, including children in public or private institutions or other care facilities, are educated with children who are nondisabled, and that special classes, separate schooling, or other removal of children with disabilities from the regular educational environment occurs only if the nature or severity of the disability is such that education in regular classes with the use of supplementary aids and services cannot be achieved satisfactorily.

Prior to the COVID-19 pandemic, for schools that did not offer virtual instruction to all children, special education and related services provided virtually in the child's home was generally considered one of the most restrictive environments, as it typically provided little or no opportunity for the child to be educated with nondisabled peers. Virtual learning provided during the pandemic may be deemed less restrictive if it is available to all children and provides the child with a disability meaningful opportunities to be educated and interact with nondisabled peers in the regular education environment.

H. Resolving Disagreements Regarding a Child's Educational Program

The Department encourages parents and LEAs to work collaboratively, in the best interests of children, to resolve any disagreements that may occur when working to provide a positive educational experience for all children, including children with disabilities, especially in light of the COVID-19 pandemic. To this end, IDEA and its implementing regulations provide specific options for resolving disputes between parents and public agencies, which can be used in a manner consistent with our shared goals of improving results and achieving better outcomes for children with disabilities. Part B of IDEA provides parents with the following options for resolving disagreements about their child's education program: state complaints, mediation, and due process complaints. Any individual or organization, including one from another state, may file a state complaint to resolve allegations that an LEA or SEA has violated a requirement of Part B of IDEA.

Question H-1: If a parent disagrees with the IEP team's decision regarding compensatory services, can they still file a due process complaint or state complaint?

Answer: Generally, yes. Although the use of IEP teams to reach decisions regarding compensatory services is intended to remedy the failure to provide appropriate services in order to address the needs of the child and to mitigate the need for additional dispute resolution procedures, like any other IEP team decision or proposal, the parent has a right to disagree with the IEP team's decision and to use IDEA's dispute resolution procedures. These include the state complaint procedures pursuant to 34 C.F.R. §§ 300.151 through 300.153; mediation procedures pursuant to 34 C.F.R. § 300.506; and the due process complaint and due process hearing procedures under 34 C.F.R. §§ 300.507 through 300.516.[94] IDEA establishes specific timelines, or permits states to establish timelines, for filing a due process complaint to request a due process hearing or for filing a state complaint. It is important that parents review the state's procedural safeguards notice to ensure they understand the applicable timelines for using these dispute resolution procedures.

Question H-2: May states continue to convene mediation sessions, resolution meetings, and due process hearings virtually, even when schools return to in-person, face-to-face instruction?

Answer: While a face-to-face meeting may be preferable when attempting to resolve disputes that may arise regarding the education of a child with a disability, IDEA and its implementing regulations permit alternative means of participation, upon agreement by the parties (34 C.F.R. § 300.328). Thus, a state may continue to conduct mediation sessions, subject to the parties' agreement, through alternative means, such as video conferences or conference calls, if the state's procedures do not prohibit mediations from occurring in this manner.

Similarly, an LEA may continue to offer to use alternative means for the parties' participation in a resolution meeting, such as video conferences or conference calls, subject to the parties' agreement. With respect to due process hearings on due process complaints, a state could continue to allow video conferences or conference calls to be used, if a hearing officer concludes that such procedures are consistent with legal practice in the state (34 C.F.R. § 300.511(c)(1)(iii)). A hearing conducted virtually must ensure a parent's right to an impartial due process hearing consistent with all requirements in 34 C.F.R. §§ 300.511 through 300.515. This includes the parent's right to open the hearing to the public consistent with 34 C.F.R. § 300.512(c)(2). If applicable, a state-level review of a hearing

---

94. Also, see Questions and Answers on IDEA Part B Dispute Resolution Procedures (July 2013). The Center for Appropriate Dispute Resolution in Special Education (CADRE), an OSEP-funded technical assistance center, has developed a series of guides and companion videos to assist parents in understanding IDEA's dispute resolution procedures. These materials are available on CADRE's web site.

decision can continue to be conducted virtually if consistent with state procedures. See <u>IDEA Part B Dispute Resolution in COVID-19 Environment</u> (June 22, 2020).

2.2.7

UNITED STATES DEPARTMENT OF EDUCATION

WASHINGTON, DC 20202

OSEP QA 21-07

RETURN TO SCHOOL ROADMAP: CHILD FIND, REFERRAL, AND ELIGIBILITY UNDER PART C OF THE INDIVIDUALS WITH DISABILITIES EDUCATION ACT (IDEA)

October 29, 2021

The Office of Special Education and Rehabilitative Services (OSERS) in the US Department of Education (herein referred to as the Department) has received requests from a diverse group of stakeholders asking that the Department clarify expectations and requirements for implementing the Individuals with Disabilities Education Act (IDEA) in light of the many challenges of the COVID-19 pandemic and as more schools and programs are returning to in-person services. These inquiries address a range of topics, such as meeting timelines, ensuring implementation of initial evaluation and reevaluation procedures, determining eligibility for early intervention, special education and related services, and providing the full array of early intervention services and special education and related services that children with disabilities need in order to receive a free appropriate public education (FAPE).[95] The purpose of the Return to School Roadmap IDEA guidance documents,[96] which focus on school and

---

95. Free appropriate public education means special education and related services that (1) are provided at public expense, under public supervision, and without charge; (2) meet the standards of the state educational agency (SEA), including the requirements of IDEA; (3) include an appropriate preschool, elementary school, or secondary school education in the state involved; and (4) are provided in conformity with an individualized education program that meets the requirements of 34 C.F.R. §§ 300.320 through 300.324. 34 C.F.R. § 300.17.
96. Other than statutory and regulatory requirements included in this Q&A document, the contents of this guidance do not have the force and effect of law and are not meant to bind the public. This document is intended only to provide clarity to the public regarding existing requirements under the law or agency policies. The Department has determined

program reopening efforts and in-person service delivery, is to support the full implementation of IDEA requirements. The documents also serve to clarify that, regardless of the COVID-19 pandemic, or the mode of intervention or instruction, children with disabilities are entitled to FAPE, and infants and toddlers with disabilities and their families are entitled to appropriate IDEA Part C services. It is also important to note that in order to fully implement IDEA requirements, communications with limited English proficient parents must be made in their native language.

The Department is issuing this guidance to state lead agencies (state LAs), early intervention service (EIS) providers, parents, and other stakeholders to reaffirm the importance of appropriate implementation of the child find obligations under Part C of the IDEA. Under Part C of the IDEA, each state LA and its EIS providers are responsible for implementing a child find system that identifies, locates, and evaluates, as early as possible, all infants and toddlers with disabilities, birth to age 3, who may require early intervention services. These child find and related requirements are reflected in the IDEA and its implementing regulations in 20 U.S.C. § 1435(a)(5)-(6) and 34 C.F.R. §§ 303.313, 303.115, 303.116, and 303.300 through 303.322.

State Early Intervention Child Find Systems

The Department understands that, during earlier stages of the COVID-19 pandemic response, programs were not open for in-person activities, and fewer infants and toddlers were in early care and education programs and had fewer pediatrician visits. During this time, data indicate that referrals to the IDEA Part C early intervention system decreased.[97] While referrals to Part C have increased, they are still not back to pre-pandemic levels, and the COVID-19 pandemic is still impacting a number of communities. As the nation enters this new stage of the COVID-19 pandemic, state LAs should consider enhancing and refocusing their child find efforts to make sure that they are sufficiently robust to ensure the appropriate referral, evaluation, and identification of all infants and toddlers who may have a disability under IDEA Part C. State LAs and EIS providers should utilize existing data systems to identify those primary referral sources that saw the biggest decrease in referrals during the pandemic and consider targeting strategies to increase child find efforts with these sources. State LAs should also consider refocusing their public awareness activities, under 20 U.S.C. § 1435(a)(6) and 34 C.F.R. §§ 303.116 and 303.301, by using a

---

that this document provides significant guidance under the Office of Management and Budget's Final Bulletin for Agency Good Guidance Practices, 72 Fed. Reg. 3432 (January 25, 2007). The questions and answers in this document are not intended to be a replacement for careful study of IDEA and its implementing regulations. The IDEA, its implementing regulations, and other important documents related to IDEA and the regulations are found at https://sites.ed.gov/idea/.

97. States reported to OSEP in their Federal Fiscal Year (FFY) 2019 state performance plans/annual performance reports (SPP/APRs) for the period July 1, 2019, through June 30, 2020, IDEA Section 618 data and through other sources that the number of children referred to Part C of the IDEA decreased.

variety of methods to inform the public including posters, pamphlets, displays, billboards, toll-free numbers, websites, videos, TV, radio, newspaper releases, and advertisements to effectively reach populations of children who may have been under identified during earlier stages of the pandemic.

In addition, state LAs and EIS providers should examine equity issues that may exist in the child find identification process, including equity issues that predate the pandemic. This includes analyzing data to examine if there are communities where there are limited referrals or if there are disparities in the economic status or race and ethnicity of families referred to Part C. Based on these data, state LAs and EIS providers should identify specific outreach strategies to connect with these typically underserved communities. The IDEA Part C statute and regulations specifically identify many subpopulations where coordination with other organizations is crucial to an effective child find process.[98] These include in 34 C.F.R. § 303.302(b) the identification of Native American infants and toddlers residing on reservations; infants and toddlers who are homeless, in foster care, and wards of the state; infants and toddlers identified under the Child Abuse Prevention and Treatment Act (CAPTA) in substantiated cases of abuse or neglect; and at-risk infants and toddlers who have been identified as directly affected by illegal substance abuse or withdrawal symptoms resulting from prenatal drug exposure.

Under IDEA Part C, a comprehensive child find system includes the following:

- Public awareness program (34 C.F.R. §303.301);
- Child find activities including coordination with other relevant state agencies (34 C.F.R. § 303.302);
- Referral procedures, including referral timeline (7 days), (34 C.F.R. § 303.303) and post-referral timeline (45 days) (34 C.F.R. § 303.310);
- Screening procedures (at the state's option) (34 C.F.R. § 303.320);
- Procedures for evaluation of the child and assessment of the child and family (34 C.F.R. § 303.321); and
- Procedures for when there is a determination that a child is not eligible (34 C.F.R. § 303.322).
- Referral procedures (34 C.F.R. § 303.303)

Primary referral sources must refer a child to Part C within seven days of when the child is identified as being potentially eligible for IDEA Part C services (34 C.F.R. 303.303(a)(2)(i)). If the state LA or EIS provider determines that a child is suspected of having a disability, IDEA Part C requires, upon receipt of parental consent, a timely, comprehensive, multidisciplinary evaluation to determine the child's eligibility.

---

98. The state must ensure that the child find system is coordinated with specific agencies, including the state agency responsible for administering CAPTA, the State Early Hearing Detection and Intervention system, the Home Visiting program under Maternal and Child Health, child care programs, and the Children's Health Insurance Program. See 34 C.F.R. § 303.302.

If the child is not determined eligible after an evaluation is conducted or if the child is not evaluated, the state LA must ensure that prior written notice is provided to the parent under 34 C.F.R. § 303.421, which informs the parent of dispute resolution options under 34 C.F.R. § 303.430.

If the child is determined eligible, the initial child and family assessment must be conducted, and the initial individualized family service plan (IFSP) meeting must be held within 45 days of referral (34 C.F.R. §§ 303.310 and 303.321). This timeline requires the following occur within 45 days of a child's referral: (1) any screening offered by the state; (2) the initial evaluation; (3) the initial child and family assessment; and (4) the initial IFSP meeting. The 45-day timeline requirement includes two allowable exceptions: (1) the child or parent is unavailable to complete one of the following—the screening (if applicable), the initial evaluation, the initial assessments of the child and family, or the initial IFSP meeting due to exceptional family circumstances that are documented in the child's early intervention records; or (2) the parent has not provided consent for the screening (if applicable), the initial evaluation, or the initial assessment of the child, despite documented, repeated attempts by the state LA or EIS provider to obtain parental consent. If the child is determined eligible under 34 C.F.R. § 303.321(a)(1)(ii), an initial child and family-directed assessment is conducted to identify the child's unique strengths and needs as well as the family's resources, priorities and concerns and supports and services and supports to enhance the family's capacity to meet the developmental needs of the child (34 C.F.R. § 303.321(c)(2)).

The state LA may also adopt screening procedures, consistent with the requirements of 34 C.F.R. § 303.320, to screen children under the age of 3 who have been referred to the Part C program to determine whether they are suspected of having a disability. Screening (if a state has adopted such procedures) requires parental notice and consent within the 45-day timeline. As part of the screening process, at a parent's request and with parental consent, the EIS provider must conduct an initial evaluation of the infant or toddler even if the results of the screening do not identify the child as suspected of having a disability.

The Office of Special Education Programs (OSEP), which is responsible for administering the federal IDEA Part C formula grants program, has developed a model Child Find Self- Assessment (CFSA) as a tool for state IDEA Part C programs to assess their child find system for identifying, locating, and evaluating all infants and toddlers with disabilities and developmental delays. OSEP strongly encourages states to utilize the CFSA as a tool to assist with implementing best practices for child find.

Frequently Asked Questions

Q1: What is the responsibility of the state LA and its EIS providers if a referral was received, but the parent was not contacted due to the COVID-19 pandemic?

A1: The Department realizes that, during the COVID-19 pandemic, some families were not contacted due to multiple circumstances (office closures, stay-at-home orders, etc.), but the state LA and its EIS providers should give immediate and high priority to identifying these children and contacting their parents. States must also collect and report data on these referrals, including data on any noncompliance with 34 C.F.R. §303.310, under Indicator 7 (45-Day Timeline) in their State Performance Plan / Annual Performance Report (SPP/APR). Further, in circumstances where noncompliance is identified, the state LA must ensure that each individual case of noncompliance is corrected, unless the child is no longer within the jurisdiction of the EIS program and provider, consistent with OSEP Memorandum 09-02 (OSEP Memo).[99]

If the child is now over age 3, the Department strongly encourages the state LA and EIS providers to provide parents with information about the IDEA Part B program and to work closely with the state educational agency (SEA) and local educational agencies (LEAs) in these circumstances to help those agencies meet their respective child find responsibilities under Part B of the IDEA. State LAs and EIS providers should use their data systems and review their child find policies and procedures to ensure that parents of all children who were referred and not contacted receive appropriate information and, where appropriate, evaluations and services.

Q2: What should the state LA and its EIS providers do if the parent declined to consent to an evaluation to determine their child's eligibility or the parent consented to an evaluation and the child was determined eligible, but then the parent declined Part C services?

A2: If a parent declined to either consent to an evaluation to determine eligibility for Part C or declined consent for the provision of Part C services after their child was determined eligible, the state LA and EIS provider are not required to conduct an evaluation or provide services under IDEA Part C. State LAs and EIS providers should have clear and complete records that document the parent's decision to decline the evaluation or Part C services offered (34 C.F.R. §303.310(c)(1)). In both situations, however, the parent's decision to decline consent to an evaluation or decline consent to Part C services may have potentially been due to the pandemic.

As communities move forward in responding to the pandemic, the Department highly encourages state LAs and EIS providers to follow up with these families to determine if circumstances have changed and if families are now interested in having their infant or toddler evaluated or receive early intervention services. For those families who did not provide consent to evaluate, programs should consider sending a communication to parents, including child find materials, that acknowledges family situations and priorities may have shifted and that state LA and EIS providers remain

---

99. OSEP Memo 09-02 provides guidance regarding the steps states must take to report on the correction of noncompliance in the APR required under Sections 616 and 642 of the IDEA.

committed to supporting the child and family. In situations when the child was found eligible for Part C services, but the parent declined consent to the provision of services, the Department encourages state LA and EIS providers to reengage the parent to develop and/or implement the IFSP.

In circumstances where the child has since turned 3, state LAs and EIS providers should provide parents with information about the IDEA Part B program as well as information about the LEA responsible for serving the child, as appropriate. The Department also encourages state LAs to develop a coordinated response to the pandemic to ensure that EIS providers are prepared to broadly identify other state and local resources and share information with families about additional resources and supports available in the state, including those funded under the American Rescue Plan.

Q3: What is the responsibility of the state LA and its EIS providers if a referral was made and the parent provided consent to an evaluation, but the child's evaluation was not conducted?

A3: State LAs and EIS providers may have been unable to conduct an evaluation due to circumstances related to the COVID-19 pandemic (e.g., stay-at-home orders and physical distancing requirements prevented an in-person evaluation). If the child was referred and the parent consented to an evaluation, but the evaluation was not conducted as required within 45 days of referral, regardless of the reason, state LAs and EIS providers must conduct the evaluation as soon as possible to determine the child's eligibility under IDEA Part C assuming the child is under 3 years of age. The IDEA Part C regulations at 34 C.F.R. § 303.321(a)(1) require that once parental consent has been obtained, if the child is suspected of having a disability, the child must receive a timely, comprehensive, multidisciplinary evaluation unless the child's eligibility is established by medical or other records under 34 C.F.R. § 303.321(a)(3)(i).

The Department strongly encourages states to prioritize the longest pending requests for evaluation. If the child is determined eligible after the evaluation, the child and family assessments and the initial IFSP meeting must also be conducted as soon as possible (assuming the child is under 3 years of age). The state must document any applicable exceptional family circumstances in the child's early intervention records. See 34 C.F.R. §303.310(b)-(c). States must also collect and report data on these evaluations, including data on any noncompliance with 34 C.F.R. §303.321(a)(i), under Indicator 7 (45-Day Timeline) in their SPP/APR. Further, in circumstances where noncompliance is identified, the state LA must ensure that each individual case of noncompliance is corrected, unless the child has turned 3 or is no longer within the jurisdiction of the EIS program and provider, consistent with "OSEP Memo 09-02."[100]

---

100. OSEP Memo 09-02 provides guidance regarding the steps states must take to report on the correction of noncompliance in the APR required under Sections 616 and 642 of the IDEA.

If the child is now over the age of 3, the Department strongly encourages state LAs and EIS providers to provide parents with information about the IDEA Part B program as well as contact information for the LEA responsible for serving the child, as appropriate. The state LA and EIS providers should work closely with the IDEA Part B SEA and LEAs in these circumstances to help those agencies meet their respective child find responsibilities under Part B of the IDEA. It is important for state LAs to collaborate with EIS providers, LEAs, local childcare programs, home visiting programs, and Head Start and Early Head Start programs to ensure that parents of children who were referred but not evaluated receive information about these and other available programs and services.

Q4: May the state LA and its EIS providers conduct a virtual (i.e., not in-person) screening or evaluation of the infant or toddler if a parent requests it instead of an in-person screening or evaluation?

A4: As state LA and EIS providers return to in-person services, they should also prepare to return to in-person screening and evaluations. If, however, a parent requests that a screening or evaluation be conducted virtually, the state LA must determine first if its policies permit virtual screenings and/or evaluations. Additionally, the state must determine if the screening or evaluation instruments would yield valid results if they are administered virtually.

Under 34 C.F.R. § 303.320, the lead agency may adopt screening procedures to determine if a child referred to Part C is suspected of having a disability. Not all states have adopted procedures to permit screening under Part C of the IDEA. Assuming a state has adopted policies and has screening or evaluation instruments that can be administered remotely, the state LA and its EIS providers may be able to offer parents the flexibility of conducting the screening or evaluation remotely. State LAs, EIS providers, and the qualified personnel conducting the evaluation should exercise judgment in assessing whether the suspected disability may be identified through screening and/or evaluations conducted virtually rather than in person. The state LA and its EIS providers may also determine eligibility based on existing medical or other records in lieu of conducting an evaluation under 34 C.F.R. § 303.321(a)(3)(i).

If after a screening is conducted and a child is suspected of having a disability, or if the parent requests an evaluation during the screening process, an evaluation must be conducted to determine eligibility once parental consent for the evaluation is obtained. If the parent consents to a screening and the screening indicates that the child is not suspected of having a disability, the state LA or EIS provider must provide notice under 34 C.F.R. § 303.421 that describes the parent's right to request an evaluation.

The state LA and EIS providers must ensure that any screening and evaluation tools that are administered virtually meet standards for technical adequacy and are nondiscriminatory in implementation under 34 C.F.R. § 303.321(a)(4). The state LA should implement these tools consistently and appropriately to minimize over- or under-identification of infants and toddlers with disabilities for early intervention services. The state LA's child find responsibilities under 34 C.F.R. § 303.302 are to locate and identify eligible children under Part C of the IDEA as early as possible and to coordinate with other state agencies and programs, including those that administer the foster care, CAPTA, and homeless programs.

2.2.8

UNITED STATES DEPARTMENT OF EDUCATION

WASHINGTON, DC 20202

OSEP QA 21-08

RETURN TO SCHOOL ROADMAP: PROVISION OF EARLY INTERVENTION SERVICES FOR INFANTS AND TODDLERS WITH DISABILITIES AND THEIR FAMILIES UNDER PART C OF THE INDIVIDUALS WITH DISABILITIES EDUCATION ACT (IDEA)

October 29, 2021

The Office of Special Education and Rehabilitative Services (OSERS) in the US Department of Education (herein referred to as the Department) has received requests from a diverse group of stakeholders asking that the Department issue new guidance interpreting requirements of the Individuals with Disabilities Education Act (IDEA) in light of the many challenges of the COVID-19 pandemic and as more schools and programs are returning to in-person services. Topics include meeting timelines; ensuring implementation of initial evaluation and reevaluation procedures; determining eligibility for early intervention, special education, and related services; and providing the full array of early intervention services and special education and related services that children with disabilities need in order to receive a free appropriate public education (FAPE).[101] Similarly, stakeholders have inquired about the implications of delayed evaluations and early intervention services to infants and toddlers with disabilities and their families served under IDEA Part C.[102] The purpose of the Return

---

101. Free appropriate public education means special education and related services that (1) are provided at public expense, under public supervision, and without charge; (2) meet the standards of the SEA, including the requirements of IDEA; (3) include an appropriate preschool, elementary school, or secondary school education in the state involved; and (4) are provided in conformity with an individualized education program that meets the requirements of 34 C.F.R. §§ 300.320 through 300.324. 34 C.F.R. § 300.17.
102. States reported to OSEP in their Federal Fiscal Year (FFY) 2019 State Performance Plans / Annual Performance Reports (SPP/APR) for the period July 1, 2019, through

to School Roadmap IDEA guidance documents,[103] which focus on school and program reopening efforts and in-person service delivery, is to support the full implementation of IDEA requirements. The documents also serve to clarify that, regardless of the COVID-19 pandemic, or the mode of intervention or instruction, children with disabilities are entitled to FAPE, and infants and toddlers with disabilities and their families to appropriate IDEA Part C services.

As the nation addresses the impact of the COVID-19 pandemic and state lead agencies (state LAs) and local early intervention service (EIS) providers are faced with making decisions about service delivery, the Department has received questions related to the provision of early intervention services. The questions in this document are intended to provide guidance and to identify the relevant regulatory requirements and options for flexibility for the state LA and EIS providers when faced with unprecedented programmatic circumstances. Furthermore, the Department recognizes that the generally home-based nature of IDEA Part C services presents a complicated set of considerations for state LAs and EIS providers in providing IDEA Part C services during the COVID-19 pandemic.

Part C of the IDEA provides funds to a state LA to make early intervention services available to all eligible infants and toddlers with disabilities and their families living within the state. Early intervention services are provided in conformity with the child's individualized family services plan (IFSP) developed by the child's IFSP team, which includes the parent, consistent with the requirements in 34 C.F.R. §§ 303.342 through 303.346. This document supplements the guidance released by the Department in October 2020, regarding the implementation of IDEA Part C services during the COVID-19 pandemic.

The Office of Special Education Programs' (OSEP's) analysis of states' IDEA federal fiscal year 2018 Section 618 data,[104] reported prior to the COVID-19 pandemic, highlighted that certain populations, including American Indian, Alaska Native, and Black or African American infants and toddlers, were less likely to be screened, referred for services, and served under Part C of the IDEA than all racial and ethnic groups combined.

The Department recommends that states address how the COVID-19 pandemic has increased the disparity in accessing early intervention services and create systems to identify and address these inequities. With

---

June 30, 2020, IDEA Section 618 data and through other sources that the number of children referred to Part C of the IDEA decreased.

103. Other than statutory and regulatory requirements included in this Q&A document, the contents of this guidance do not have the force and effect of law and are not meant to bind the public. This document is intended only to provide clarity to the public regarding existing requirements under the law or agency policies. The questions and answers in this document are not intended to be a replacement for careful study of IDEA and its implementing regulations. The IDEA, its implementing regulations, and other important documents related to IDEA and the regulations are found at https://sites.ed.gov/idea/.

104. See the 2020 Annual Report to Congress on the Individuals with Disabilities Education Act.

funding from the American Rescue Plan for IDEA Part C, now is the time for states to implement infrastructure changes and enhance implementation capacity to support EIS providers in implementing evidence-based practices to address the disparities in the state's early intervention system from screening, eligibility, and service delivery all the way through transition. These activities could include improving data systems so they can be used to help identify and measure equity challenges and ensure that families with limited English proficiency, families from low-income backgrounds, and families of color have access to high-quality early intervention services through targeted outreach, resources, and supports. Building a strong equitable system also requires a diverse workforce with the capacity to effectively support families with a variety of backgrounds.

IDEA acknowledges the importance of parents and other family members in supporting a child's development. To be able to make sound decisions about their child's involvement in early intervention, and their own involvement, parents should be fully informed about what will take place and where, what is being proposed, and much more.[105] Parents who would like additional support in understanding IDEA's requirements may contact their local regional parent training and information centers (PTIs) for direct assistance and referrals to other organizations and to gain skills to effectively participate in the education and development of their children. There are more than 100 PTIs in the United States and Territories that provide training, resources, and support on a wide variety of topics. Parents can locate the appropriate PTI for their area at <u>Find Your Parent Center</u>.[106]

This document focuses on the development and implementation of individualized family services plans (IFSPs). An IFSP is the written plan for providing early intervention services to an infant or toddler with a disability and the infant's or toddler's family. The IFSP must be developed by the child's IFSP team, which includes the parent, in accordance with the procedures outlined in 34 C.F.R. §§ 303.342, 303.343, and 303.345, and include the content required in 34 C.F.R. § 303.344.

The inclusion of these resources is not intended to reflect their importance, nor is it intended to endorse any views expressed, or products or services offered, by these entities. These resources may include materials that contain the views and recommendations of various subject-matter experts as well as hypertext links, contact addresses, and websites to information created and maintained by other public and private organizations. The opinions expressed in any of these materials do not necessarily reflect the positions or policies of the Department. The Department does not control or guarantee the accuracy, relevance, timeliness, or completeness of any outside information included in the materials that may be provided by these resources.

---

105. See Building the Legacy for Our Youngest Children with Disabilities: <u>Module 10: Introduction to Procedural Safeguards</u> (March 2015).
106. This document contains examples of resources that are provided for the user's convenience.

Frequently Asked Questions

Question 1: What are the state LA or EIS providers' responsibilities for ensuring that IFSP teams address the ongoing impact of the COVID-19 pandemic on the child and family when developing the initial IFSP?

Upon referral, the state LA or EIS provider must, within 45 days of referral, conduct (1) any screening, if applicable;[107] (2) the initial evaluation to determine the child's eligibility under Part C of IDEA; (3) the initial child and family assessment; and (4) the initial IFSP meeting to develop the IFSP with the IFSP team, which includes the parent. The evaluation of the child must identify the levels of functioning in all five developmental areas (physical, cognitive, communication, adaptive, and social or emotional) under 34 C.F.R. § 303.321. Furthermore, under 34 C.F.R. § 303.321(a)(2) and (c), EIS providers must assess the child's unique strengths and needs, as well as conduct a family-directed assessment to identify the family's resources, priorities, and concerns and the supports and services necessary to help the family meet the needs of their infant or toddler with a disability. Additionally, under 34 C.F.R. § 303.321(a)(2) and (c), EIS providers must assess the child's unique strengths and needs, as well as conduct a family-directed assessment to identify the family's resources, priorities, and concerns, as well as the supports and services necessary to help the family meet the developmental needs of their infant or toddler with a disability. Finally, under 34 C.F.R. § 303.344(a), when developing the IFSP, the IFSP team must include a statement of the child's level of functioning in all five developmental areas, based on the information from the child's evaluation and assessments conducted under 34 C.F.R. §303.321.

The challenges of the pandemic have impacted the physical, social, and emotional health of families across the nation. Some families have faced an increase in joblessness, homelessness, food insecurity, and health challenges related to the COVID-19 pandemic. A child's development and the family's capacity to support the needs of an infant or toddler with a disability can be adversely impacted by these types of traumatic stress. IFSP teams should consider the full impacts of the pandemic on each child and family and include social-emotional and behavioral supports in the development and implementation of the initial IFSP. It is important that all early intervention services, including social-emotional, behavioral, and mental health supports, are culturally relevant, meaningful to the child and family, provided by qualified personnel, based on peer-reviewed research (to the extent practicable), and necessary to meet the unique needs of

---

107. The state LA may adopt screening procedures, consistent with the requirements of 34 C.F.R. § 303.320, to screen children under the age of 3 who have been referred to the Part C program to determine whether they are suspected of having a disability. Screening (if a state has adopted such procedures) requires parental notice and consent and must be performed within the 45-day timeline. At a parent's request and with parental consent, the EIS provider must conduct an initial evaluation of the infant or toddler even if the results of the screening do not identify the child as suspected of having a disability.

the child and the family to achieve the desired results or outcomes under 34 C.F.R. § 303.344(d).

Question 2: What are the state LAs and EIS providers' responsibilities to ensure that IFSP teams address the ongoing impact of the COVID-19 pandemic on the child and family after the initial IFSP has been developed?

Answer: Under 34 C.F.R. § 303.342(b), a periodic review of the IFSP must be conducted minimally at six months or more frequently as conditions warrant. The COVID-19 pandemic's impact on the child and family may warrant a periodic review of the IFSP prior to the six-month or annual review dates.

As part of the periodic review of the IFSP, EIS providers must conduct ongoing assessment under 34 C.F.R. § 303.321(c) of the child's unique strengths and needs. The periodic review must also include a family-directed assessment to identify the family's resources, priorities, and concerns and the supports and services necessary to help the family meet the developmental needs of their infant or toddler with a disability. The qualified personnel conducting initial assessments should take into consideration the specific impact of the COVID-19 pandemic on both the needs of the child and the resources and capacity of the child's family.

The IFSP team, which includes the parent, must identify on the IFSP, under 34 C.F.R. § 303.344(d), any changes needed in the services, including frequency, delivery, method, or setting, to address the child's needs and outcomes. The state LA or EIS provider must ensure that services identified on the IFSP are provided to the child and family.

Question 3: What are the state LAs and EIS providers' responsibilities to infants and toddlers with disabilities and their families who did not receive some or all of the early intervention services in their IFSPs due to circumstances related to the COVID-19 pandemic?

Answer: The state LA or EIS provider must review its data and other information, such as information provided by a child's family, to determine whether and which eligible children did not receive services identified on their IFSPs, and take appropriate actions based on the results of the review. If IFSP services have not been provided in conformity with the IFSP, the state LA or EIS provider may need to conduct a periodic review of the IFSP in order to determine the current needs of the child and family (34 C.F.R. § 303.342(b)). As part of that periodic review by the IFSP team, under 34 C.F.R. § 303.344(c), the IFSP must include a statement of the child's progress toward achieving the results or outcomes identified in the IFSP and whether modifications to the IFSP are necessary.

Additionally, the IFSP team may determine whether and to what extent compensatory services may be needed to address service disruptions due to the COVID-19 pandemic.[108] The IFSP team may determine that com-

---

108. Under IDEA, courts have awarded compensatory services as an equitable remedy to address the needs of the infant or toddler with a disability and the family. Likewise, the

pensatory services are necessary to mitigate the impact of disruptions and delays in providing appropriate services to the child. IFSP teams must ensure decisions about compensatory services are individualized based on updated assessment information for the child and family under 34 C.F.R. §§ 303.340 through 303.344.

The state LA must also report data on any noncompliance under 34 C.F.R. § 303.342(a) and (e) under Indicator 1 (Timely Receipt of Services) in their SPP/APR and correct each individual case of noncompliance, unless the child is no longer within the jurisdiction of the EIS program and provider, consistent with OSEP Memorandum 09-02 (OSEP Memo).[109]

Question 4: What are the state LAs and EIS providers' responsibilities for infants and toddlers with disabilities and their families who, due to circumstances related to the COVID-19 pandemic, received services under an interim IFSP?[110]

Answer: Under certain circumstances, early intervention services for an eligible child and the child's family may begin before the evaluation and assessments are completed, especially when those services have been determined to be needed immediately by the child and the child's family. The required evaluations and assessments, however, must still be completed within the 45-day timeline in 34 C.F.R. § 303.310.

State LAs and EIS providers that utilized interim IFSPs[111] due to circumstances related to the COVID-19 pandemic and did not complete the full evaluation and develop an initial IFSP within timelines required under 34 C.F.R. § 303.310 must still complete the evaluations (although late), convene an IFSP team meeting to review the results, and revise the IFSP as needed. OSEP strongly encourages state LAs and EIS providers to prioritize those infants and toddlers who have been served through an interim IFSP for the longest period of time.

Interim IFSPs that exceed 45 days would constitute noncompliance unless there are documented exceptional family circumstances. The LA or EIS provider must also report the data on any noncompliance with 34 C.F.R. § 303.310 under Indicator 7 (45-Day Timeline) in their SPP/APR

---

state complaint procedures provide for compensatory services as an available remedy when there is a finding of a failure to provide appropriate services under IDEA in order to address the needs of the infant or toddler with a disability and his or her family (34 C.F.R. 303.432(b)(1)). It is the Department's position that, generally, many of the same types of individualized and child-centered deliberations that are appropriate for an IFSP team meeting discussing the infant's or toddler's and family's IFSP would be appropriate when considering the need for, and extent of, compensatory services.

109. OSEP Memo 09-02 provides guidance regarding the steps states must take under Sections 616 and 642 of the IDEA to report on the correction of noncompliance in the APR.
110. An interim IFSP may be put into place with parental consent under 34 C.F.R. § 303.345 to provide IDEA Part C services before the evaluation or assessment is completed and, in addition, must include the name of the responsible service coordinator, consistent with 34 C.F.R. § 303.344(g). The service coordinator will implement the interim IFSP and coordinate with any other agencies or people as appropriate.
111. The requirements for an interim IFSP are in 34 C.F.R. §§ 303.310(c) and 303.345.

and correct each individual case of noncompliance, unless the child is no longer within the jurisdiction of the EIS program and provider, consistent with OSEP Memo 09-02.

Question 5: What should the IFSP team consider if a parent requests that early intervention services are provided virtually[112] as a method of delivery?

Answer: The child's IFSP team (including the parent) must determine whether delivering the service virtually is an appropriate methodology for each service identified on the IFSP. Prior to the COVID-19 pandemic, some states permitted IFSP services to be delivered virtually. During various stages of the pandemic, states have allowed infants and toddlers with disabilities and their families to receive IFSP services virtually. Some parents may wish to continue to receive some or all IFSP services virtually. The state LA and its EIS providers may be able to provide IFSP services virtually depending on the state's policies and procedures, whether the services can be effectively provided on a virtual basis, and the individualized determination made by the child's IFSP team. Early intervention services must be tailored to meet the unique needs of the individual child and family (34 C.F.R. § 303.344(d)).

Question 6: What options are available to parents, state LAs, and EIS providers to resolve disputes under IDEA Part C?

Answer: OSEP encourages parents, state LAs, and EIS providers to work collaboratively, in the best interest of infants and toddlers with disabilities, to resolve disagreements that may occur when providing positive early intervention experiences. When there are disputes over Part C requirements, however, parents are entitled to exercise their rights to state dispute resolution options under Part C of IDEA.

Under 34 C.F.R. § 303.421(a), parents must receive prior written notice a reasonable time before the state LA or an EIS provider proposes, or refuses, to initiate or change the identification, evaluation, or placement of their infant or toddler, or the provision of early intervention services to the infant or toddler with a disability and that infant's or toddler's family. Under 34 C.F.R. §303.421(b)(3), this notice must include information about all dispute resolution options. These include the right to (1) file a state complaint regarding an alleged violation of any requirement of Part C of IDEA; (2) request mediation to resolve any matter under Part C; and (3) file a due process complaint regarding the identification, evaluation, or

---

112. Virtual service delivery is also referred to as teleintervention, remote early intervention, remote learning, telehealth, telemedicine, telepractice, teletherapy, virtual home vision, or virtual learning. This method of delivery primarily engages audio or video technology to connect EIS providers with parents and/or caregivers in ways that support their child's development throughout their daily activities and routines ("Remote Service Delivery and Distance Learning," Early Childhood Technical Assistance Center, December 1, 2021, https://ectacenter.org/topics/disaster/tele-intervention.asp).

placement of their infant or toddler or the provision of early intervention services to their child and family.[113]

Question 7: What are the state LA or EIS providers' responsibilities if an infant or toddler with a disability did not receive timely transition services due to circumstances related to the COVID-19 pandemic?

Answer: Under 34 C.F.R. § 303.209(a)(1)(ii), states are required to ensure a smooth transition for infants and toddlers with disabilities under the age of 3 and their families who are exiting the Part C early intervention program. If the LA determines that a toddler with a disability is not potentially eligible for Part B preschool services, the lead agency, with the approval of the family of that toddler, makes reasonable efforts to convene a conference among the lead agency, the family, and providers of other appropriate services for the toddler to discuss service options that the toddler may receive (34 C.F.R. § 303.209(c)(2)). The transition plan in the IFSP includes, consistent with 34 C.F.R. §303.344(h), as appropriate, steps for the toddler with a disability and his or her family to exit from the Part C program and any transition services that the IFSP Team identifies as needed by that toddler and family. A transition conference or meeting to develop the transition plan must meet the IFSP meeting requirements in 34 C.F.R. §§ 303.342(d) and (e) and 303.343(a).

The state LA or EIS provider must review its data and other information (such as information provided by a child's family) to determine whether and which eligible children did not receive transition services and take appropriate actions, even if such children are now 3 years old or older. Additionally, if an eligible child did not receive transition services, the state LA must report data on any noncompliance with 34 C.F.R. § 303.209 under Indicator 8 (Early Childhood Transition) in its SPP/APR and correct each individual case of noncompliance, unless the child is no longer within the jurisdiction of the EIS program and provider, consistent with OSEP Memo 09-02.

Under 34 C.F.R. § 303.342(b), the state LA or EIS provider may need to conduct a periodic review of the IFSP to determine if transition services were not provided. As part of that periodic review, under 34 C.F.R. § 303.344, the IFSP team may also consider, on an individualized basis, whether and to what extent compensatory services may be needed to address service delays and disruptions due to the COVID-19 pandemic. IFSP teams must ensure decisions about compensatory services are based on any transition needs identified and services not provided to the child and family.

Question 8: What systemic actions should the state LA or EIS provider take to address transition activities that were not completed within the

---

113. The Center for Appropriate Dispute Resolution in Special Education (CADRE), an OSEP-funded technical assistance center, has developed a series of guides and companion videos to assist parents in understanding IDEA's dispute resolution procedures. These materials are available on CADRE's website.

required timeline or that were delayed due to circumstances related to the COVID-19 pandemic?

Answer: At a systemic level, the Department expects that state LAs and state educational agencies ensure that EIS providers and local educational agencies meet all applicable transition requirements and timelines by utilizing their data systems and reviewing their child find policies and procedures to complete required transition activities that were not completed due to the COVID-19 pandemic. This includes reengaging families with whom they may have lost contact and completing timely transition services for all infants, toddlers, and children determined to be eligible for early intervention and special education. States must collect and report data on these referrals under Part C Indicator 8 (Early Childhood Transition) and Part B Indicator 12 (Effective Transition) in their SPP/APR.

EIS providers should identify a system to prioritize and resolve any overdue transition services while simultaneously adhering to current timelines for children exiting Part C services. States can use IDEA Part C funds (both the regular IDEA Part C funds and the supplemental Part C funds appropriated under the American Rescue Plan Act) and funds provided to states through the Elementary and Secondary School Emergency Relief and Governor's Emergency Education Relief funds to complete overdue transition activities. It is crucial that toddlers and their families exiting the Part C program experience a smooth and effective transition to the child's next program or other appropriate services, including services that may be identified for a child who is no longer eligible to receive IDEA Part C or Part B services.

In considering how to prioritize services, EIS providers may consider the following: conducting activities to address the transition needs of children who are the oldest (e.g., turned 3 sooner than others with overdue transition services); analyzing and triaging the reasons for overdue transition services; and identifying mitigation strategies, including utilizing fiscal resources to support timely transition.

As the impact of the COVID-19 pandemic continues, states might consider expanding IDEA Part C services to include at-risk populations. States might also consider expanding IDEA Part C services to include infants or toddlers who would be at risk of experiencing a substantial developmental delay if early intervention services were not provided to the infant or toddler. Additionally, states might consider infrastructure improvements within its Part C system, as well as specialized professional development for EIS providers to address needs related to early childhood mental health (ECMH) diagnosis and treatment for all children and families, especially underserved populations.

Question 9: What resources are available to support the safe return to in-person services to reduce the spread of COVID-19?

Answer: The Centers for Disease Control and Prevention (CDC) provides COVID-19 guidance for early care and education (ECE) programs, including child care centers, home-based programs and family child care, Head Start, and other pre-kindergarten programs. CDC's guidance includes strategies that ECE programs can use to reduce the spread of COVID-19 and maintain safe operations.

Key takeaways include the following:

- Vaccination is currently the leading public health prevention strategy to end the COVID-19 pandemic. Promoting vaccination among eligible individuals can help early care and education (ECE) programs protect staff and children in their care, as well as their families.
- Most ECE programs serve children under the age of 12 who are not yet eligible for vaccination at this time. Therefore, this guidance emphasizes implementing layered COVID-19 prevention strategies (e.g., using multiple prevention strategies together) to protect children and adults who are not fully vaccinated.
- COVID-19 prevention strategies remain crucial to protect people, including children and staff, who are not fully vaccinated, especially in areas of moderate to high community transmission levels.
- Masks should be worn indoors by all individuals (ages 2 and older) who are not fully vaccinated. ECE settings may implement universal mask use in some situations, such as if they have increasing, substantial, or high COVID-19 transmission in their ECE program or community, and while they serve a population not yet eligible for vaccination.

CHAPTER 3

A Primer on Dispute Resolution under the IDEA and Section 504

3.1 Dispute Resolution
    3.1.1 State Complaint Resolution
    3.1.2 The Due Process Hearing
3.2 Special Education Disputes in the Federal Court System
    3.2.1 The US District Court
    3.2.2 The US Courts of Appeals
    3.2.3 The US Supreme Court
3.3 Published and Unpublished Decisions
3.4 Researching Cases Online

The Individuals with Disabilities Education Act (IDEA) contains mechanisms by which parents and school district administrators can settle disputes regarding the special education of students with disabilities. Two avenues of dispute resolution are particularly germane to our purposes in this textbook: the state education agency's (SEA) complaint resolution process (CRP) and the due process hearing (DPH). We will not cover two other dispute resolution mechanisms included in the IDEA—mediation and the resolution session—because they are less formal and are mechanisms to resolve disputes before they reach the level of the DPH.

3.1 Dispute Resolution

The purposes of both the state complaint procedures (SCP) and DPH are similar (i.e., to resolve disputes regarding an IDEA-eligible student's special education) the way the two systems work are significantly different. Zirkel (2020) describes the SCP system as investigative and the DPH system as adjudicative. We next describe the two systems of dispute resolution.

3.1.1 State Complaint Resolution[1]

Regulations to the IDEA require that each state adopt a procedure whereby a student's parents can file a complaint against a school district regarding the special education provided to their child. A student's parents or any other person or organization, except for a student's school district, may file a complaint with the SEA. The complaint must be filed within one year of the date in which the violation occurred, although states may extend this timeline. When the complaint is received, officials in the SEA must investigate the allegations. The school district being investigated must also be given an opportunity to respond to the parents' allegations, and the parents must be given an opportunity to amend their complaint. If SEA officials determine a formal investigation is needed, an on-site investigation in the district will be conducted.

After the complaint is filed, the SEA has 60 days in which SEA officials must issue a written decision in which they (a) provide the details of their independent determination, (b) present their findings of fact and conclusions, and (c) give their rationale for arriving at their decision. If it is found that the school district failed to provide appropriate services, the SEA report must detail the district's failure, include corrective actions that address the student's needs (e.g., compensatory services), and detail the actions the school district should take to prevent similar situations from occurring in the future.

The SEA's CRP may be preferred by some parents because attorneys are not required, final decisions are usually made more quickly, and it is less financially and emotionally taxing (Zirkel, 2020). Additionally, the CRP process requires little involvement of a student's parents. Moreover, Zirkel asserts that CRPs tend to be in a more parent-friendly format. The CRP mechanism does not include the right to confront and cross-examine witnesses, and there is no mandated right to appeal the decision on the SEA unless the right exists in the laws of the state in which the CRP is conducted.

According to comments to the 2006 regulations to the IDEA there is no federally guaranteed right to judicial review of the CRP decision.

> The regulations neither prohibit nor require the establishment of procedures to permit an LEA or other party to request reconsideration of a State complaint decision. We have chosen to be silent in the regulations about whether a State complaint decision may be appealed because we believe States are in the best position to determine what, if any, appeals process is necessary to meet each State's needs, consistent with State law. (IDEA Regulations Comments, 2006, p. 46607)

If a student's parents do not agree with the finding in the CRP, they may file for a DPH. The ruling of the DPH may be appealed to state or federal court.

---

1. Regulations to the IDEA addressing the state complaint system may be found at 34 C.F.R. § 300.151 to 300.153.

3.1.2 The Due Process Hearing[2]

The DPH is the most well known of the IDEA's dispute solution systems. Although either parents or school district officials may file for a due process hearing, most commonly requests for hearings are brought by a student's parents. School officials or parents may file for a DPH within two years of when the parents knew or should have known of a violation (34 C.F.R. 300.507[a][2]). Readers should note that states may set its own time frame regarding the statute of limitation. Additionally, dispute resolution under Section 504 is the same as is required under the IDEA. Unlike the IDEA, however, Section 504 puts the responsibility for all DPHs on the local educational agency (LEA).

An impartial hearing officer (IHO) presides over a DPH. The IHO cannot be employed by a school district or the SEA that is involved in the education of the student or have any personal or professional interest that could interfere with his or her objectivity (34. C.F.R.§ 300.511[c]). The IHO must understand state and federal laws and have the ability to render and write decisions using acceptable legal practices. The role of the IHO is to listen to the arguments of both sides and applies to the specific facts of the case to the law in deciding the case. The possible remedies that an IHO may order include injunctive relief, compensatory education, or tuition reimbursement, but probably not attorney's fees.

The issues heard in a DPH may include any issue related to the identification, evaluation, or educational placement of a student with a disability, or the provision of free appropriate public education (FAPE) to the student (34 C.F.R. 300.507[a]). Both parties in the DPH process have the rights that a litigant has in a hearing in a court, such as the right to (a) retain and be represented by an attorney, (b) present evidence, (c) examine and cross-examine witnesses, (d) obtain written or electronic verbatim record of the hearing, and (e) obtain written or electronic records of the findings of fact and the decision (34 C.F.R. 300.512[a][1-5]). A DPH is very much like a court trial except that it is less formal. The decision must be made within 45 days of the end of the hearing. The ruling of the IHO is final; however, either party has the right to appeal within 90 days of the final ruling. Readers should note these timelines can be different depending on state laws.

In most states, called one-tier states, the appeal of a DPH is made to a state or federal court. In a few states, which are called two-tier states, an appeal of a DPH ruling is made to the SEA. The decision of the SEA can then be appealed to state or federal court. Most appeals are to the federal courts, so we next examine appeals to these courts. Prior to filing an appeal, parents must exhaust their administrative remedies, which means in a one-tier state the parents must have gone through the DPH and in a two-tier state the parents must have gone through the DPH and the state

---

2. Regulations to the IDEA addressing the state complaint system may be found at 34 C.F.R. § 300.507 through 300.516.

review. There are exceptions to the exhaustion requirement when going through the procedures would be inadequate or futile.

3.2 Special Education Disputes in the Federal Court System

The federal court system is a hierarchy. Figure 3.1 depicts the hierarchy of the federal courts. Similarly, state courts are also hierarchical (see Figure 3.2), which includes the US district court, US circuit courts of appeals, and the US Supreme Court. Appeals of a ruling from the DPH go to the first level of federal courts: the US district court. Appeals from the US district courts go to the US courts of appeals, also called the appellate or circuit courts, in their jurisdiction. The final appeal is to the US Supreme Court, the court of last resort.

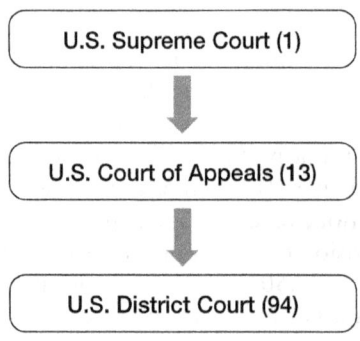

Figure 3.1. Federal Court System

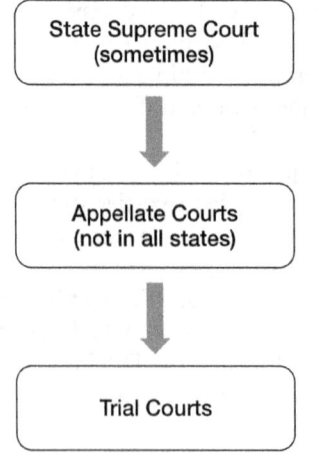

- State-level courts have the ability to resolve both state and federal claims
- State supreme court decisions can be appealed directly to the U.S. Supreme Court on issues of federal law.

Figure 3.2. Typical State Court System

3.2.1 The US District Court

There are 94 federal district courts in the United States. Every state has at least one district court, and some states have as many as four. In most circumstances, federal district courts, which are sometimes called trial courts, hear the facts of the case, apply the law, and issue a ruling. Often, in the federal district court a jury will be present to hear the facts of the case and issue a ruling.

When an IHO ruling is appealed to the US district court, however, the judge reviews the facts as determined by the IHO, determines if the IHO applied the law correctly, and either affirms or overturns the ruling of the IHO. In *Board of Education of the Hendrick Hudson Central School District v. Rowley* (1982), the US Supreme Court noted that the IDEA's requirement that a reviewing court receive the records from the administrative proceedings (i.e., the DPH) "carries the implied requirement that due weight shall be given to these proceedings" (*Board of Education v. Rowley*, 1992, p. 208). This essentially means that the district court judge acts more as an appellate judge would act because unless the judge determines that the IHO made errors, the facts are considered fixed, and the judge determines if the IHO applied the law correctly. If a district court judge determines the IHO incorrectly determined the facts, the judge may review the case without giving deference to the IHO's ruling. This is referred to hearing the case *de novo*,[3] which means the district court judge decides the case without deferring to the IHO's ruling.

Decisions from federal district courts do not create precedent outside of its jurisdiction. So, for example, a ruling from the US district court in South Carolina would not be controlling on the US district court in Arkansas. Nonetheless, judges in the district court in Arkansas could certainly choose to follow the ruling of the district court in South Carolina, if a judge found that ruling persuasive.

In an appeal of a special education DPH to a federal district court, the attorneys for the parents and the school district will write arguments, called briefs, and submit them to the federal district court judge. The party that loses will typically claim the DPH was not conducted properly, the IHO misapplied the law, or both issues. The task of the federal court judge will then be to determine if the law was applied correctly by the IHO. The judge will either affirm or overturn the ruling of the IHO. The losing party may then file an appeal with the next highest court in the federal court hierarchy, the US courts of appeals.

3.2.2 The US Courts of Appeals

The next highest level of courts, immediately above the US district courts and immediately below the US Supreme Court, is the US circuit court of appeals for the various circuits. The 94 US district court jurisdictions are

---

3. The Latin phrase *de novo* means "starting anew."

divided up into 12 judicial circuits.[4] Each of these circuits has an appellate court that hears appeals from the US district court. Table 3.1 depicts these jurisdictions, and Figure 3.3 presents the geographic boundaries of the jurisdiction.

A US court of appeals hears appeals of rulings from the US district court in its jurisdiction. For example, the US Court of Appeals for the Fourth Circuit would hear appeals from the US district court for South Carolina because South Carolina is in the Fourth Circuit (i.e., Maryland, North Carolina, South Carolina, Virginia, and West Virginia). The Fourth Circuit court would not hear cases from the US district court in Pennsylvania because the Pennsylvania court is in the jurisdiction of the US Court of Appeals for the Sixth Circuit.

Rulings from the US courts of appeals set precedent for the lower courts within its jurisdictions. For example, a ruling from the US Court of Appeals for the Third Circuit will be binding on all the lower courts in the Third Circuit (i.e., the US district court for the districts of Delaware,

TABLE 3.1 **Circuit and District Court Jurisdictions.**

Circuit	Jurisdiction
1st	Maine, Massachusetts, New Hampshire, Puerto Rico, Rhode Island
2nd	Connecticut, New York, Vermont
3rd	Delaware, New Jersey, Pennsylvania, Virgin Islands
4th	Maryland, North Carolina, South Carolina, Virginia, West Virginia
5th	Louisiana, Mississippi, Texas
6th	Kentucky, Ohio, Michigan, Tennessee
7th	Illinois, Indiana, Wisconsin
8th	Arkansas, Iowa, Minnesota, Missouri, Nebraska, North Dakota, South Dakota
9th	Alaska, Arizona, California, Guam, Hawaii, Idaho, Montana, Nevada, Northern Mariana Islands, Oregon, Washington
10th	Colorado, Kansas, New Mexico, Oklahoma, Utah, Wyoming
11th	Alabama, Florida, Georgia
12th (DC)	Washington, DC
13th (Federal)	Washington, DC (specialized courts)

---

4. There is a 13th appellate court called the Court of Appeals for the Federal Circuit. This court has nationwide jurisdiction to hear specialized cases such as trademarks, patents, and international trade.

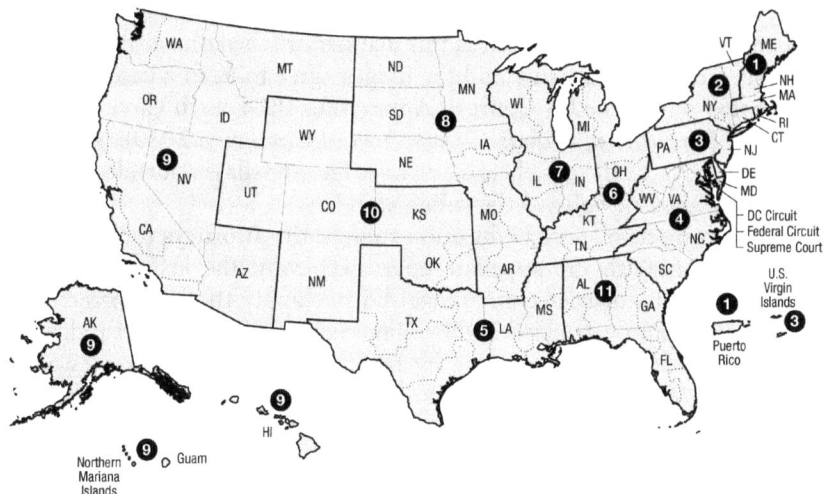

Figure 3.3. Boundaries of the US Courts of Appeals and the US District Court

New Jersey, Pennsylvania, and the Virgin Islands). On the other hand, rulings from the US Court of Appeals for the Third Circuit would not be binding on the US district court for the district of Arkansas because Arkansas is in the jurisdiction of the US Court of Appeals for the Eighth Circuit (i.e., the districts of Arkansas, Iowa, Minnesota, Missouri, Nebraska, North Dakota, and South Dakota). Because of the importance of the appellate courts, rulings from this level of courts often have persuasive authority and are adopted by other courts in other jurisdictions even though they are not binding. An example of an appellate court ruling in special education that had great persuasive authority was *Daniel R. R. v. State Board of Education* (1989). Although the ruling of the US Court of Appeals for the Fifth Circuit only had binding or controlling authority on lower courts in Louisiana, Mississippi, and Texas, the decision was eventually adopted by the US Court of Appeals for the Second Circuit (Connecticut, New York, and Vermont), the US Court of Appeals for the Third Circuit (Delaware, New Jersey, Pennsylvania), the US Court of Appeals for the Tenth Circuit (Colorado, Kansas, Oklahoma, New Mexico, Utah, Wyoming), and the US Court of Appeals for the Eleventh Circuit (Alabama, Florida, Georgia).

Appellate courts do not have juries, hear witnesses, hear new witnesses, or retry cases. Rather, appellate courts review the procedures and rulings of the district courts and determine if the law was applied correctly. A US circuit court is composed of several judges (numbers of judges differ by circuit) who are divided into panels of three. Most cases appealed to the circuit courts will be heard and ruled on by these panels of three judges. Rarely, a case will be heard by all the judges on a court of appeals; a process called hearing a case *en banc*.[5] In an *en banc* hearing, the full

---

5. *En banc* is a French term meaning "in the bench."

court makes the ruling. This typically occurs when the court believes a significant issue needs to be heard in this manner or when one or both parties requests an *en banc* hearing and the judges agree to it. In a case reviewed in this text out of the US Court of Appeals for the Fourth Circuit (*R.S. v. Board of Directors of Woods Charter School Company*, 2020), an appeal was made to have the case heard *en banc*. The appellate court decided not to hear the case *en banc* so the ruling stood.

With respect to special education rulings, the attorneys for both sides will file briefs with the appellate court. Typically, the losing party will contend that the district court judge did not apply the law correctly or, in the case of an overturned DPH ruling, that the district court judge did not properly consider the ruling by the IHO. All the cases reviewed in this text were out of the US courts of appeals. A party that loses at the appellate level may file an appeal with the highest court in the land, the US Supreme Court.

3.2.3 The US Supreme Court

The US Supreme Court is the highest court in the land. Rulings from the Supreme Court are bidding in all jurisdictions. Each year the Supreme Court receives 8,000 appeals of rulings out of the US circuit courts of appeals. These appeals ask the court to hear the case. This appeal is called a Petition for a Writ of Certiorari. This petition, typically written by attorneys for a party not satisfied with the decision of the appellate court, essentially asks the Supreme Court to request that a lower court send up records of a case for review. Often, the Supreme Court will ask the solicitor general of the United States, the fourth-highest-ranking official in the US Department of Justice, to file a brief in the case expressing the views of the US government in the case.

The petition will also ask the court to answer a question or two of major importance in the case. The Supreme Court is not required to hear cases that are appealed to it. In fact, the High Court grants certiorari and generally hears less than 1% of the cases appealed to it. Generally, the US Supreme Court will hear cases of significance or cases that represent a split or disagreement among the circuits. If the Supreme Court justices decide to hear a case, called granting the petition for certiorari, the case is placed on the docket. Attorneys for the petitioner and respondent are then given a limited amount of time in which they are to write a brief limited to 50 pages. After the original briefs are filed, both parties may write shorter briefs responding to the written arguments of the other party. The US solicitor general will also file a brief representing the views of the federal government. Additionally, if the Supreme Court allows it, parties not directly involved with the case, but who are nonetheless interested in its outcome, may file friend of the court briefs, called *amicus curiae*. The Supreme Court will then schedule oral arguments. During oral arguments, the petitioner and respondent have approximately 30 minutes each to present their case. Typically, the justices will pepper the attorneys with questions during their presentations. After the allotted hour, oral arguments will end, and the justices will proceed to conference to discuss the case. After the case has been decided, the senior justice in the majority will assign a justice to write the majority opinion. If a justice agrees with the outcome of the case but not the rationale for arriving at it, he or she may write a concurring opinion. Any justice may write a dissenting opinion.

There have only been 12 special education cases ruled on by the US Supreme Court (13 if you count a decision that ended in a tie). These cases are of tremendous importance to special educators throughout the United States because rulings by the Supreme Court are binding on all lower courts and DPHs in the country. The cases we review is this annual are the highest federal court cases heard regarding students with disabilities and federal law in 2021. No cases were heard by the US Supreme Court in 2021.

3.3 Published and Unpublished Decisions

In this annual, readers will notice some cases are listed with a citation (e.g., 959 F.3d 519). The citation means that the case is published in a federal reporter. When a case is chosen for publication, the case becomes binding precedent, sometimes called mandatory or controlling authority, in that court and in the district courts in the circuit in which the published case was heard. Attorneys may cite the case in the brief they submit to a court. The case may also have persuasive authority in other circuits and in district courts outside of the circuit with the published case. Some cases are listed with a Federal Appendix number (e.g., 808 F. App'x 19), an "unpublished" label, or both. Cases that appear in the Federal Appendix are where rulings of the US court of appeals that have not been selected for publication in the *Federal Reporter* may appear. These cases do not generate binding precedent but may be persuasive. Persuasive cases may also be cited by attorneys in certain circumstances.

3.4 Researching Cases Online

With the availability of online resources, today's school employees are more legally literate about special education laws, policies, and procedures and are better able to identify legal issues, identify applicable laws or legal standards, and apply relevant legal rules to solve legal dilemmas. Since many of the legal sources involving children with disabilities originated in federal statutory laws, it is a good place to begin your search of special education–related legal information. Federal and state statutes are readily available in both print and online versions. Federal statutes are located in the *United States Code (USC)*, the official version. Federal statutes are organized by topic or subject and are published in the *United States Code* as a series of volumes. All three of the leading federal statutes impacting students with disabilities can be found in specific titles of the *United States Code*, including the Individuals with Disabilities Education Act, Section

504 of the Rehabilitation Act of 1973, and the Americans with Disabilities Act (ADA). For example, the Individuals with Disabilities Education Act (IDEA) can be found in Title 20 (Education) of the *United States Code*; Section 504 of the Rehabilitation Act of 1973 can be found in Title 29 (Labor Statutes); and the Americans with Disabilities Act (ADA) can be found under Title 42 (Public Health and Welfare).

Due to significant advances in the accessibility of online legal information, there are many online resources providing free access to the *United States Code*, allowing users to browse or search by a specific title, chapter, or section. The official web page of the *United States Code* can be found on the govinfo website: https://www.govinfo.gov/app/collection/USCODE.

Additionally, the *United States Code* can be accessed online through a variety of nongovernmental websites, including Cornell's Legal Information Institute (LII) (https://www.law.cornell.edu/uscode/text) or FindLaw's *United States Code* online sites (https://codes.findlaw.com/us/).

Regulations are published in the *Code of Federal Regulations* (CFR). State laws and regulations are generally available online from the websites of their states. Legal citations are easy to read. The first number indicates the volume number where the case, statute, or regulation is located; the abbreviation refers to the book or series in which the material may be found; the second number indicates the page on which a case begins or the section number of a statute or regulation; the last part of a citation includes the name of the court, for lower court cases, and the year in which the dispute was resolved. For instance, the citation for *Barnett v. Memphis City School System*, 294 F. Supp.2d 924 (W.D. Tenn. 2003) can be found in volume 294 of the *Federal Supplement, Second Series* beginning on page 924. The case was resolved at the federal trial court in the Western Division of Tennessee.

Like federal statutes, the federal regulations, the *Code of Federal Regulations* (CFR) are all available online. Two useful online resources for accessing the federal regulations relating to special education include (1) *Electronic Code of Federal Regulations* (e-CFR), (https://www.ecfr.gov), a currently updated version of the *Code of Federal Regulations* (CFR); and (2) the US Department of Education's IDEA website detailing both the statute and regulations (https://sites.ed.gov/idea/statuteregulations/#regulations).

Individual state statutes and regulations often organize their statutes based on subject (e.g., education). In many states, you can find specific websites that provide access to specific state statutes and regulations. For example, Cornell's Legal Information Institute (LII) allows you to search education statutes by individual state (https://www.law.cornell.edu/wex/table_education) or jurisdiction type (https://www.law.cornell.edu/states/listing).

The internet has made finding legal cases at the federal, state, and local levels much more accessible. Today, for example, legal opinions are accessible daily from official federal and state court websites as well as secondary websites, including Google Scholar, FindLaw, and Justica. Many of the legal cases profiled in this book can be found online on the Google Scholar website (https://scholar.google.com), which includes both federal and state legal opinions (see figure 3.1). From the main Google Scholar search page, select the radio button for "Case law." Type your case citation or case name in the search box and click the Search button. Keyword searches of the full text of case opinions may also be conducted from this screen. Searches may be limited to federal courts and/or to particular state courts. The United States courts website provides access to US Supreme Court, US courts of appeals, and US district court websites. Table 3.2 lists online resources for searching federal- and state-level court decisions or rulings. Additionally, open access websites, including Cornell's Legal Information Institute (LII) and Google Scholar, allow users to search federal and state legal cases individually or together (Yell, 2019). Beginning in 2001, the Public Access to Court Electronic Records (PACER) website (https://www.pacer.gov/findcase.html) became available, allowing users to retrieve individual legal cases online from both federal appellate- and district-level jurisdictions. Currently, there is a maximum charge of $3.00 for online access to any single court case document other than name searches, reports that are not case specific, and transcripts of federal court proceedings. Table 3.3 provides leading online resources of special education statutes, regulations, and administrative agency policy and guidance documents. Increasingly, there are a growing number of secondary online legal resources related to special education law and policy. One such example of a secondary online resource for special education law and policy are blogs. Blogs are online discussions on a particular topic and involve informal diary-style text entries, often referred to as posts. Online blog posts are usually displayed in chronological order. Table 3.4 lists some of the leading special education law and policy blogs, including the SPEDLAW blog (https://spedlawblog.com), which was created by the authors of this book.

TABLE 3.2. Online Resources for Searching Special Education Federal- and State-Level Caselaw

Name	Website
Case Law Access Project (Harvard University) (Provides access to all US official published case law)	https://case.law/
Cornell's Legal Information Institute (LII) (Cornell Law School) (Provides primary legal materials, legal encyclopedia, and the Supreme Court Bulletin)	https://www.law.cornell.edu/
Google Scholar	https://scholar.google.com
Justia	https://law.justia.com/
Oyez	http://www.oyez.org
PACER (Public Access to Court Electronic Records) (*Note*: there is a nominal fee associated with accessing legal case information)	https://www.pacer.gov/
Public Library of Law	https://www.fastcase.com/
US Supreme Court	http://supremecourt.gov
US Courts	http://uscourts.gov

TABLE 3.3. **Online Resources of Special Education Statutes, Regulations, and Administrative Agency Policy and Guidance Documents**

Name	Website
Americans with Disabilities Act's (ADA) Homepage	https://www.ada.gov/pubs/ada statute08.htm
Cornell Legal Information Institute (CII): State Law Resources by Jurisdiction	https://www.law.cornell.edu/states/listing
e-CFR (Electronic Code of Federal Regulations)	https://www.ecfr.gov
US Department of Education, Office of Special Education Programs (OSEP) policy letters and guidance to support the implementation of the Individuals with Disabilities Education Act (IDEA)	https://sites.ed.gov/idea/policy-guidance/
US Department of Education, IDEA Statute and Regulations	https://sites.ed.gov/idea/statuteregulations/
US Department of Labor—Section 504 of the Rehabilitation Act of 1973	https://www.dol.gov/oasam/regs/statutes/sec504.htm
US House of Representatives, Office of the Law Revision Counsel	http://uscode.house.gov
50 State Survey of Special Education Laws and Regulations (Franklin County Law Library)	https://fclawlib.libguides.com/specialeducation/50statesurvey

TABLE 3.4. **Online Blogs of Special Education Legal Information**

Name	Website
Disability Scoop: Politics and Law Blog	http://www.disabilityscoop.com/politics/
Education Law Prof Blog	https://lawprofessors.typepad.com/education_law/
SpedLawBlog	https://spedlawblog.com/
The Wrightslaw Law to Special Education Law and Advocacy	https://www.wrightslaw.com/blog/

CHAPTER 4

Topics Covered by US Courts of Appeals in 2021

4.1 504 Implementation
    4.1.1 Ninth Circuit
        4.1.1.1 R.D., a minor, by and through her personal representatives, Catherine DAVIS and Sean DAVIS; et al., Plaintiffs-Appellants, v. LAKE WASHINGTON SCHOOL DISTRICT, a municipal corporation, Defendant-Appellee

4.2 Attorney's Fees
    4.2.1 Ninth Circuit
        4.2.1.1 Melissa GORDON; Robert GORDON, Plaintiffs-Appellees, v. LOS ANGELES UNIFIED SCHOOL DISTRICT, Defendant-Appellant Melissa GORDON; Robert GORDON, Plaintiffs-Appellants, v. LOS ANGELES UNIFIED SCHOOL DISTRICT, Defendant-Appellee
        4.2.1.2 Matthew C. OSKOWIS, individually and on behalf of E.O., Plaintiff-Appellant, v. SEDONA-OAK CREEK UNIFIED SCHOOL DISTRICT # 9, Defendant-Appellee

4.3 Cause of Action
    4.3.1 Fifth Circuit
        4.3.1.1 T.O. v. FORT BEND INDEPENDENT SCHOOL DISTRICT

4.4 Charter Schools
    4.4.1 Third Circuit
        4.4.1.1 HATIKVAH INTERNATIONAL ACADEMY CHARTER SCHOOL, Appellant v. EAST BRUNSWICK TOWNSHIP BOARD OF EDUCATION; A.K. & R.K. on behalf of H.K.

4.5 Child Find
4.5.1 Second Circuit
4.5.1.1 K.B., on behalf of S.B. v. KATONAH LEWISBORO UNION FREE SCHOOL DISTRICT

4.5.2 Third Circuit
4.5.2.1 A.B., through his parent KATINA B., Appellants v. ABINGTON SCHOOL DISTRICT, Respondents

4.5.3 Ninth Circuit
4.5.3.1 Debra LEGRIS; Aviana LEGRIS, Plaintiffs-Appellants, v. CAPISTRANO UNIFIED SCHOOL DISTRICT, a local educational agency, Defendant-Appellee

4.5.4 Tenth Circuit
4.5.4.1 J.N., as mother and NEXT FRIEND OF M.N., a minor v. JEFFERSON COUNTY BOARD OF EDUCATION

4.6 Coronavirus
4.6.1 Fifth Circuit
4.6.1.1 E.T., J.R., S.P., M.P., E.S., H.M., & A.M. v. PAXTON

4.7 Corporal Punishment
4.7.1 Fifth Circuit
4.7.1.1 T.O. v. FORT BEND INDEPENDENT SCHOOL DISTRICT

4.8 Deliberate Indifference
4.8.1 Fifth Circuit
4.8.1.1 Rosie Phillips, next friend of J.H. v. Stephen W. Prator, for the Caddo Parish Sheriff's Office

4.8.2 Ninth Circuit
4.8.2.1 Claudia HERRERA; Cesar ORTIZ, Plaintiffs-Appellants, v. LOS ANGELES UNIFIED SCHOOL DISTRICT, a public entity; Jose HUERTA; Jose LOPEZ; DOES; LOS ANGELES UNIFIED SCHOOL DISTRICT, Defendants-Appellees, and COUNTY OF LOS ANGELES, Defendant

4.8.2.2 R.D., a minor, by and through her personal representatives, Catherine DAVIS and Sean DAVIS; et al., Plaintiffs-Appellants, v. LAKE WASHINGTON SCHOOL DISTRICT, a municipal corporation, Defendant-Appellee

4.9 Discrimination
4.9.1 Fifth Circuit
4.9.1.1 D.H.H. v. KIRBY CONSOLIDATED INDEPENDENT SCHOOL DISTRICT

4.9.1.2 HARRISON as next friend of B.F. v. KLEIN INDEPENDENT SCHOOL DISTRICT

4.10 Eligibility
4.10.1 Fifth Circuit
4.10.1.1 D.H.H. v. KIRBY CONSOLIDATED INDEPENDENT SCHOOL DISTRICT

4.11 Emotional Disturbance
4.11.1 Fifth Circuit
4.11.1.1 D.H.H. v. KIRBY CONSOLIDATED INDEPENDENT SCHOOL DISTRICT
4.11.1.2 LEIGH ANN H. as parent, guardian, and next friend of K.S. v. RIESEL INDEPENDENT SCHOOL DISTRICT

4.12 Evaluation
4.12.1 Fifth Circuit
4.12.1.1 AMANDA P. AND CASEY P., as parent/guardian/next friend of T.P. v. COPPERAS COVE INDEPENDENT SCHOOL DISTRICT
4.12.1.2 D.C. v. KLEIN INDEPENDENT SCHOOL DISTRICT

4.13 Fourth Amendment Rights
4.13.1 Fifth Circuit
4.13.1.1 J.W. v. Paley

4.14 Free Appropriate Public Education
4.14.1 Second Circuit
4.14.1.1 A.R., on behalf of a class of those similarly situated v. CONNECTICUT STATE BOARD OF EDUCATION

4.14.2 Third Circuit
4.14.2.1 Eileen ESPOSITO; Louis ESPOSITO; Kyle MATULLO, Appellants v. RIDGEFIELD PARK BOARD OF EDUCATION

4.14.3 Sixth Circuit
4.14.3.1 Nestor ALVAREZ, individually and on behalf of K.A. v. SWANTON LOCAL SCHOOL DISTRICT

4.15 Frivolous Lawsuit
4.15.1 Ninth Circuit
4.15.1.1 Matthew C. OSKOWIS, individually and on behalf of E.O., Plaintiff-Appellant, v. SEDONA-OAK CREEK UNIFIED SCHOOL DISTRICT # 9, Defendant-Appellee

4.16 Exhaustion of Administrative Remedies
4.16.1 Third Circuit
4.16.1.1 Thomas AHEARN, as parents and natural guardians of Louis AHERN, Eileen AHEARN, as parents and natural

guardians of Louis AHERN, Appellants v. EAST STROUDSBURG AREA SCHOOL DISTRICT; COLONIAL INTERMEDIATE UNIT 20

4.16.1.2 T.R., a minor, individually, by and through her parent, Barbara GALARZA, and on behalf of all others similarly situated; Barbara GALARZA, individually, and on behalf of all others similarly situated; A.G., a minor, individually, by and through his parent, Margarita PERALTA, and on behalf of all others similarly situated; Margarita PERALTA, individually, and on behalf of all others similarly situated; L.R.; D.R., a minor, individually, by and through her parent, Madeline PEREZ, and on behalf of all others similarly situated; J.R.; Madeline PEREZ, individually, and on behalf of all others similarly situated; R.H., a minor, individually, by and through his parent, Manqing LIN, and on behalf of all others similarly situated; Manqing LIN, individually, and on behalf of all others similarly situated v. SCHOOL DISTRICT OF PHILADELPHIA

4.16.2 Fifth Circuit

4.16.2.1 Lela Logan, individually and on behalf of her minor child L.L. v. MORRIS JEFF COMMUNITY SCHOOL

4.16.3 Sixth Circuit

4.16.3.1 PEREZ v. STURGIS PUBLIC SCHOOLS; STURGIS PUBLIC SCHOOLS BOARD OF EDUCATION

4.16.4 Ninth Circuit

4.16.4.1 D.D., a minor, by and through his guardian ad litem, Michaela INGRAM, Plaintiff-Appellant, v. LOS ANGELES UNIFIED SCHOOL DISTRICT, Defendant-Appellee

4.16.4.2 D.O., by and through his guardian ad litem Sonya WALKER, Plaintiff-Appellee, v. ESCONDIDO UNION SCHOOL DISTRICT, Defendant-Appellant

4.16.4.3 STUDENT A, by and through PARENT A, her guardian; STUDENT B, by and through PARENT B, his guardian; STUDENT C, by and through PARENT C, his guardian; STUDENT D, by and through PARENT D, her guardian; STUDENT E, by and through PARENT E, her guardian, on behalf of themselves and all others similarly situated, Plaintiffs-Appellants, v. SAN FRANCISCO UNIFIED SCHOOL DISTRICT; Vincent MATTHEWS, in his official capacity as the Superintendent for the San Francisco Unified School District, Defendants-Appellees

4.17 Harassment

4.17.1 Fifth Circuit

4.17.1.1 Harrison as next friend of B.F. v. KLEIN INDEPENDENT SCHOOL DISTRICT

4.18 Homebound
4.18.1 Sixth Circuit
4.18.1.1 Nestor ALVAREZ, individually and on behalf of K.A. v. SWANTON LOCAL SCHOOL DISTRICT

4.19 Identification
4.19.1 Fifth Circuit
4.19.1.1 Amanda P. and Casey P., as parent/guardian/next friend of T.P. v. Copperas Cove Independent School District
4.19.1.2 D.C. v. KLEIN INDEPENDENT SCHOOL DISTRICT

4.20 IEP
4.20.1 Second Circuit
4.20.1.1 BOARD OF EDUCATION OF THE YORKTOWN CENTRAL SCHOOL v. C.S., Individually and on Behalf of M.S., a Minor, S.S., Individually and on Behalf of M.S., a Minor

4.20.2 Ninth Circuit
4.20.2.1 CAPISTRANO UNIFIED SCHOOL DISTRICT, Plaintiff-Appellant/Cross-Appellee, v. S.W. and C.W., on behalf of their minor child, B.W., Defendants-Appellees/Cross-Appellants

4.21 Independent Educational Evaluations
4.21.1 Ninth Circuit
4.21.1.1 L.C., a minor, by and through his Guardian Ad Litem Ausencia CRUZ, Plaintiff-Appellee, v. ALTA LOMA SCHOOL DISTRICT, a Local Educational Agency, Defendant-Appellant

4.22 Initial IEP
4.22.1 Third Circuit
4.22.1.1 NORTHFIELD CITY BOARD OF EDUCATION v. K.S., on behalf of L.S., Appellant

4.23 IQ Testing
4.23.1 Third Circuit
4.23.1.1 Eileen ESPOSITO; Louis ESPOSITO; Kyle MATULLO, Appellants v. RIDGEFIELD PARK BOARD OF EDUCATION

4.24 Judicial Review
4.24.1 Tenth Circuit
4.24.1.1 C.W. by and through his parents B.W. and C.B. v. DENVER COUNTY SCHOOL DISTRICT NO. 1

4.25 Jurisdiction
4.25.1 Tenth Circuit
4.25.1.1 C.W. by and through his parents B.W. and C.B. v. DENVER COUNTY SCHOOL DISTRICT NO. 1

4.26 Maintenance of Program
    4.26.1 Third Circuit
        4.26.1.1 Y.B., on behalf of S.B.; F.B., on behalf of S.B. v. HOWELL TOWNSHIP BOARD OF EDUCATION

4.27 Masks
    4.27.1 Sixth Circuit
        4.27.1.1 G.S., by and through his parents and next friends, Brittany and Ryan Schwaigert, et al., v. GOVERNOR BILL LEE
        4.27.1.2 M.B., parent of minor S.B. et al., v. Governor William Lee, KNOX COUNTY BOARD OF EDUCATION

4.28 Mootness
    4.28.1 Fourth Circuit
        4.28.1.1 Johnson on behalf of A.J. and T.S. v. CHARLOTTE MECKLENBERG SCHOOL BOARD OF EDUCATION

4.29 Paraprofessional
    4.29.1 Ninth Circuit
        4.29.1.1 Claudia HERRERA; Cesar ORTIZ, Plaintiffs-Appellants, v. LOS ANGELES UNIFIED SCHOOL DISTRICT, a public entity; Jose HUERTA; Jose LOPEZ; DOES; LOS ANGELES UNIFIED SCHOOL DISTRICT, Defendants-Appellees, and COUNTY OF LOS ANGELES, Defendant

4.30 Private School Reimbursement
    4.30.1 Ninth Circuit
        4.30.1.1 CAPISTRANO UNIFIED SCHOOL DISTRICT, Plaintiff-Appellant/Cross-Appellee, v. S.W. and C.W., on behalf of their minor child, B.W., Defendants-Appellees/Cross-Appellants

4.31 Procedural Matters
    4.31.1 Tenth Circuit
        4.31.1.1 C.W. by and through his parents B.W. and C.B. v. DENVER COUNTY SCHOOL DISTRICT NO. 1

4.32 Procedural Violations
    4.32.1 Ninth Circuit
        4.32.1.1 L.C., a minor, by and through his Guardian Ad Litem Ausencia CRUZ, Plaintiff-Appellee, v. ALTA LOMA SCHOOL DISTRICT, a Local Educational Agency, Defendant-Appellant

4.33 Qualified Immunity
    4.33.1 Fifth Circuit
        4.33.1.1 J.W. v. Paley

4.34 Referral
4.34.1 Fifth Circuit
4.34.1.1 Leigh Ann H. as parent, guardian, and next friend of K.S. v. RIESEL INDEPENDENT SCHOOL DISTRICT

4.35 Relationship between Conduct and Disability
4.35.1 Fifth Circuit
4.35.1.1 Leigh Ann H. as parent, guardian, and next friend of K.S. v. RIESEL INDEPENDENT SCHOOL DISTRICT

4.36 Retaliation
4.36.1 Third Circuit
4.36.1.1 Shanicqua S. APONTE, Appellant v. POTTSTOWN SCHOOL DISTRICT; Ryan JACOBS; Joseph SCHROEDER, all in personal and professional capacity

4.37 Safety
4.37.1 Third Circuit
4.37.1.1 H.U.; B.U., parents and natural guardians of K.U., a minor, Appellants v. NORTHAMPTON AREA SCHOOL DISTRICT; COLONIAL NORTHAMPTON IU-20

4.38 Settlement Agreements
4.38.1 Second Circuit
4.38.1.1 Shkelqesa DERVISHI, on behalf of T.D. v. DEPARTMENT OF SPECIAL EDUCATION, in STAMFORD PUBLIC SCHOOL, STAMFORD BOARD OF EDUCATION

4.39 Sexual Assault
4.39.1 Third Circuit
4.39.1.1 H.U.; B.U., parents and natural guardians of K.U., a minor, Appellants v. NORTHAMPTON AREA SCHOOL DISTRICT; COLONIAL NORTHAMPTON IU-20

4.40 Stay Put
4.40.1 Second Circuit
4.40.1.1 ABRAMS, individually as parent and natural guardian of A.A. v. NEW YORK CITY DEPARTMENT OF EDUCATION
4.40.1.2 Alexandra FIALLOS, as parent and natural guardian of L.F. and individually, v. NEW YORK CITY DEPARTMENT OF EDUCATION

4.40.2 Third Circuit
4.40.2.1 HATIKVAH INTERNATIONAL ACADEMY CHARTER SCHOOL, Appellant v. EAST BRUNSWICK TOWNSHIP BOARD OF EDUCATION; A.K. & R.K. on behalf of H.K.

4.40.2.2 NORTHFIELD CITY BOARD OF EDUCATION v. K.S., on behalf of L.S., Appellant

4.40.2.3 Y.B., on behalf of S.B.; F.B., on behalf of S.B. v. HOWELL TOWNSHIP BOARD OF EDUCATION

4.40.3 Ninth Circuit

4.40.3.1 E.E., a minor, by and through his guardian ad litem Laura HUTCHISON-ESCOBEDO; Christopher ESCOBEDO; Laura ESCOBEDO, Plaintiffs-Counter-Defendants-Appellees, v. NORRIS SCHOOL DISTRICT, Defendant-Counter-Claimant-Appellant

4.40.3.2 S.C. by her mother and next friend, K.G., Plaintiff-Appellant, v. LINCOLN COUNTY SCHOOL DISTRICT, Defendant-Appellee

CHAPTER 5

Case Summaries by Circuit

5.1 Summary of a Ruling by the US Supreme Court

    5.1.1   Mahanoy Area School District v. B.L.

5.2 Summaries of Rulings from the US Court of Appeals for the Second Circuit[1]

    5.2.1   A.R., on behalf of a class of those similarly situated v. CONNECTICUT STATE BOARD OF EDUCATION

    5.2.2   Elizabeth ABRAMS, individually as parent and natural guardian of A.A., Dore ABRAMS, individually as parent and natural guardian of A.A., Arelis ARAUJO, individually as parent and natural guardian of Z.A., Luis ARAUJO, individually as parent and natural guardian of Z.A., Jhoana JUCA, individually as parent and natural guardian of K.A., Victor ARTEAGA, individually as parent and natural guardian of K.A., Donna CORNETT, individually as parent and natural guardian of J.B., John BURGESS, individually as parent and natural guardian of J.B., Eileen MENDEZ, individually as parent and natural guardian of A.C., Yvonne DAVIS, individually as parent and natural guardian of O.C., Claudia RIVAS, individually as parent and natural guardian of S.C., Brenda MELENDEZ, individually as parent and natural guardian of J.C., Carolyn MASON, individually as parent and natural guardian of A.D., Patrick DONOHUE, individually as parent and natural guardian of S.J.D., Neysha CRUZ, individually as parent and natural guardian of O.F., Piedad ANGAMARCA, individually as parent and natural guardian of J.G., Janice TORRES, individually as parent and natural

---

[1]. No special education cases were found for the US courts of appeals for the First, Seventh, Eighth, or DC Circuit.

guardian of A.L., Abdon LOPEZ, individually as parent and natural guardian of A.L., Shannon THOMASON, individually as parent and natural guardian of E.P., Vinnie PENNA, individually as parent and natural guardian of E.P., Alexandra VERA-FIALLOS, individually as parent and natural guardian of L.F., Nahoko MIZUTA, individually as parent and natural guardian of Y.M., Kentaro MIZUTA, individually as parent and natural guardian of Y.M., Yarely MORA, individually as parent and natural guardian of L.N., Luis NUNEZ, Sr., individually as parent and natural guardian of L.N., Plaintiffs-Appellants, v. Meisha PORTER, in her official capacity as the Chancellor of the New York City Department of Education, NEW YORK CITY DEPARTMENT OF EDUCATION, Defendants-Appellees

5.2.3 BOARD OF EDUCATION OF THE YORKTOWN CENTRAL SCHOOL v. C.S., Individually and on Behalf of M.S., a Minor, S.S., Individually and on Behalf of M.S., a Minor

5.2.4 Shkelqesa DERVISHI, on behalf of T.D. v. DEPARTMENT OF SPECIAL EDUCATION, in STAMFORD PUBLIC SCHOOL, STAMFORD BOARD OF EDUCATION

5.2.5 Alexandra FIALLOS, as parent and natural guardian of L.F. and individually, v. NEW YORK CITY DEPARTMENT OF EDUCATION

5.2.6 K.B., on behalf of S.B. v. KATONAH LEWISBORO UNION FREE SCHOOL DISTRICT

5.3 Summaries of Rulings from the US Court of Appeals for the Third Circuit

5.3.1 A.B., through his parent KATINA B., Appellants v. ABINGTON SCHOOL DISTRICT, Respondents

5.3.2 Thomas AHEARN, as parents and natural guardians of Louis AHERN, Eileen AHEARN, as parents and natural guardians of Louis AHERN, Appellants v. EAST STROUDSBURG AREA SCHOOL DISTRICT; COLONIAL INTERMEDIATE UNIT 20

5.3.3 Shanicqua S. APONTE, Appellant v. POTTSTOWN SCHOOL DISTRICT; Ryan OXENFORD; Matthew MOYER; Steven RODRIGUEZ; Brett WADE; Kim STILLWELL; Eren JACOBS; Joseph SCHROEDER, all in personal and professional capacity

5.3.4 Eileen ESPOSITO; Louis ESPOSITO; Kyle MATULLO, Appellants v. RIDGEFIELD PARK BOARD OF EDUCATION

5.3.5 H.U.; B.U., parents and natural guardians of K.U., a minor, Appellants v. NORTHAMPTON AREA SCHOOL DISTRICT; COLONIAL NORTHAMPTON IU-20

5.3.6 HATIKVAH INTERNATIONAL ACADEMY CHARTER SCHOOL, Appellant v. EAST BRUNSWICK TOWNSHIP BOARD OF EDUCATION; A.K. & R.K. on behalf of H.K.

Case Summaries by Circuit

- 5.3.7 NORTHFIELD CITY BOARD OF EDUCATION v. K.S., on behalf of L.S., Appellant
- 5.3.8 T.R., a minor, individually, by and through her parent, Barbara GALARZA, and on behalf of all others similarly situated; Barbara GALARZA, individually, and on behalf of all others similarly situated; A.G., a minor, individually, by and through his parent, Margarita PERALTA, and on behalf of all others similarly situated; Margarita PERALTA, individually, and on behalf of all others similarly situated; L.R.; D.R., a minor, individually, by and through her parent, Madeline PEREZ, and on behalf of all others similarly situated; J.R.; Madeline PEREZ, individually, and on behalf of all others similarly situated; R.H., a minor, individually, by and through his parent, Manqing LIN, and on behalf of all others similarly situated; Manqing LIN, individually, and on behalf of all others similarly situated v. SCHOOL DISTRICT OF PHILADELPHIA
- 5.3.9 Y.B., on behalf of S.B.; F.B., on behalf of S.B. v. HOWELL TOWNSHIP BOARD OF EDUCATION

5.4 Summaries of Rulings from the US Court of Appeals for the Fourth Circuit

- 5.4.1 Johnson on behalf of A.J. and T.S. v. CHARLOTTE-MECKLENBURG SCHOOL BOARD OF EDUCATION

5.5 Summaries of Rulings from the US Court of Appeals for the Fifth Circuit

- 5.5.1 Amanda P. and Casey P, as parent/guardian/next friend of T.P. v. COPPERAS COVE INDEPENDENT SCHOOL DISTRICT
- 5.5.2 D.C. v. KLEIN INDEPENDENT SCHOOL DISTRICT
- 5.5.3 D.H.H. v. KIRBYVILLE CONSOLIDATED INDEPENDENT SCHOOL DISTRICT
- 5.5.4 E.T., J.R., S.P., M.P., E.S., H.M., & A.M. v. PAXTON
- 5.5.5 Harrison as next friend of B.F. v. KLEIN INDEPENDENT SCHOOL DISTRICT
- 5.5.6 J.W. v. PALEY
- 5.5.7 Leigh Ann H. as parent, guardian, and next friend of K.S. v. RIESEL INDEPENDENT SCHOOL DISTRICT
- 5.5.8 Lela Logan, individually and on behalf of her minor child L.L. v. MORRIS JEFF COMMUNITY SCHOOL
- 5.5.9 Rosie Phillips, next friend of J.H. v. Stephen W. Prator, for the CADDO PARISH SHERIFF'S OFFICE
- 5.5.10 T.O. v. FORT BEND INDEPENDENT SCHOOL DISTRICT

- 5.6 Summaries of Rulings from the US Court of Appeals for the Sixth Circuit
  - 5.6.1 Nestor ALVAREZ, individually and on behalf of K.A. v. SWANTON LOCAL SCHOOL DISTRICT
  - 5.6.2 G.S., by and through his parents and next friends, Brittany and Ryan Schwaigert, et al., v. GOVERNOR BILL LEE
  - 5.6.3 M.B., parent of minor S.B. et al., v. Governor William Lee, KNOX COUNTY BOARD OF EDUCATION
  - 5.6.4 PEREZ v. STURGIS PUBLIC SCHOOLS; STURGIS PUBLIC SCHOOLS BOARD OF EDUCATION
- 5.7 Summaries of Rulings from the US Court of Appeals for the Ninth Circuit
  - 5.7.1 CAPISTRANO UNIFIED SCHOOL DISTRICT, Plaintiff-Appellant/Cross-Appellee, v. S.W. and C.W., on behalf of their minor child, B.W., Defendants-Appellees/Cross-Appellants
  - 5.7.2 D.D., a minor, by and through his guardian ad litem, Michaela INGRAM, Plaintiff-Appellant, v. LOS ANGELES UNIFIED SCHOOL DISTRICT, Defendant-Appellee
  - 5.7.3 D.O., by and through his guardian ad litem Sonya WALKER, Plaintiff-Appellee, v. ESCONDIDO UNION SCHOOL DISTRICT, Defendant-Appellant
  - 5.7.4 E.E., a minor, by and through his guardian ad litem Laura HUTCHISON-ESCOBEDO; Christopher ESCOBEDO; Laura ESCOBEDO, Plaintiffs-Counter-Defendants-Appellees, v. NORRIS SCHOOL DISTRICT, Defendant-Counter-Claimant-Appellant
  - 5.7.5 Melissa GORDON; Robert GORDON, Plaintiffs-Appellees, v. LOS ANGELES UNIFIED SCHOOL DISTRICT, Defendant-Appellant Melissa GORDON; Robert GORDON, Plaintiffs-Appellants, v. LOS ANGELES UNIFIED SCHOOL DISTRICT, Defendant-Appellee
  - 5.7.6 Claudia HERRERA; Cesar ORTIZ, Plaintiffs-Appellants, v. LOS ANGELES UNIFIED SCHOOL DISTRICT, a public entity; Jose HUERTA; Jose LOPEZ; DOES; LOS ANGELES UNIFIED SCHOOL DISTRICT, Defendants-Appellees, and COUNTY OF LOS ANGELES, Defendant
  - 5.7.7 L.C., a minor, by and through his Guardian Ad Litem Ausencia CRUZ, Plaintiff-Appellee, v. ALTA LOMA SCHOOL DISTRICT, a Local Educational Agency, Defendant-Appellant
  - 5.7.8 Debra LEGRIS; Aviana LEGRIS, Plaintiffs-Appellants, v. CAPISTRANO UNIFIED SCHOOL DISTRICT, a local educational agency, Defendant-Appellee

- 5.7.9 Matthew C. OSKOWIS, individually and on behalf of E.O., Plaintiff-Appellant, v. SEDONA-OAK CREEK UNIFIED SCHOOL DISTRICT #9, Defendant-Appellee
- 5.7.10 R.D., a minor, by and through her personal representatives, Catherine DAVIS and Sean DAVIS; et al., Plaintiffs-Appellants, v. LAKE WASHINGTON SCHOOL DISTRICT, a municipal corporation, Defendant-Appellee
- 5.7.11 S.C. by her mother and next friend, K.G., Plaintiff-Appellant, v. LINCOLN COUNTY SCHOOL DISTRICT, Defendant-Appellee
- 5.7.12 STUDENT A, by and through PARENT A, her guardian; STUDENT B, by and through PARENT B, his guardian; STUDENT C, by and through PARENT C, his guardian; STUDENT D, by and through PARENT D, her guardian; STUDENT E, by and through PARENT E, her guardian, on behalf of themselves and all others similarly situated, Plaintiffs-Appellants, v. SAN FRANCISCO UNIFIED SCHOOL DISTRICT; Vincent MATTHEWS, in his official capacity as the Superintendent for the San Francisco Unified School District, Defendants-Appellees

5.8 Summaries of Rulings from the US Court of Appeals for the Tenth Circuit

- 5.8.1 C.W. by and through his parents B.W. and C.B. v. DENVER COUNTY SCHOOL DISTRICT NO. 1

5.9 Summaries of Rulings from the US Court of Appeals for the Eleventh Circuit

- 5.9.1 J.N., as mother and NEXT FRIEND OF M.N., a minor v. JEFFERSON COUNTY BOARD OF EDUCATION

5.1 Summary of a Ruling by the US Supreme Court

5.1.1

Mahanoy Area School District

v.

B.L.

June 23, 2021

Note: Because this is a ruling of the Supreme Court, it will be published and is precedent for all lower courts. The ruling, previous rulings, petitions, and Amicus Curiae briefs are available at https://www.scotusblog.com/case-files/cases/mahanoy-area-school-district-v-b-l/.

Issues:

- The First Amendment in public schools
- The First Amendment and off-campus speech

Facts of the Case:

B.L. was a student in the Mahanoy Area School District in Mahanoy City, Pennsylvania. In her freshman year of high school, B.L. tried out for the cheerleading squad and made the junior varsity. Near the end of her freshman year B.L. tried out for a position on her school's varsity cheerleading squad. She was not selected for the varsity squad and instead was offered a spot on the junior varsity squad. B.L. was frustrated with the decision, especially since another freshman student made the varsity team.

When she was at a convenience store with a friend, B.L. expressed her opinion on Snapchat. Her 250 followers received both messages she posted. The first Snapchat post featured a photograph of B.L. and a friend holding up their middle fingers and was captioned "F[***] school f[***] softball f[***] cheer f[***] everything." The second post simply contained the following text: "Love how me and [the name of another student] get told we need a year of jv before we make varsity but tha[t] doesn't matter to anyone else?" and an upside down smiley face emoji.

B.L.'s friends on Snapchat included current members of the school cheerleading squad. The team member took screen shots of the Snapchat posts and circulated them to others at the school, one of whom was a daughter of the cheerleading coaches. Both the members of the cheerleading squad and students at large reportedly approached cheerleading coaches upset by what B.L. had posted. When the cheerleading coaches brought the issue to the attention of the principal of B.L.'s high school, it was decided that B.L. would be suspended from the junior varsity cheerleading squad for the coming school year.

Subsequent apologies by B.L. for her behavior were not enough to change the opinion of the school district's administration. The superintendent for the school district, the school principal, and the school's athletic director supported the decision for B.L. to remain suspended from the cheerleading squad for the year. In response, B.L.'s parents filed suit in the US District Court for the Middle District of Pennsylvania, alleging that the Mahanoy school district violated her free speech rights under the First Amendment to the Constitution. The district court found that B.L.'s First Amendment right to free speech had been violated by the school's course of action in disciplining her. As a result, the court issued a temporary restraining order and injunction against the district and ordered B.L. be put back on the JV cheerleading squad. The district court also ordered that Mahanoy's athletic director clear B.L.'s disciplinary record and pay a small sum in damages and attorney's fees for B.L.'s family.

On appeal, a panel of the US Court of Appeals for the Third Circuit affirmed the district court's ruling that Mahanoy's disciplinary action of B.L.'s profanity on social media violated the First Amendment. In the case, which at that time was titled *B.L. v. Mahanoy Area School District*, the court held that off-campus speech enjoyed the full scope of First Amendment protections. The school district filed an appeal with the US Supreme Court, which agreed to hear the case in January 2021.

Ruling of the US Supreme Court:

Justice Stephen Breyer wrote the ruling for an 8–1 Supreme Court upholding the decisions of the circuit court. He began his ruling by noting the Supreme Court's decision in *Tinker v. Des Moines Independent School District* (1969) made it clear that students do not shed their constitutional rights at the schoolhouse gate. Justice Breyer also noted that, although school districts may have ground to regulate some forms of student off-campus speech, the facts of the *Mahanoy* case were not sufficient to overcome B.L.'s rights to free expression.

Justice Breyer offered three points to consider when regulating the off-campus behavior of students. First, although the US common law doctrine of *in loco parentis* (i.e., in place of the parent) asserts that schools have the obligation to stand in as proxies for the parents or guardians of minor youth during the school day, the primary responsibility for discipline for off-campus behavior should likely fall to parents and guardians. Second, a school official's decision to regulate the off-campus expression of students should be a decision made with great care considering the breadth of expression that students may engage in. Third, the court held that schools are "nurseries of democracy" and should take a special interest in protecting the unpopular expression of students. Nonetheless, Justice Breyer wrote, there are circumstances in which schools may need to regulate the off-campus behavior of students, including situations such as those involving (a) serious bullying or harassment, (b) harm or threats of harm to students or teachers, and (c) breaches of school security devices.

Significance to Educators:

School officials must exercise care in regulating the off-campus speech of students; however, this does not mean they should not exercise limits on it. When off-campus speech or behavior involves threats, harassment, or bullying, such behaviors or speech may be prohibited. When a school district prohibits such behaviors, these prohibitions should be clearly related to a legitimate school function (e.g., protecting the safety of students or teacher) and should be written into the school disciplinary code.

5.2 Summaries of Rulings from the US Court of Appeals for the Second Circuit

5.2.1

A.R., on behalf of a class of those similarly situated

v.

CONNECTICUT STATE BOARD OF EDUCATION

US Court of Appeals, Second Circuit

5 F.4th 155

July 8, 2021

Issue:

- Under Connecticut law, whether a student with disabilities has the right to receive a free appropriate public education (FAPE) between the ages of 21 and 22 under the Individuals with Disabilities Education Act (IDEA).

Facts of the Case:

In this case, a student's mother brought a class action lawsuit on behalf of her child with a disability as well as similarly situated students with disabilities who were receiving special education. Based on Connecticut law, students with disabilities were threatened to be denied special education and related services under the IDEA by the end of the school year in which they turned 21 years of age. Since the Connecticut State Board of Education provided free public education programs, including free adult education programs to nondisabled students between the ages of 21 and 22, the parent argued that the state board of education should also provide FAPE to students with disabilities in the same age group. It is also alleged that the Connecticut State Board of Education violated the IDEA because it denied special education services based on a student's age while simultaneously providing free public education services, including GED programs allowing disabled students between the ages of 21 and 22 to obtain a high school diploma.

Ruling:

The Second Circuit Court of Appeals affirmed the decision of a prior district court ruling that the Connecticut State Board of Education denied FAPE to students with disabilities between the ages of 21 and 22. Connecticut's publicly funded adult education programs constituted "public education" under the IDEA, and the state's termination of special education for disabled students between the ages of 21 and 22 violated both the IDEA and state law. As a result, the state board of education was unable to terminate students with disabilities, on the basis of age, who have not yet received a regular high school diploma before they reach the age of 22.

Significance to Educators:

In the state of Connecticut, this case illustrates that public school districts are legally required to offer FAPE to both students with and without disabilities until they turn 22 if they have not yet earned their high school diploma. In the case, the Second Circuit Court of Appeals held that the Connecticut State Board of Education violated the rights of students with disabilities between the ages of 21 and 22 by denying them FAPE while at the same time providing free public education services to nondisabled students in the same age range. This case demonstrates the importance of knowing state law in conjunction with relevant federal laws covering students with disabilities.

5.2.2

Elizabeth ABRAMS, individually as parent and natural guardian of A.A., Dore ABRAMS, individually as parent and natural guardian of A.A., Arelis ARAUJO, individually as parent and natural guardian of Z.A., Luis ARAUJO, individually as parent and natural guardian of Z.A., Jhoana JUCA, individually as parent and natural guardian of K.A., Victor ARTEAGA, individually as parent and natural guardian of K.A., Donna CORNETT, individually as parent and natural guardian of J.B., John BURGESS, individually as parent and natural guardian of J.B., Eileen MENDEZ, individually as parent and natural guardian of A.C., Yvonne DAVIS, individually as parent and natural guardian of O.C., Claudia RIVAS, individually as parent and natural guardian of S.C., Brenda MELENDEZ, individually as parent and natural guardian of J.C., Carolyn MASON, individually as parent and natural guardian of A.D., Patrick DONOHUE, individually as parent and natural guardian of S.J.D., Neysha CRUZ, individually as parent and natural guardian of O.F., Piedad ANGAMARCA, individually as parent and natural guardian of J.G., Janice TORRES, individually as parent and natural guardian of A.L., Abdon LOPEZ, individually as parent and natural guardian of A.L., Shannon THOMASON, individually as parent and natural guardian of E.P., Vinnie PENNA, individually as parent and natural guardian of E.P., Alexandra VERA-FIALLOS, individually as parent and natural guardian of L.F., Nahoko MIZUTA, individually as parent and natural guardian of Y.M., Kentaro MIZUTA, individually as parent and natural guardian of Y.M., Yarely MORA, individually as parent and natural guardian of L.N., Luis NUNEZ, Sr., individually as parent and natural guardian of L.N., Plaintiffs-Appellants, v. Meisha PORTER, in her official capacity as the Chancellor of the New York City Department of Education, NEW YORK CITY DEPARTMENT OF EDUCATION, Defendants-Appellees

US Court of Appeals, Second Circuit

December 9, 2021

Issues:

- Stay-put provision under the IDEA
- School district's obligation to pay for private services during the COVID-19 pandemic

Facts of the Case:

The parents of 17 unrelated parents of students with traumatic brain disorders were seeking reimbursement from a New York school district to pay for private school special education services offered to students with traumatic brain disorders offered during the COVID-19 pandemic. The parents argued that the stay-put provision under the IDEA legally required the district to pay for special education services their children received from their private special education schools during the early months of the COVID-19 pandemic. In this case, the parents were seeking payment from the district for certain special education services that their children received during the period of extended closures of public schools during spring 2020.

Ruling:

The Second Circuit Court of Appeals affirmed the ruling of a prior district court that the parents' request for the district to pay for private school special education services during the early months of the COVID-19 pandemic was denied. The Second Circuit agreed that the IDEA's stay-put provision legally requires a district to maintain a student's current educational placement while a dispute is ongoing or pending. In this case, the students' educational placements were not in any jeopardy. As such, the parents were seeking reimbursements for certain special education services their children received during the public school closures of spring 2020. The Second Circuit reasoned that since the students were at no risk of losing their pendency placement while the disputes regarding past payments continued, the district did not abuse its discretion in denying an injunction under the IDEA's stay-put provision.

Significance to Educators:

Pendency is the IDEA's primary method of preventing the disruption of a student with a disability's education when a district and parents disagree on the special education and related services that are recommended in an IEP (individualized education program). As this case illustrates, a school district's legal obligation to pay for private school services during the pendency of one or more IDEA-related disputes often depends on whether the student's placement is in jeopardy. In many instances, if a district can provide evidence that a particular student received special education services despite these services not being paid by the district, there is a good probability that a court will delay a payment order for these special education services. In this particular case, the fact that the 17 students were still attending their respective private school placement increased the district's claim that immediate payment of these private special education school services was unnecessary.

5.2.3

BOARD OF EDUCATION OF THE YORKTOWN CENTRAL SCHOOL

v.

C.S., Individually and on Behalf of M.S., a Minor, S.S., Individually and on Behalf of M.S., a Minor

990 F.3d 152

US Court of Appeals, Second Circuit

March 3, 2021

Issue:

- Whether a school district can unilaterally alter a student's Individualized Education Plan (IEP) during the IDEA's 30-day resolution period

Facts of the Case:

A New York school district brought legal action under the Individuals with Disabilities Education Act (IDEA) against the parents of a 12-year old middle school student who had numerous disabilities, including attention deficit hyperactivity disorder (ADHD) and Tourette's syndrome. The district is seeking the reversal of a state review officer (SRO) decision ordering the school district to provide tuition reimbursement for the student's private school tuition.

The student's original IEP prepared for the student and presented to the parents indicated incorrectly that the student would be placed in a 12-student classroom. The parents deemed this placement insufficient for their child. Instead, the parents believed that the district would actually provide a 15-student classroom placement, which the parents also deemed insufficient and then enrolled their child in a private school. When the parents filed a due process complaint, the district sought to unilaterally amend the student's original IEP to reflect that the student would be in a 15-student classroom.

A previous ruling by a district court ruled that the district did not effectively amend the student's IEP and denied the student a free appropriate public education (FAPE). Based on the district's failure to obtain the parents' written agreement to the change in the student's IEP, the district was ordered to reimburse the parents for their child's private school tuition.

Ruling:

The Second Circuit Court of Appeals affirmed the prior ruling of the district court ruling that a school district may not unilaterally amend a student's IEP during the IDEA's 30-day resolution period. As such, the district awarded the parents tuition reimbursement for the student's private school costs. The Second Circuit ruling stressed that the IEP is a collaborative process with procedural protections for parents. The district's failure to obtain parental agreement to proposed changes to the student's IEP prevented the district from arguing that the amended IEP would have offered FAPE.

Significance to Educators:

This legal case provides the legal rationale why a district cannot unilaterally amend a student's IEP during the 30-day resolution period under the IDEA following a parent's filing of a due process complaint. The IDEA's 30-day mediation period is a time for reaching consensus between school officials and parents. The IDEA needs to be a collaborative process requiring the participation of parents in all aspects surrounding the identification, evaluation, and educational placement of their child, including the entire contents of the student's IEP. The Second Circuit ruling indicates that districts in the states of New York, Connecticut, and Vermont must base their FAPE determinations on the student's IEP that originally prompted the parents' due process complaint.

5.2.4

Shkelqesa DERVISHI, on behalf of T.D.

v.

DEPARTMENT OF SPECIAL EDUCATION, in STAMFORD PUBLIC SCHOOL, STAMFORD BOARD OF EDUCATION

US Court of Appeals, Second Circuit

March 1, 2021

-Unpublished-

Issue:

- Settlement agreements under the IDEA

Facts of the Case:

On behalf of her autistic son, a parent sued a local board of education claiming that the student with disabilities was denied a free appropriate public education (FAPE) under the IDEA. More specifically, the parent argued that she was entitled to reimbursement for a home-based applied behavioral analysis (ABA) therapy program. Based on the terms of the settlement agreement, the parent was requesting in excess of $400,000 for the time she spent providing at-home ABA therapy to her son. While the district agreed to reimburse the parent for certain expenses specified in the settlement agreement, it denied the parent's requests for reimbursement for other expenses, including reimbursement for home-based ABA therapy, YMCA services, transportation costs for the student, and compensatory education. Additionally, there were disputes between the district and parent regarding the meaning of some terms in the settlement agreement—namely, the definition of "ABA services" and "autism consulting services," both of which the district originally agreed to pay.

Ruling:

While the Second Circuit Court of Appeals agreed that the parent was legally entitled to reimbursement for expenses related to the behavior analyst's services, she was not entitled to receive reimbursement for any of the home-based APA therapy services that she provided. According to the Second Circuit, the district did not properly define "autism consulting services" or specific parameters for reimbursement in the settlement agreement. Rather, the district's written settlement agreement only required reimbursement for ABA therapy by "qualified providers." The Second Circuit maintained that the parent was not a board certified behavior analyst and the parent's only training consisted of other trained ABA providers working with her son.

Significance to Educators:

This case highlights the importance of appropriately defining terms and detailing the parameters of parental reimbursement in a settlement agreement involving the IDEA. While the district ultimately did not have to reimburse the parent in excess of $400,000 for at-home ABA therapy–related costs, the district's failure to define several key terms in the settlement agreement resulted in largely preventable litigation costs as well as the lost time necessary to prepare the district's case for court proceedings.

5.2.5

Alexandra FIALLOS, as parent and natural guardian of L.F. and individually,

v.

NEW YORK CITY DEPARTMENT OF EDUCATION

840 F. App'x 662

US Court of Appeals, Second Circuit

March 25, 2021

Issue:

- The stay-put provision under the IDEA

Facts of the Case:

The parent of a nonverbal student with a traumatic brain injury alleged her son was denied a free appropriate public education (FAPE) because a New York school district violated the IDEA's stay-put provision based on a failure to fund the student's unilateral private school placement when an independent hearing officer (IHO) ordered the district to do so. As a result, the parent is seeking tuition reimbursement to the private school where her son was unilaterally placed.

Ruling:

The Second Circuit Court of Appeals affirmed a prior decision by a district court denying the parent's request for tuition reimbursement to a private school specializing in students with traumatic brain injuries. The Second Circuit ruled that the district did not violate the student's stay-put rights under the IDEA. Instead, the Second Circuit held that the events causing the parent to initiate a legal suit against the district were highly unlikely to occur in the future. In order to successfully demonstrate a violation of the IDEA's stay-put provision, a parent needs to demonstrate a sufficient likelihood that they and the student would suffer a similar wrong(s) in the future. For example, the court held that the injury to the parent could only reoccur if the student was transferred out of the private school identified as the stay-put placement, unilaterally placed in another school, and received a favorable administrative decision indicating that the new school will be the student's pendency placement.

Significance to Educators:

In order to legally satisfy an alleged violation of the IDEA's stay-put provision, a parent must prove that it is highly likely that they will suffer a certainly impending future injury. In this case, the district demonstrated that it was highly unlikely for the student to transfer to another private school and an independent hearing officer (IHO) to declare that particular private school be the student's stay-put placement.

5.2.6

K.B., on behalf of S.B.
v.
KATONAH LEWISBORO UNION FREE SCHOOL DISTRICT

847 Fed. App'x. 38

US Court of Appeals, Second Circuit

February 26, 2021

Issue:

- The child find obligation under the IDEA

Facts of the Case:

The parent of a student with an emotional disability filed legal suit against a New York school district alleging that it violated the "child find" obligation under the IDEA based on its failure to promptly identify a student as someone with an emotional disability requiring special education and related services. Based on the academic progress of the high school student with a bipolar disorder during her four-month stay in a psychiatric hospital and her subsequent return to school, the district made the decision that the student did not need extended school year (ESY) services under the IDEA in order to satisfy the free appropriate public education (FAPE) provision under the IDEA. The parent is seeking tuition reimbursement for the student's private summer program. The district maintains that there is no evidence involving this student to substantiate any child find violation under the IDEA.

Ruling:

The Second Circuit Court of Appeals affirmed the decision of a prior district court that the district did not violate the child find obligation under the IDEA. In this case, the Second Circuit held that the district only has to make ESY services available to the student if he or she needs them to receive FAPE. The court indicated that evidence supported the determination that the student did not need special education services during the summer to receive an educational benefit. For example, the student did not lose any credits during her hospitalization and was on track to graduate on time. As a result, the court held that the district had no legal obligation to evaluate the student for an emotional disability until it learned of her hospitalization. In their ruling, the court also noted that the student's IEP in the junior year of high school would have satisfied the FAPE provision under the IDEA. As a result, the parent was not entitled to receive any reimbursement for the student's summer private school placement.

Significance to Educators:

In order to demonstrate a violation of the child find obligation under the IDEA, parents are legally required to demonstrate by a preponderance of the evidence that school officials significantly overlooked signs of the student's disability and were negligent in ordering testing or there was no rational justification for not deciding to perform a student evaluation. Since a child find violation under the IDEA is procedural, a person(s) making such a claim must establish that the child find violation impacted the student's right to a free appropriate public education (FAPE), significantly impacted the parents' opportunities to participate in the decision-making process, and caused a deprivation in the student's educational benefits.

5.3 Summaries of Rulings from the US Court of Appeals for the Third Circuit

5.3.1

A.B., through his parent KATINA B., Appellants
v.
ABINGTON SCHOOL DISTRICT, Respondents
841 F. App'x 392
US Court of Appeals, Third Circuit
20-1619
January 8, 2021

Issue:

- When a parent asks a vague question regarding services, does that trigger a child find violation?

Facts of the Case:

The student was diagnosed with autism spectrum disorder and received special education services pursuant to an individualized education program (IEP) from the district from the first through fourth grades. The parent was dissatisfied with the services the student received and enrolled him in a private school. After the child attended the private school for a year, the parent e-mailed the district and stated she was interested in finding out what programs the district can offer.

The district responded, describing in general terms what special education services were available for students.

A year went by before the parent then e-mailed the district stating it had not offered an appropriate program and placement, leaving the parent with no other option but to continue the enrollment in the private school for the next school year and requested that the school district fund the tuition. The district responded stating it did not believe it had an obligation to fund the tuition, since the parent unilaterally withdrew him and had not requested or completed district reenrollment.

The parents filed for a due process hearing. The hearing officer found that the parent's "vague questions" to administrators did not convey a clear interest in enrolling the student in a district special education program for either school year at issue. The hearing officer also found that while the student remained eligible for special education services due to his previous classification, the parent's inquiry did not place the district on notice that it had a duty to evaluate and propose programming. The hearing officer explained that, absent such notice, the district was not required to reimburse tuition.

Ruling:

The Third Circuit affirmed the decision of the hearing officer. Vague statements do not trigger a duty of the school district to initiate an evaluation for a student.

Significance to Educators:

Whenever a parent makes a request for services, evaluation, change, or an IEP meeting, the district should keep detailed records of the request and respond in a timely fashion. All requests, including vague ones, should be taken seriously.

5.3.2

Thomas AHEARN, as parents and natural guardians of Louis AHERN, Eileen AHEARN, as parents and natural guardians of Louis AHERN, Appellants

v.

EAST STROUDSBURG AREA SCHOOL DISTRICT; COLONIAL INTERMEDIATE UNIT 20

848 F. App'x 75

US Court of Appeals, Third Circuit

March 5, 2021

Issue:

- Exhaustion of administrative remedies

Facts of the Case:

During the 2013–2014 school year, the student attended school in a class for students with autism after being identified as an individual with an intellectual disability, autism, and speech and language impairment. The district developed a staff action for an emergency plan called "SAFE Plan" in order to redirect him and keep him on task during the school day. The district, however, allegedly failed to follow the plan. Specifically, the parents alleged that, on one occasion, their son was restrained and placed in handcuffs by a school resource officer. On another occasion, the student was allegedly locked in a school bathroom (where he caused harm both to himself as well as items in the room). At no time prior to treating the student this way, did the district call the parents and/or 911 as in indicated in the SAFE Plan.

The parents filed a state court action against the district, alleging, among other things, violations of the Fourteenth Amendment and Section 504 of the Rehabilitation Act, 29 U.S.C. § 504. After the district had removed the case to the district court and moved to dismiss for failure to exhaust administrative remedies under the Individuals with Disabilities Education Act (IDEA), the parents filed an amended complaint. In their amended complaint, they advanced a Fourteenth Amendment claim pursuant to 42 U.S.C. § 1983 and a disability discrimination claim under Section 504. Defendants again moved to dismiss for failure to exhaust administrative remedies.

It is undisputed that the parents did not exhaust administrative remedies under the IDEA. The parents, however, argue that the IDEA's exhaustion mandate did not apply to their child's claims because (1) the rights recently afforded by the Supreme Court in *Knick v. Township of Scott*, 139 S. Ct. 2162 (2019) to property owners to a federal forum for claims of unconstitutional treatment at the hands of state officials should be extended to students and families who claim the deprivation of constitutional rights in a school setting; and (2) the district court erred in its application of the *Fry* test.

The parents further argue that exhaustion was not required under *Fry* because neither of the alleged incidents "had anything to do with the Student's educational program." They also contend that "had the Student been handcuffed or locked in a bathroom at a public facility other than the school, he could have raised the same claims against a separate entity" and that any "adult individual who had been handcuffed without justification and/or locked in a bathroom would have a right to bring a claim for mistreatment." See, for example, Fry, 137 S. Ct. at 756 ("First, could the plaintiff have brought essentially the same claim if the alleged conduct had occurred at a public facility that was not a school—say, a public theater or library? And second, could an adult at the school—say, an employee or visitor—have pressed essentially the same grievance? When the answer to those questions is yes, a complaint that does not expressly allege the denial of a FAPE is also unlikely to be truly about that subject; after all, in those other situations there is no FAPE obligation and yet the same basic suit could go forward"). Furthermore, the parents contend that exhaustion should be excused as futile because the relief they seek (i.e., money damages) is not allowed under the IDEA.

Ruling:

The court agreed the crux or gravaman of the parents' complaint was the denial of FAPE, and therefore, they needed to exhaust their administrative remedies.

Significance to Educators:

Make sure the issue, when FAPE is at issue, is it first addressed in administrative courts. Other issues may be addressed in other courts.

5.3.3

Shanicqua S. APONTE, Appellant

v.

POTTSTOWN SCHOOL DISTRICT; Ryan OXENFORD;
Matthew MOYER; Steven RODRIGUEZ; Brett WADE;
Kim STILLWELL; Eren JACOBS; Joseph SCHROEDER,
all in personal and professional capacity

842 F. App'x 806

US Court of Appeals, Third Circuit

January 15, 2021

Issue:

- Retaliation

Facts of the Case:

A fourth-grade student labeled as eligible for special education and related services as a student with an emotional disturbance was described as inconsolable after a behavioral incident that caused the school to go into a lockdown. The student stated that he had stopped taking his medication. The principal called child welfare authorities for assistance.

The parent claimed that the principal called child welfare authorities as a retaliation for her advocacy and her Section 504 claim.

Ruling:

The three-judge panel affirmed the lower court's ruling that the principal was not acting in a retaliatory manner. Specifically, the call by the principal was a direct response to the events of the day.

Significance to Educators:

Document all concerns that you have of a child. Respond directly to the behaviors that a child manifests when there is an incident. Do not let a retaliation claim prevent action. But be sure that the actions that are engaged in are documented and supported by the evidence.

5.3.4

Eileen ESPOSITO; Louis ESPOSITO; Kyle MATULLO, Appellants

v.

RIDGEFIELD PARK BOARD OF EDUCATION

US Court of Appeals, Third Circuit

20-2246

May 18, 2021

Issues:

- FAPE
- IQ testing

Facts of the Case:

The student entered the second grade in 2005 with a language disorder. Following an assessment, the student received services within the district for the next decade. The parent waived the reevaluation in 2008 and 2012. In 2015, they met with school officials to develop an IEP for his final school year. The proposed IEP provided for daily individualized language arts instruction, periodic speech-language consultation, and counseling twice a month. The parent consented to the IEP and additional psychological and education assessments to assist with the student's postgraduation transition planning. Unexpectedly, those tests showed a precipitous drop in the student's intellectual abilities, in the "Borderline Range of Cognitive Ability," and an IQ score of 76 (5th percentile), far below his 2005 test results (35th percentile). The district did not change the 2015–2016 IEP.

An outside expert hired by the parents stated the student was dyslexic and that he had "low engagement and experience with literacy." In 2017, after the student completed school, the parents filed a due process petition alleging the district denied the student a FAPE from 2005 through 2016. The administrative law judge (ALJ) limited the remedial period to the 2015–2016 school year, also finding the board knew or reasonably should have known of the injury no earlier than 2015. After a hearing, the ALJ found the student had received a FAPE in 2015–2016 and dismissed the parents' petition.

K.M. challenges the latter conclusion and argues that, having timely filed his petition within two years of when he knew or should have known (the KOSHK date), he is entitled to compensatory education for a period equal to the period of deprivation. In other words, his entire academic career at the district from 2005 through 2016.

Ruling:

The ALJ did not clearly err in finding the district did not know, and could not have reasonably known, of potential IDEA violations until the July

2015 reevaluation. Between 2005 and 2015, the student and the district had reason to believe the student was making sufficient progress in school. Further, as noted, the student was never tested between 2005 and 2015 because the parent knowingly waived reevaluations in 2008 and 2012. The student does not identify evidence suggesting the board should have otherwise discovered potential problems prior to the July 2015 tests. The ALJ thus properly limited the student's potential remedy to the 2015–2016 academic year.

Significance to Educators:

Keep detailed records of a student's progress in their program. Consider reevaluating every three years and make sure you have data to document a student's performance.

5.3.5

H.U.; B.U., parents and natural guardians of K.U., a minor, Appellants

v.

NORTHAMPTON AREA SCHOOL DISTRICT; COLONIAL NORTHAMPTON IU-20

US Court of Appeals, Third Circuit

October 15, 2021

Issues:

- Safety
- Sexual assault

Facts of the Case:

In December 2017, the student was sexually assaulted by a fellow student in a school van. The parents sued on her behalf under 42 U.S.C. § 1983. At the time of the assault, the student was a fifteen-year-old student who, because of her various neurological disorders, attended a school for children with special needs. She was transported along with three or four other students who rode the van daily with her, accompanied by two staff members: a driver and a monitor. Both staff members received TACT2 "[t]herapeutic aggressive control training," addressing "how to . . . de-escalate a student's aggressive behavior." TACT2 training does not cover peer-to-peer sexual contact specifically, but all drivers and monitors were instructed in their Employee Manual to "enforce assertive discipline" on school transportation and to "physical[ly] restrain[]" students if it is necessary to "protect the child or other children on the vehicle."

The students in the van had assigned seats, with the student normally sitting alone. At some point in December 2017, however, the student asked if she could move and sit next to another student. At the time, the other student was twelve or thirteen years old and had a history of violent contact with his peers, including punching and throwing objects at them. He had also threatened extreme violence against peers and the school. The driver, unaware of this history and never having observed the other student engage in violence or sexual misconduct, permitted the seat change. The change was unproblematic for several days, but at some point in late December, the other student sexually assaulted the student on the van ride home from school. He groped her, forced her hand down his pants, and made her perform oral sex on him. A few days later, the student reported the assault to a teacher.

The assault wrought a severe psychological toll on the student. In the weeks that followed, she twice attempted suicide by overdosing. She also attempted to get off the school van while it was moving. She has experienced increased depression, anxiety, and difficulties with trust, especially of males. The parents later brought this action on her behalf. In their complaint, the parents asserted that the district and the private school had violated the student's substantive due process rights under a state-created danger theory. The parents alleged that the student's substantive due process rights were violated because the bus monitor's approval of the seating change "caused the student to be in a more vulnerable position" seated next to a "violent, unpredictable" student.

Ruling:

Here, the only state actor plaintiffs identify is the monitor, who approved the student's request to sit with the other student in the van ("Consequently, we ask whether the other student's assaulting the student was foreseeable to the monitor and conclude that it was not. The monitor was unaware of the other student's past behavioral problems documented in his school records. The monitor did not have actual or constructive knowledge about the other student's history"). She had never observed the other student engage in any sexual misconduct in the school van, nor was she aware of any past incident of sexual assault on school transportation. Thus, the risk of serious harm was not foreseeable, and the plaintiffs are left unable to satisfy this element of the state-created danger test announced in *Bright v. Westermoreland County* (443 F.3d 276, 3rd Cir. 2006). Therefore, the district was not liable for the problems that occurred.

Significance to Educators:

Ensure staff are trained in monitoring students as a part of transportation and that the staff are also trained in safely supervising students with behavior problems.

5.3.6

HATIKVAH INTERNATIONAL ACADEMY CHARTER SCHOOL,
Appellant

v.

EAST BRUNSWICK TOWNSHIP BOARD OF EDUCATION;
A.K. & R.K. on behalf of H.K.

US Court of Appeals, Third Circuit

August 19, 2021

Issues:

- Stay-put provision
- Charter schools

Facts of the Case:

The student is a fifth grader who has been diagnosed attention deficit hyperactivity disorder, oppositional tendencies, and developmental delays. The student attended a public charter school in New Jersey. The parents unilaterally moved the student to a private school, and the charter and the parents agreed on an individualized education program (IEP) that kept the student at the private school. The local school district, the student's resident school district, challenged this IEP in state administrative proceedings.

The dispute is whether the financial responsibility for the student's pendent placement costs rests with the resident school district or the student's former charter school under the Individuals with Disabilities Education Act (IDEA) and N.J. Stat. Ann. § 18A:36A-11, when the student's former charter school implemented the IEP that placed the student at a private school. The district court concluded that financial responsibility for the student's tuition costs rested with the charter school but ordered the district to pay for his transportation costs.

The charter school contends the district is responsible for the student's pendent placement costs under the IDEA's stay-put rule. The Third Circuit Court agreed that the stay-put rule requires that "during the pendency of any proceedings conducted pursuant to this section, unless the State or local educational agency and the parents otherwise agree, the child shall remain in the then-current educational placement of the child" (20 U.S.C. § 1415(j)). This rule is protective in nature and reflects Congress's policy choice that all children with disabilities remain in their current educational placement until the dispute about their placement is resolved, "regardless of whether their case is meritorious or not." The stay-put rule consequently functions as an "automatic preliminary injunction," and the "usual prerequisites to injunctive relief are not required."

Ruling:

We hold that financial responsibility for all pendent placement costs rests entirely with the resident school district. We therefore will reverse in part and remand.

The court stated it had previously explained in disputes between parents and school districts that the financial responsibility for a student's pendent placement costs lies with the resident school district. The IDEA itself does not specify which party must pay for the student's stay-put costs. See 20 U.S.C. § 1415(j). But it is "well established" that the resident school district must fund a student's private placement if it is the educational setting the student's current IEP prescribes. This financial obligation "arises automatically" when the private school is the student's pendent placement. The obligation arises automatically from a determination that the private school is the protected status quo during the period in which the dispute resolution process is ongoing. Consequently, financing goes hand in hand with pendent private school placement. A party therefore does not need to request separately reimbursement for the student's stay-put costs.

To the extent the IDEA and our case law are not dispositive of cost allocation in this situation, New Jersey law is. New Jersey law explicitly extends the resident school district's financial obligations to costs associated with an IEP that a charter school implements. In other words, New Jersey's decision to give charter schools the authority to implement IEPs while leaving financial responsibility with the resident school district means that any tension stemming from the separation of financial responsibility and decision-making authority is an apparently deliberate policy choice. Congress has imposed a significant financial burden on states and school districts that participate in [the] IDEA, New Jersey too has placed this burden on resident school districts. Although "we are mindful of the financial burden which will, in some instances, be borne by local school districts," our IDEA case law and the language of N.J. Stat. Ann. § 18A:36A-11(b) require that the resident school district pay for the student's pendent placement costs, even if the student's former charter school created and implemented the current IEP. Because we conclude that the district bears the burden of the student's pendent placement costs under the stay-put rule, we will reverse the district court's order with respect to the student's tuition costs and remand nonetheless must fund his pendent placement cost. The ALJ ordered the district to reimburse the charter school for the student's costs from the date of his IEP.

Significance to Educators:

As the local educational agency of residence, the district remained responsible for funding the student's placement as required by New Jersey law.

5.3.7

NORTHFIELD CITY BOARD OF EDUCATION
v.
K.S., on behalf of L.S., Appellant
847 F. App'x 130
US Court of Appeals, Third Circuit
March 30, 2021

Issues:
- Stay-put provision
- Initial IEP

Facts of the Case:

The student needed regular therapy because of childhood trauma so when she began attending the district as a fifth grader, her mother, the parent, told the school of her daughter's emotional difficulties. She informed a teacher that the student had "a history of trauma" and was "having a little difficulty adjusting to her new surroundings," and she told a school counselor that the student had "engaged in self-harm."

That fall the student did well in most of her classes and showed writing talent, but she struggled in math. When the parent reached out to her math teacher for help, the teacher found her a math tutor and offered "to help her anytime during the school day."

The next semester, the student still struggled, so in late January, the parent asked the school to evaluate her daughter for special education. But after looking at her grades and talking with her teachers, the school decided that she did not have a disability and did not need special education. Though she had a C in math, she was doing well in her other classes. She did, however, have some emotional problems. Sometimes, she acted out. She did not get along with certain classmates, and the parent thought she might be depressed. The school put the student into a program to address those emotional issues. She started meeting with a social worker a few times a week.

By April, the student had grown "very depressed." She was "often tearful," did not like going to class, and did not want to see her friends. She also admitted that she was cutting herself with a paper clip. Worried about her safety, the social worker encouraged the parent to take her to a hospital for a psychiatric evaluation immediately. The student ended up staying at a hospital for five days.

When she returned, the school had a transition plan in place: The social worker would meet the student for counseling every day. The school would let her avoid other students by eating lunch in the library and arriving to each class late. And it would move her English and math classes to the morning so that she could go to an outpatient facility in the afternoon.

The school also reevaluated the student for special education. Because her emotional problems had grown severe enough to interfere with her education, the school classified her as "emotionally disturbed." It also developed an IEP for the next school year. Under the program, the student would get to retake tests, use a calculator and reference aids in class, and have extra time on assignments. She would also have frequent counseling sessions and a special math class. That summer, a psychiatrist diagnosed her with anxiety, depression, and posttraumatic stress disorder.

But before the next school year started, the parent filed an administrative complaint. The parent charged the school with violating the IDEA. The parent claimed that the program did not do enough for the student's emotional needs, and blamed the school for not catching the student's problems earlier. When the new school year arrived, the school did not implement the student's program but kept her in general education. But it provided an aide to sit with her throughout the school day.

After a hearing, the administrative law judge (ALJ) found that the program was fine and the school acted reasonably in waiting to evaluate and classify the student, but the judge decided that the district should have implemented the program instead of keeping her in general education. The ALJ awarded the student compensatory education for the special math classes that were missed. The district court agreed that the district had classified the student in time and provided a proper program. But it reversed the grant of compensatory education, holding that federal law barred implementing the program after the parent sued. The parent then appealed alleging that the district should have implemented the program.

Ruling:

The parent faults the school for not putting the student into her planned special education after she sued. But it could not. Once a parent sues, the school "shall" leave the student in her "current educational placement" until the suit is over (20 U.S.C. § 1415(j)). This is known as the "stay-put rule." To be sure, a school and parent can agree to move the student to her new placement (20 U.S.C. § 1415(j)). But if they do not agree, as here, the school must keep the "educational status quo," whether that is general education or a program. *Ridley v. School District*, 744 F.3d at 118; see *Drinker ex rel. Drinker v. Colonial Sch. Dist.*, 78 F.3d 859, 867 (3d Cir. 1996).

For the student, the district court found the status quo was general education. The district had planned to put the student into a program for sixth grade. But she had no program in fifth grade. Because the parent sued over the summer, the district court reasoned, the student's program was her projected placement, not her current one. It says nothing about what counts as a current placement when a child is between programs or does not yet have one in place. The court stated the district acted appropriately.

Significance to Educators:

The stay-put provision is fairly straightforward. Implement the current agreed upon placement until there is closure on the litigation or the parties agree otherwise. Make sure to talk with your counsel about the current appropriate program for the student.

5.3.8

T.R., a minor, individually, by and through her parent, Barbara GALARZA, and on behalf of all others similarly situated; Barbara GALARZA, individually, and on behalf of all others similarly situated; A.G., a minor, individually, by and through his parent, Margarita PERALTA, and on behalf of all others similarly situated; Margarita PERALTA, individually, and on behalf of all others similarly situated; L.R.; D.R., a minor, individually, by and through her parent, Madeline PEREZ, and on behalf of all others similarly situated; J.R.; Madeline PEREZ, individually, and on behalf of all others similarly situated; R.H., a minor, individually, by and through his parent, Manqing LIN, and on behalf of all others similarly situated; Manqing LIN, individually, and on behalf of all others similarly situated

v.

SCHOOL DISTRICT OF PHILADELPHIA

US Court of Appeals, Third Circuit

July 9, 2021

Issue:

- Exhaustion of administrative remedies

Facts of the Case:

The School District of Philadelphia oversees hundreds of public schools providing educational programs to hundreds of thousands of enrolled students. Given the size and diversity of such enrollment, there are some enrolled students within the school district—and parents of enrolled students—who have limited English proficiency (LEP), meaning English is not their primary language so that they have a "limited ability to read, write, speak, or understand English." The demand for interpreters often exceeds the number of staff available so that "not all employee requests for translation are fulfilled." District employees can also call and request interpretation services from the Language Line—a telephonic interpretation service.

In August 2015, parent 1 and her ward, student 1, and parent 2 and her child, student 2—the original plaintiffs—filed a complaint against the district. Importantly, student 1 and student 2 had exhausted administrative remedies and received decisions from a due process hearing officer. After the hearing officer had found that parent 1 and parent 2 were each "denied meaningful parental participation," he awarded compensatory education to student 1 and student 2.

There were other parents who also had students eligible and have LEP, but have not exhausted their administrative remedies. They joined in a lawsuit against the district. The complaint alleges the district "has adopted a systemic policy of failing to provide sufficient interpretation services and to timely and completely translate IEP process documents and regular education forms." While the complaint acknowledges that the district has provided some translation services at IEP team meetings, it asserts that the district's "incomplete, inconsistent effort has not and cannot facilitate the requisite meaningful parent participation."

As for relief, the complaint requests, inter alia, that the district court "order that the [school] district adopt and implement a new written special education plan and [school] district policy to provide legally mandated translation and sufficient interpretation services to members" of the classes and "[o]rder that the [school] district timely translate and deliver all IEP process documents to all members of the parent class and the student class as needed in the appropriate native language in advance of IEP meetings to ensure meaningful participation." The plaintiffs do not seek individualized damages or remedies.

Ruling:

The plaintiffs did not pursue the administrative process established by the IDEA for resolving claims of procedural violations and FAPE denials. Because the plaintiffs' IDEA claim does not fit within a systemic exception to exhaustion, the court will not excuse such a failure to exhaust. The district court lacked jurisdiction to address the plaintiffs' IDEA claim. The district court also could not decide the plaintiffs' remaining non-IDEA claims because they too sought relief for the denial of a FAPE.

The IDEA establishes a detailed administrative mechanism for resolving disputes about whether an educational agency has complied with the IDEA. See 20 U.S.C. § 1415. This mechanism includes procedures for the filing of complaints (see § 1415(b)(6)-(7)), mediation (§ 1415(e)), impartial due process hearings conducted by a hearing officer (§ 1415(f)), and appeals of hearing officer findings to the state educational agency (§ 1415(g)). The IDEA also provides that after these administrative proceedings have concluded, an aggrieved party may bring a civil action in a state court or United States district court (§ 1415(i)(2)). This detailed statutory regime makes it "clear . . . that Congress intended plaintiffs to complete the administrative process before resorting to federal court" (Komninos v. Upper Saddle River Bd. of Educ., 13 F.3d 775, 778 (3d Cir. 1994), citing Smith v. Robinson, 468 U.S. 992, 1011-12 (1984)).

Despite the IDEA's administrative exhaustion requirement, the Third Circuit has acknowledged that a plaintiff's failure to exhaust may be excused "where: (1) exhaustion would be futile or inadequate; (2) the issue presented is purely a legal question; (3) the administrative agency cannot grant relief; [or] (4) exhaustion would cause severe or irreparable harm" (D.E. v. Cent. Dauphin Sch. Dist., 765 F.3d 260, 275 (3d Cir. 2014)), citing Komninos, 13 F.3d at 778 (analyzing futility exception). "Absent the existence of any of those exceptions, failure to exhaust will deprive a federal court of subject matter jurisdiction."

The Third Circuit has also stated that exhaustion is not required where plaintiffs "allege systemic legal deficiencies and, correspondingly, request system-wide relief that cannot be provided (or even addressed) through the administrative process" (Beth V. by Yvonne V. v. Carroll, 87 F.3d 80, 89 (3d Cir. 1996)). Yet the court has suggested that this exception—the "systemic exception"—"merely flows implicitly from, or is in fact subsumed by, the futility and no-administrative-relief exceptions." Id. (remanding to district court to determine whether plaintiffs' claim fell within any recognized exception to exhaustion).

Significance to Educators:

A court may not grant class status without the exhaustion of remedies; however, this does not relieve a district of its obligation to provide a FAPE and ensure meaningful parental participation. Work to ensure meaningful parental participation on all levels and in all meetings discussing a child's educational programming.

5.3.9

Y.B., on behalf of S.B.; F.B., on behalf of S.B.
v.
HOWELL TOWNSHIP BOARD OF EDUCATION
US Court of Appeals, Third Circuit
July 19, 2021

Issues:

- Stay-put provision
- Maintenance of program

Facts of the Case:

The student is a 12-year-old boy diagnosed with Down syndrome. As a result, he "shows delays in cognitive, social, and motor areas." The district determined it could not provide the student an IDEA-mandated free appropriate public education (FAPE) at its own public schools, so it crafted an IEP that placed the student at a private school and reimbursed the parents for associated costs.

In November 2016, shortly after the student's IEP was renewed for another year—including the provision providing for his placement at the private school—the family moved homes and transferred the student from district 1 to district 2. District 2's staff reviewed the district 1 IEP and met with the student and the parents and informed the parents "that [the student's] IEP can be implemented in [district 2's special education] where [the student] will receive a free appropriate public education in the least restrictive environment." Despite this assurance, the parents continued to send the student to the private school.

In July 2017, more than seven months after district 2 informed the parents it would provide the student a FAPE in accordance with his IEP, the parents requested a due process hearing. The parents challenged district 2's refusal to implement the student's IEP—which the parent argued required the student's continued attendance at the private school regardless of district 2's ability to provide the services the IEP called for—and asserted that district 2 must reimburse the parents for the student's private school tuition.

Ruling:

There are two provisions at issue in this case. The "stay-put" provision provides that "during the pendency" of certain administrative and legal proceedings, "unless the State or local educational agency and the parents otherwise agree, the child shall remain in the then-current educational placement of the child" (20 U.S.C. § 1415(j)). The IDEA's intrastate transfer provision, on the other hand, provides that a school district receiving an intrastate transfer student with a previously existing IEP "shall provide ... a free appropriate public education, including services comparable to those described in the previously held IEP, in consultation with the parents until such time as the [new district] adopts the previously held IEP or develops, adopts, and implements a new IEP" (20 U.S.C. § 1414(d)(2)(C)(i)(I), emphasis omitted). In a broad sense, then, both provisions discuss the procedural safeguards afforded to students during periods of educational transition. Unlike the "stay-put" provision—which requires the continued implementation of the child's original IEP—the intrastate transfer provision requires only that the new district provide "services comparable" to those in the child's most recent IEP.

The court must first determine which of these two competing provisions—each requiring something different from district 2 (the "same" IEP under the "stay-put" provision, or "comparable services" under the intrastate transfer provision)—governs this case. The appellant argues the "stay-put" provision controls, while district 2 claims the intrastate transfer provision applies. The court agrees with district 2 and holds that in a voluntary intrastate transfer, the "stay-put" provision does not apply, and the new school district need only provide "services comparable" to those the student had been receiving under the IEP in effect before the transfer.

Significance to Educators:

Read the IEP of all new students very carefully. Consider whether the services required by a student can reasonably be provided in the local school district, and work to provide them. Also, read the IEP very carefully to ensure the district is responsible for implementing a defective IEP.

5.4 Summaries of Rulings from the US Court of Appeals for the Fourth Circuit

5.4.1

Johnson on behalf of A.J. and T.S.

v.

CHARLOTTE-MECKLENBURG SCHOOL BOARD OF EDUCATION

US Court of Appeals, Fourth Circuit

December 20, 2021

Issues:
- Mootness in IDEA litigation
- Jurisdiction

Facts of the Case:

Stephanie Johnson withdrew her two daughters, A.J. and T.S., from the Charlotte-Mecklenburg School District in North Carolina. She also filed an administrative complaint alleging that the school district had violated her daughters' rights under the IDEA, including their right to a free appropriate public education (FAPE). She sought prospective services, new IEPs, and compensatory services. Mrs. Johnson failed to obtain these remedies in the hearing in which an administrative law judge (ALJ) concluded that she failed to provide sufficient evidence to support her assertions. Mrs. Johnson then filed a civil action in the federal district court and withdrew her daughters from the Charlotte-Mecklenburg School District. Because Mrs. Johnson failed to include a request for compensatory services, the district court dismissed her case as moot because her daughters were no longer enrolled in the Charlotte-Mecklenburg School District. Mrs. Johnson then appealed the ruling of the federal district court to the US Court of Appeals for the Fourth Circuit.

Ruling:

The circuit court affirmed the lower court's decision, agreeing that Mrs. Johnson's withdrawal of her children from the Charlotte-Mecklenburg School District rendered moot her request for prospective relief. Additionally, the circuit court held that because district court proceedings under the IDEA were original civil actions, Mrs. Johnson's failure to specify that she was seeking compensatory education or to include allegations from which the court could infer that she sought compensatory education she did not present a live controversy to the court.

Significance to Educators:

According to the US Court of Appeals for the Fourth Circuit, federal courts are prohibited from issuing advisory opinions and from deciding issues that will not affect the rights of the parties of the case. Because federal courts lack jurisdiction when the issues are no longer live or parties lack a legal interest in the outcome, and because the court cannot grant relief to the prevailing party, the case must be declared moot and dismissed.

5.5 Summaries of Rulings from the US Court of Appeals for the Fifth Circuit

5.5.1

Amanda P. and Casey P., as parent/guardian/next friend of T.P.

v.

COPPERAS COVE INDEPENDENT SCHOOL DISTRICT

US Court of Appeals, Fifth Circuit

March 1, 2021

838 F. App'x 104

(Per court order, this decision is not for publication and is not precedent)

Issues:

- Identification and evaluation
- Placements

Facts of the Case:

T.P. was an elementary student receiving special education services under the IDEA. He was diagnosed with autism and attention deficit hyperactivity disorder (ADHD). T.P. and his family moved from North Carolina to Texas, where he was enrolled in the Copperas Cove Independent School District. T.P.'s parents requested that their son be tested for dyslexia. He was screened and then received full testing, in which it was recommended that he receive general education dyslexia services.

When T.P.'s parents became dissatisfied with the special education services he was receiving, they filed for a due process hearing alleging that the school district had failed to provide their son with a FAPE. A special education hearing officer concluded that T.P.'s parents had failed to show that the school district had denied him a FAPE. T.P.'s parents filed a suit in federal district court. The parents and the school district moved for summary judgment. The federal district court denied the parents' motion but granted the school district's motion. The district court concluded that T.P.'s parents had not shown that the school district had neither committed procedural not substantive violations in developing and implementing the student's IEP. The parents filed a suit in the US Court of Appeals for the Fifth Circuit alleging that the federal district had committed a number of errors in arriving at their ruling.

Ruling:

The US Circuit Court of Appeals for the Fifth Circuit affirmed the federal district court's ruling. Upon reviewing the brief, records, and oral evidence, the circuit court was not convinced that such violations occurred.

Significance to Educators:

In a footnote to the decision, the US Court of Appeals for the Fifth Circuit noted that the sides had different views of the US Supreme Court's ruling in *Endrew F. v. Douglas County School District*. The circuit court noted that the FAPE educational benefit announced by the High Court in the *Endrew F.* ruling was that to meet its substantive burden under the IDEA, a school must offer a program reasonably calculated to enable a student to make progress appropriate in light or his or her circumstance. This standard aligned with the FAPE standard developed by the Fifth Circuit Court in *Cypress-Fairbanks Independent School District v. Michael F.* (118 F. 3d 245, 1997). In this case, the Fifth Circuit Court analyzed whether a student had received a FAPE using the following four factors: (1) was the student's educational program individualized on the basis of the student's assessment and performance, (2) was a student's program carried out in a coordinated and collaborative manner by key stakeholders, (3) was the student's program in the least restrictive environment, and (4) did the student receive positive academic and nonacademic benefits?

5.5.2

D.C.
v.
KLEIN INDEPENDENT SCHOOL DISTRICT
US Court of Appeals, Fifth Circuit
June 17, 2021

(Per court order, this decision is not for publication and is not precedent)

Issues:
- Identification and evaluation
- Denial of FAPE

Facts of the Case:

D.C. was an elementary student with a specific learning disability in reading comprehension. Soon after he began first grade in the Klein Independent School District in Texas, his teachers realized he was struggling with reading comprehension and fluency. The school provided him with some accommodations, but he continued to struggle with reading. When D.C. was in fifth grade, the school personnel conducted an evaluation and told his parents that he was eligible for special education services. An IEP was developed for D.C. but did not include specialized interventions in reading comprehension. He showed only marginal improvements.

The parents filed a due process complaint, alleging that the school district unreasonably delayed evaluating D.C. for special education eligibility, and delayed providing D.C. with an appropriate special education program. The hearing officer concluded that the Klein Independent School District had failed to provide D.C. with a FAPE by violating its child find duty. The hearing officer found that although the school district had reason to suspect that D.C. had a disability and needed special education services by April 2017, district personnel failed to evaluate him until June 2018.

The hearing officer also found that D.C.'s IEP did not provide FAPE because the program (a) was not individualized and it did not address his reading comprehension problems, (b) did not provide services in the LRE, (c) was not developed in a collaborative manner, and (d) did not provide D.C. with sufficient academic benefit because he made only minimal progress in reading. The hearing officer ordered the school district to modify D.C.'s IEP to provide 45 minutes a day of reading instruction using a research-based reading comprehension program and also awarded D.C. 180 hours of compensatory education services.

The parents then filed in federal district court, seeking attorney's fees and costs because they had prevailed in the hearing. Attorneys for the school district counterclaimed seeking reversal of the award of compensatory education, asserting that the hearing office had made errors in the ruling. Both parties moved for summary judgment. A magistrate judge reviewed the motions and recommended to grant the student's motion and deny the district's motion. The federal district court affirmed the hearing officer's order regarding the violation of child find and the inadequacy of the IEP and awarded D.C. attorney's fees. The school district appealed to the US Court of Appeals for the Fifth Circuit.

Ruling:

First, the Fifth Circuit Court agreed with the hearing officer and the district court that the Klein Independent School District had violated the child find requirement of the IDEA. The court noted that there is a "reasonable time" requirement to child find to identify, locate, and evaluate students with a suspected disability. Moreover, the court's inquiry examined (a) the date the child find requirement was triggered due to notice of suspected disability, (b) the date the child find duty was ultimately satisfied, and (c) the reasonableness of the delay between the two dates.

Second, the Fifth Circuit Court agreed with the hearing officer and the district court that the Klein Independent School District had violated the FAPE requirements of the IDEA in D.C.'s IEP. The court used the test it had developed in *Cypress-Fairbanks Independent School District v. Michael F.* (118 F. 3d 245, 1997) to determine the adequacy of D.C.'s IEP. Finding that a student's IEP must "produce progress not regression or trivial educational advancement" and that "demonstrated educational benefit must be meaningful" the circuit court concluded that "D.C. did not receive meaningful educational benefits from his IEP."

The attorneys for the school district countered that after D.C.'s IEP was implemented he passed all his classes, therefore, the decisions of the hearing officer and district court regarding FAPE should be overturned. The circuit court disagreed, finding that the fact that D.C. passed all his classes was not particularly significant, noting that the Supreme Court in *Endrew F.* specifically rejected the notion that a student is receiving FAPE merely because he or she is passing from grade to grade. Rather, the circuit court noted that the development for a student with disabilities should be measured with respect to the individual student.

Significance to Educators:

If a student has a 504 plan or is in a school's multidisciplinary system it is important to track the student's progress. If a student does not make progress, that should be considered a red flag that he or she may need to be evaluated for special education services. In these situations, district personnel should move quickly to evaluate for special education, or if they believe evaluation is not necessary, document their reasoning for not evaluating in a procedural safeguards notice to the parent. Additionally, when a student has an IEP, ensure that school personnel collect data on student progress and make changes to instruction when he or she is failing to make progress.

5.5.3

D.H.H.
v.
KIRBYVILLE CONSOLIDATED INDEPENDENT SCHOOL DISTRICT
US Court of Appeals, Fifth Circuit
October 22, 2021
(Per court order, this decision is not for publication and is not precedent)

Issues:
- Evaluation
- Need for special education
- Discrimination
- Emotional disturbance

Facts of the Case:

D.H.H. was a high school student in the Kirbyville Consolidated Independent School District. She obtained mostly good grades in school, but her behavior had been inconsistent both in and out of school. When D.H.H. was in eighth grade, her parents requested that she receive a comprehensive evaluation for special education services, services under Section 504, or both. After conducting an evaluation, school personnel determined that D.H.H. was not eligible for special education services.

When the evaluations were being conducted, D.H.H.'s parents filed a due process complaint alleging that the school district had failed to identify her as a student with a disability. The hearing officer dismissed the claim under 504 because of lack of subject matter jurisdiction and conducted the hearing on the IDEA claim. Ultimately, the hearing officer concluded that D.H.H. was not a student with a disability but ordered the school district to reimburse D.H.H.'s parents for a private evaluation. D.H.H.'s parents than filed a second due process complaint. A new hearing officer, noting that D.H.H. has improved her behavior and was doing well in school, determined that D.H.H. was not eligible for special education services. Before filing for the second due process hearing, D.H.H.'s parents filed a lawsuit in federal district court appealing the first hearing officer's decision. Both D.H.H.'s parents and the school district filed for summary judgment. The federal district court referred the case to a magistrate judge, who issued a report and recommendations in the case. The district court adopted the magistrate judge's recommendations and held for the school district on all claims. D.H.H.'s parents timely appealed to the US Court of Appeals for the Fifth Circuit.

Ruling:

The Fifth Circuit Court noted that binding precedent required that, in 504 discrimination cases, the offending party must have intentionally discriminated via bad faith or gross misjudgment. Noting that D.H.H.'s parents' claims were based entirely on the school district's decision not to find D.H.H. a student with a disability and had provided no evidence of intentional discrimination, therefore, the claim was dismissed.

Significance to Educators:

When school district personnel conduct an evaluation, it should be thorough and accurate, and it should address all of a student's needs. Moreover, district personnel should be willing and able to demonstrate the appropriateness of their evaluation and eligibility determination. Keeping good documentation is very important.

5.5.4

E.T., J.R., S.P., M.P., E.S., H.M., & A.M.
v.
PAXTON
US Court of Appeals, Fifth Circuit
December 1, 2021

Issue:

- Coronavirus litigation

Facts of the Case:

Governor Abbott of Texas issued an executive order that prohibited any governmental entity, including a school district, or governmental official to require any person to wear a face covering. The executive order also superseded local governmental authorities from requiring face masks. Two weeks after the executive order was issued, a group representing seven children with various disabilities and health impairments filed an action in federal district court on behalf of their children. In their complaint, the parents sought a declaration that the executive order violated the Americans with Disabilities Act (ADA), the Rehabilitation Act, the Individuals with Disabilities Education Act, and the American Rescue Plan and that the enforcement of the ban denied their children a quality education because of their disabilities. They also sought a preliminary and permanent injunction prohibiting Texas attorney general Ken Paxton from enforcing the ban.

Attorney General Paxton filed a motion to dismiss alleging that the parents lacked standing and alternatively that they had failed to exhaust their administrative remedies before filing their suit. After holding a bench trial, the district court issued an opinion finding that the plaintiffs had standing to sue Attorney General Paxton and that the executive order violated the ADA and Rehabilitation Act. Based on these findings, the district court permanently enjoined the attorney general from enforcing the executive order prohibiting public school districts from banning face masks. The attorney general sought an emergency stay of the district court's injunction.

Ruling:

The US Court of Appeals for the Fifth Circuit concluded that the attorney general demonstrated a strong likelihood of success on the merits of the case because it was unlikely that the plaintiffs had standing to pursue their claims. Additionally, the attorney general had to demonstrate that the stay (a) was necessary to prevent irreparable harm, (b) would not harm the medically vulnerable students who sought universal masking as a disability accommodation, and (c) would serve the public interest. Finding that the attorney general met all four elements, the Fifth Circuit Court granted the stay of the federal district court's order pending the appeal on its merits.

Significance to Educators:

Educators have struggled to keep up with the ever changing rules regarding COVID-19 and masking. Because of the differences among states regarding mask mandates, educators would be advised to consult with their attorneys prior to making decisions regarding mask mandates in their schools.

5.5.5

Harrison as next friend of B.F.
v.
KLEIN INDEPENDENT SCHOOL DISTRICT
US Court of Appeals, Fifth Circuit

April 7, 2021

Issues:

- Harassment
- Retaliation
- Elements of a discrimination action

Facts of the Case:

The plaintiff, Nichole Harrison, was the mother of B.F., an elementary student with multiple physical and cognitive disabilities. During the time period of this case (2016–2017; 2017–2018; 2018–2019), B.F. attended two elementary schools in the Klein Independent School District. In July 2018, B.F.'s mother filed suit alleging disability discrimination against the school district and certain school personnel in violation of the Americans with Disabilities Act (ADA) and Section 504 of the Rehabilitation Act. Additionally, the mother asserted that the school district had failed to provide reasonable accommodations to B.F. also violating the ADA and Section 504. Also B.F.'s mother alleged that her son had suffered abuse and harassment at the hands of school staff.

When school officials became aware of the abuse and harassment, they promptly investigated the incidences and took appropriate action, which included termination of the involved employees. The mother, Nichole Harrison, filed suit in federal district court. Following a hearing in 2020, the federal district court granted the school district's motion for summary judgment and dismissed B.F.'s claims with prejudice. B.F.'s mother filed an appeal.

Ruling:

According to the US Court of Appeals for the Fifth Circuit, to show discrimination under the ADA and Section 504, B.F.'s mother had to establish that (a) B.F. was a qualified individual with disability under Section 504/ADA, (b) the school excluded B.F. from participation in, or denied the benefits of, services, programs, or activities for which the school was responsible; B.F. was excluded, denied the benefits, or discriminated against because of his disability; and (d) the exclusion, denial of benefits, or discrimination against B.F. was intentional. Additionally, to show that the school district had failed to make reasonable accommodations for his disability, B.F.'s mother had to show that school district personnel knew of B.F.'s disabilities and limitations but failed to make reasonable accommodation for his limitations.

The Fifth Circuit Court also noted that school officials had immediately investigated instances of abuse and neglect and took appropriate remedial actions. The court also explained that the standard of deliberate indifference is a high bar to meet. The Fifth Circuit Court affirmed the federal district court's dismissal of Harrison's claims.

Significance to Educators:

In situations in which abuse or harassment is suspected, school officials must act promptly to investigate. Such actions, if made in good faith, will be helpful in proving that deliberate indifference did not occur. To obtain relief under Section 504, school personnel would need to be aware of potential abuse or harassment and fail to act.

5.5.6

J.W.
v.
PALEY

US Court of Appeals, Fifth Circuit

June 23, 2021

(Per court order, this decision is not for publication and is not precedent)

Issues:
- Fourth Amendment rights
- Qualified immunity

Facts of the Case:

J.W. was a 17-year-old student in special education attending the Mayde Creek High School in the Katy Independent School District. He got into a fight with another student, damaged some furniture, and attempted to leave the school. Teachers who witnessed the incident notified the school's assistant principal, who notified the school resource officer (SRO), Elvin Paley, to help keep J.W. in the building. Paley's body cam shows him tasing J.W. The tasing continues as J.W. was lying on the ground. Emergency medical services and the school nurse were called. J.W. was taken to the hospital and subsequently missed several months of school. J.W. contended that he suffered from severe anxiety and posttraumatic stress disorders as a result of the tasing. J.W.'s mother filed a number of claims against the Katy Independent School District and Elvin Paley the SRO in federal district court. The school district filed for summary judgment, which the district court granted on all claims except the Section 1983 claims against Elvin Paley for using excessive force under the Fourth Amendment. Paley filed an appeal with the US Circuit Court for the Fifth Circuit.

Ruling:

The Fifth Circuit Court had previously held that students cannot assert substantive due process claims against school officials based on disciplinary actions. Additionally, in one case the Fifth Circuit Court rejected Fourth Amendment claims that involved student discipline. The court, thus, ruled in favor of Elvin Paley.

Significance to Educators:

School resource officers should not use physical force with students unless absolutely necessary in situations that pose physical harm to students or staff. The law regarding Fourth Amendment and substantive due process claims against school officials when using discipline is different depending on the circuit in which one resides. Nonetheless, the SRO's continuing tasing a student after he had fallen to the ground and ceased struggling raise questions about the legality of his actions.

5.5.7

Leigh Ann H. as parent, guardian, and next friend of K.S.

v.

RIESEL INDEPENDENT SCHOOL DISTRICT

US Court of Appeals, Fifth Circuit

November 22, 2021

Issues:

- Referral
- Need for evaluation
- Emotional disturbance and learning disability
- Relationship between misconduct and disability

Facts of the Case:

K.S. was a student in the Riesel Independent School District in Texas. K.S. had gone through elementary and high school with mixed academic success and a spotty disciplinary record. When he began to have behavioral difficulties in third grade his mother, Leigh Ann H., had K.S. evaluated by a private psychologist. The psychologist reported that K.S. was in the average range of intellectual functioning and may have had learning disabilities in reading and written expression. The psychologist recommended that K.S. be considered for special education in learning disabilities and possibly emotional disturbance. School district personnel were not provided the report until K.S. was in 11th grade.

During his middle and high school years, K.S.'s academic record was mixed although he generally performed acceptably. His behavior, however, was more of a problem with K.S. being suspended once and being transferred to the school district's disciplinary alternative school for 30 days. When he was in 10th grade, K.S. received 26 disciplinary referrals. In 11th grade, the number of K.S.'s disciplinary referrals dropped to two through March.

In March 2016, his mother referred K.S. for a full individual evaluation. The evaluation concluded that K.S. qualified for special education for learning disabilities in math and reading fluency. He was not evaluated for an emotional disturbance. An IEP was developed for K.S., which included a transition plan. K.S.'s mother was concerned that her son was not receiving the accommodations in his IEP, so she filed for a due process hearing. The school district responded by conducting another evaluation of K.S., although they did not conduct a behavioral assessment because school personnel considered his behavior within the average range. The school developed a new IEP, which was very similar to the old IEP but added an adjust goal in mathematics.

Prior to the due process hearing, an incident occurred on school grounds in which he was charged with assault. A manifestation determination was held in which it was decided that there was no relationship between K.S.'s learning disability and the behavioral incident. The team recommended that K.S. be sent back to the school district's disciplinary alternative school. The school district then held a manifestation review in which it was determined that there was no relationship between K.S.'s disability and misconduct and that there was no failure to implement K.S.'s IEP.

In the hearing, K.S. and his mother alleged that the school district had failed (a) to properly identify and evaluate K.S., (b) to provide K.S. with a FAPE, (c) to provide prior written notice, and (d) to educate K.S. in the least restrictive environment. A hearing office found in favor of the Riesel School District on all counts. K.S. and his mother appealed the administrative decisions to the US District Court for the Western District of Texas.

K.S. and his mother also filed a request for a second due process hearing challenging the procedural and substantive adequacy of the manifestation determination. When the second hearing officer also ruled in favor of the Riesel School District, Mrs. H. and K.S. returned to the federal district court, which consolidated the two appeals and referred the case to a magistrate judge for review and recommendations. The magistrate judge issued a report recommending that the federal district court find for the Riesel School District. The federal district court adopted his recommendations in full, and K.S. and his mother filed a timely appeal with the US Court of Appeals for the Fifth Circuit. They sought compensatory education for K.S. and reimbursement for their private evaluation.

Ruling:

Noting that unless the circuit court found clear error in the district court's finding, it would not reverse, the court ruled for the Riesel Independent School District. The court held that K.S. and his mother did not meet their burden of proof in the administrative hearing. The court cited the previous decision in *Cypress-Fairbanks Independent School District v. Michael F.* (118 F.3d 245, 5th Cir. 1997) that the "party attaching the appropriateness of an [individualized education program] . . . bears the burden of showing why [it was] . . . inappropriate under the IDEA" (p. 253).

The circuit court refused to overrule the finding that the school district had no reason to suspect that K.S. had a disability early in the student's academic career because K.S.'s mother had never expressed a concern to the school district nor had K.S.'s teachers ever expressed concerns. The court also noted that K.S.'s educational record displayed no consistent record of failure, and although he did have disciplinary problems, that did not give rise to a reasonable suspicion of an emotional disturbance.

The Fifth Circuit also applied the five-factor test developed in *Cypress-Fairbanks Independent School District v. Michael F.* (118 F.3d 245, 5th Cir. 1997) to determine if K.S.'s program conferred a FAPE, in affirming the decision of the federal district court.

Significance to Educators:

Because a student exhibits disciplinary problems does not necessarily mean that a student should be automatically evaluated for the presence of an emotional disability. Nonetheless, such problems should serve as an alert for school district personnel to monitor a student's behavior. Moreover, if a student's parents or teacher express concerns over a student's academic or functional performance, such concerns must be taken seriously and should probably lead to an evaluation.

5.5.8

Lela Logan, individually and on behalf of her minor child L.L.

v.

MORRIS JEFF COMMUNITY SCHOOL

US Court of Appeals, Fifth Circuit

September 28, 2021

(Per court order, this decision is not for publication in official or permanent law reports)

Issues:

- Exhaustion required
- Exhaustion of administrative remedies

Facts of the Case:

In 10th grade, L.L. began attending school in the Morris Jeff Community School, a charter school in Louisiana. L.L. had an IEP and a behavior intervention plan (BIP). Following a serious behavioral incident, L.L. was arrested and handcuffed, and he later entered a behavioral treatment center. Following the incident, L.L.'s mother, Lela Logan, sued the school in federal district court for violation of the ADA and Rehabilitation Act, breach of the IEP contract, and negligent implementation of L.L.'s BIP. Mrs. Logan filed suit in court without first pursuing the administrative procedures required by the IDEA (i.e., a due process hearing). The school moved for dismissal for failing to exhaust administrative remedies. The district court granted the motion and dismissed Logan and L.L.'s complaint. An appeal was filed with the US Court of Appeals for the Fifth Circuit.

Ruling:

The circuit court noted that the IDEA established formal dispute resolution procedures that a plaintiff must exhaust before going to court, and neither the ADA nor the Rehabilitation Act have such a requirement. Moreover, to prevent an end run around the IDEA's exhaustion requirement by using other law to litigate a student with disabilities' right to a FAPE, the Fifth Circuit further noted that Congress extended the exhaustion requirement to any suit under other federal laws that sought relief that was also available under the IDEA. When a complaint seeks to find that a student's instruction plan is inadequate or that a student is not receiving appropriate services, it is likely that the complaint seek relief that is available under the IDEA.

The Fifth Circuit also cited the US Supreme Court's ruling in *Fry v. Napoleon* (137 S. Ct. 748) that a court should examine if the substance or "gravamen" of a student's complaint to determine the purpose of the complaint. The High Court proposed two questions that needed to be answered by a court: (a) Could the plaintiff had brought the same claim at a public facility such as a library or a theater that was not a school? and (b) Could any adult, such as employee or visitor, have brough the same complaint? It the answer is no to both these questions, the exhaustion requirement probably applies. Because the crux of L.L.'s complaint involved the student's IEP and BIP, the exhaustion requirement applied. The judgment of the district court was affirmed.

Significance to Educators:

When school officials face discrimination complaints from parents under Section 504 or Title II of the ADA, if the complaints refer more to a student's services under the IDEA, it is likely that the parents will need to exhaust administrative remedies before going to court.

5.5.9

Rosie Phillips, next friend of J.H.

v.

Stephen W. Prator, for the CADDO PARISH SHERIFF'S OFFICE

US Court of Appeals, Fifth Circuit

September 28, 2021

(Per court order, this decision is not for publication and is not precedent)

Issues:

- Deliberate indifference
- Violations of the Americans with Disabilities Act and Section 504 of the Rehabilitation Act

Facts of the Case:

J.H. was a student in Northwood High School in Shreveport, Louisiana. J.H. was diagnosed as severely autistic and was nonverbal. He received special education services in a self-contained classroom with other students who had severe and profound disabilities. In August 2017, J.H. became upset, left the special education classroom, and lingered in the classroom. The school called a sheriff's deputy to the scene. J.H.'s behavior escalated, and the deputy tased him. J.H.'s mother, Rosie Phillips, sued in federal court on behalf of her son, alleging violations of Title II of the Americans with Disabilities Act (ADA) and Section 504 of the Rehabilitation Act. The defendant in the lawsuit was Sheriff Stephen Prator, which meant the suit was against the Sheriff's Office. J.H.'s mother asserted that the Sheriff's Office failed to accommodate J.H.'s disability and intentionally discriminated against her son because of his disability. The district court dismissed J.H.'s claims. Rosie Phillips appealed to the US Court of Appeals for the Fifth Circuit arguing that the district court erred in holding that she failed to state a claim for intentional discrimination.

Ruling:

The Fifth Circuit Court noted that, because the case was only in the pleading stage and the facts were yet to be determined, the question was not whether there was evidence to support the allegation of intentional discrimination but, rather, whether the complaint plausibly alleged such discrimination. The court has also had to consider the complaint involving Deputy Nunnery, who tased J.H., and Sheriff Prator, pointing out that both the ADA and the Rehabilitation Act are vicarious liability statutes meaning that the Sheriff's Office could be held liable for the actions of an employee. The Fifth Circuit Court agreed with the district court that Phillips did not plausibly allege that Sheriff Prator's conduct amounted to intentional discrimination but that it was possible that Deputy Nunnery knew that in the situation that occurred an accommodation was necessary. Moreover, the court noted, Nunnery did not take any actions to de-escalate the situation such as speaking in a calm voice, giving clear and concise directions, providing J.H. adequate personal space, or consulting with other adults on the scene who knew J.H. Rosie Phillips alleged Nunnery's actions were intentional. Given this information the court concluded that Nunnery understood the limitations imposed by J.H.'s autism and chose not to accommodate them. Because Rosie Phillips stated a plausible claim of intentional discrimination against the Sheriff's Office based on Deputy Nunnery's conduct, the Fifth Circuit Court allowed Rosie Phillips to proceed to the evidence-gathering phase of her lawsuit. Thus, the Fifth Circuit Court affirmed the judgment of the district court in part and reversed in part.

Significance to Educators:

Many school districts across the country hire local police to provide security services in schools. In such situations, it is important that these police officers be trained in proper responses when addressing problems posed by students with disabilities. Moreover, police officers in schools should only be called upon in emergency situations, and not in regular disciplinary situations.

5.5.10

T.O.
v.
FORT BEND INDEPENDENT SCHOOL DISTRICT
US Court of Appeals, Fifth Circuit

September 28, 2021

(Per court order, this decision is not for publication and is not precedent)

Issues:
- Corporal punishment
- Cause of action

Facts of the Case:

T.O. was a first grader at the Hunters Glen Elementary School in the Fort Bend Independent School District. T.O. was diagnosed with attention deficit hyperactivity disorder (ADHD) and oppositional defiant disorder (ODD) and received services through a behavior intervention plan (BIP). The services provided to T.O. included a behavioral aide. The plan called for oral redirection and placement in a quiet area whenever he misbehavior and praise when T.O. exhibited appropriate behavior.

One day T.O. misbehaved and his aide took him out into the hallway and told him to sit there until he calmed down. A fourth-grade teacher, Angela Abbott, was walking down the hallway and offered to assist the behavioral aide. The aide explained that the situation was under control, but when T.O. yelled that he wanted to get back in the classroom, Abbott stepped between T.O. and the classroom door. T.O. then tried to push Abbott away from the door, striking her in the leg, whereupon Abbott seized T.O. by the neck, slammed him to the floor, and held him in a choke hold for several minutes. She released T.O. after being asked to do so by his behavioral aide. The Fort Bend School District investigated the incident on three occasions, but Abbott was not disciplined.

T.O.'s parents sued Abbott under Section 1983 and the school district for disability discrimination under the ADA and Section 504. Abbott and the school district moved to dismiss all claims. A magistrate judge reviewed the case and issued recommendations to the US District Court of the Southern District of Texas. The magistrate concluded that Abbott was entitled to qualified immunity because her use of force was not a constitutional violation under a previous decision by the US Court of Appeals for the Fifth Circuit, *Fee v. Herndon* (900 F.2d 804, 5th Cir. 1990). The ruling in *Fee*, which is at odds with the law in other circuits and has been criticized, recognized that "corporal punishment is a deprivation of substantive due process when it is arbitrary, capricious, or wholly unrelated to the state goal of maintaining an atmosphere conducive to learning. . . .

[Punishment does] not implicate the due process clause if the forum state affords adequate post-punishment civil or criminal remedies for the student to vindicate legal transgressions" (*Fee*, 1990, p. 808). The magistrate also concluded that T.O. had failed to state a claim for disability discrimination against the school district. The district court adopted the magistrate judge's recommendations in full, dismissing all of T.O.'s claims, and denying the plaintiffs leave to file a second amended complaint. T.O.'s parents filed a timely appeal challenging the dismissal of their Section 1983 and nondiscrimination claims. They also appealed the denial of their motion to file a second amended complaint.

Ruling:

The US Court of Appeals for the Fifth Circuit, relying largely on its previous ruling in *Fee*, affirmed all the rulings of the federal district court. Interestingly enough, two of the judges filed a concurring opinion in which they repeated their call for an *en banc* (i.e., all 12 judges in a circuit hear a case) rehearing of the *Fee* ruling. The judges called the *Fee* rule unjust and completely out of step with rulings by the US Courts of Appeals for the Second, Third, Fourth, Sixth, Seventh, Eighth, Ninth, Tenth, and Eleventh Circuits. The concurring judges also noted that the US Supreme Court will eventually be called upon to resolve this dramatically lopsided split in the circuits. The judges concluded that the US Circuit Court of Appeals should fix the error announced in *Fee* before the US Supreme Court has to fix it.

Significance to Educators:

The decision in *T.O. v. Fort Bend Independent School District* is the law in the Fifth Circuit's jurisdiction of Louisiana, Mississippi, and Texas. The ruling, which is based on the previous Fifth Circuit decision in *Fee*, is out of step with every other circuit court in the country, and may certainly had a different result in these other circuits. Nonetheless, even in the states of Louisiana, Mississippi, and Texas, this decision should not be interpreted to mean that discipline of students with disabilities, no matter how severe, will automatically be permissible if there is an educational purpose behind the discipline. Such actions may expose school districts and educators to potential liability under IDEA, ADA, and Section 504 and may inflict damage on students. The so-called intervention in this case escalated the situation and subjected the school district to two years of litigation.

5.6 Summaries of Rulings from the US Court of Appeals for the Sixth Circuit

5.6.1

Nestor ALVAREZ, individually and on behalf of K.A.

v.

SWANTON LOCAL SCHOOL DISTRICT

US Court of Appeals, Sixth Circuit

June 3, 2021

-Unpublished-

Issues:

- Homebound instruction and services under the IDEA
- Denial of FAPE

Facts of the Case:

A parent of an Ohio high school student with speech apraxia and a mild intellectual disability alleged that his daughter was denied a free appropriate public education (FAPE) by only providing her with four hours of home instruction each week. The district temporarily placed the student with multiple disabilities on a home-based program to address concerns of the student's parents regarding her interactions with another male classmate. The parents refused to send the student back to school after the student's father confirmed that his daughter and a male student were texting one another.

Ruling:

The Sixth Circuit of the US Court of Appeals affirmed the decision of a prior district court ruling in favor of the district. The district proposed sending the student to another school; however, the Sixth Circuit indicated that the parents and their attorney failed to respond to the district's offer for the student to attend another school.

Significance to Educators:

As this case illustrates, a district may successfully avoid liability for an allegedly inadequate home-based program by showing that the district was attempting to serve the best interests of the student with disabilities. In this case, the district did not violate the FAPE provision of the IDEA. Instead, the court argued that the delay in returning the student back to a school-based program was caused by the conduct of the student's parents and attorney and not by the actions of the district.

5.6.2

G.S., by and through his parents and next friends, Brittany and Ryan Schwaigert, et al.,

v.

GOVERNOR BILL LEE

US Court of Appeals, Sixth Circuit

August 23, 2021

-Unpublished-

Issue:

- Public school mask mandates for medically vulnerable students

Facts of the Case:

Tennessee's governor, Bill Lee, argued that the state's public schools should have a parental opt-out option for medically vulnerable students not requiring them to wear face masks indoors. At the time, Tennessee was already imposing a universal mask mandate for K–12 students enrolled in public schools. Governor Lee maintained that Tennessee K–12 public schools could safely accommodate medically vulnerable students without requiring the wearing of masks indoors. In this case, Governor Lee attempted to stay, or delay, enforcement of a federal court order mandating the use of masks allowing medically vulnerable students to attend public schools safely. The federal court highlighted that those students with disabilities are especially susceptible to COVID-19 and that mandatory mask policies are necessary to maintain the safety of these students.

Ruling:

Based on the ruling of the Sixth Circuit Court of Appeals, Tennessee's Governor Lee was required to comply with the federal court order mandating the use of masks indoors for medically vulnerable students in the state's K–12 public schools. According to the Sixth Circuit, Governor Lee needed to show that the temporary stay of requiring masks for medically vulnerable students was necessary to prevent irreparable harm and served the public interest. Moreover, the court argued that Governor Lee was unable to show any evidence about the unreasonableness of mandatory mask mandates for students or identify any viable alternatives to mandatory masking that would have been equally effective in protecting medically vulnerable students.

Significance to Educators:

This case illustrates well that there exists a high legal bar for state officials, including state governors, to delay enforcement of a federal court order without being able to demonstrate with evidence that the delay is necessary to prevent irreparable harm to others, the delay would not cause as much harm to others, and the delay in enforcement would serve the overall public interest. Based on the Sixth Circuit's ruling, Governor Lee was unable to succeed on the merits needed to delay the federal court order prohibiting him from allowing parents of medically vulnerable students to opt out of a district's public school mask mandate. It was suggested by the Sixth Circuit that Governor Lee could potentially have successfully obtained a temporary stay of the federal court order by identifying viable alternatives to mandatory student masking that were equally effective at protecting medically vulnerable students from contracting COVID-19.

5.6.3

M.B., parent of minor S.B. et al.,

v.

Governor William Lee, KNOX COUNTY BOARD OF EDUCATION

US Court of Appeals, Sixth Circuit

December 20, 2021

-Unpublished-

Issue:

- Public school mask mandates for medically vulnerable students

Facts of the Case:

A Tennessee public school district is appealing a preliminary court injunction requiring the enforcement of a universal mask mandate to accommodate medically vulnerable students in the state's public schools.

Ruling:

The US Court of Appeals for the Sixth Circuit denied the district's motion to stay, or temporarily delay the enforcement of the court injunction while its appeal is pending.

Significance to Educators:

While school districts may opt to legally challenge a court-issued injunction requiring mandator masking in K–12 public schools, the district should be prepared to enforce the mandatory masking requirements if a court allows the injunction to remain in place based on the ongoing litigation. In this particular case, the district failed to prove that medically vulnerable students can have equal access to public education through virtual learning. As such, the district is required to implement the court-ordered mask mandate as a reasonable accommodation when it faces Section 504 and Americans with Disabilities Act (ADA) claims.

5.6.4

PEREZ

v.

STURGIS PUBLIC SCHOOLS; STURGIS PUBLIC SCHOOLS BOARD OF EDUCATION

3 F.4th 236

US Court of Appeals, Sixth Circuit

June 25, 2021

Issue:

- Exhaustion of administrative remedies under the IDEA

Facts of the Case:

A 23-year-old student with a hearing impairment brought legal action alleging that a Michigan public school district discriminated against him by not providing resources necessary for him to fully participate in class, in violation of the Americans with Disabilities Act (ADA) as well as Michigan state law. The student sued the district for emotional distress that he allegedly suffered as a result of the district's failure to meet his special education needs under the ADA. Prior to the student's lawsuit, the district was involved in a settlement of an IDEA due process complaint.

Ruling:

The Sixth Circuit Court of Appeals upheld an earlier district court's dismissal of the student's ADA claim. The Sixth Court's reasoning is that the district's settlement of a previous IDEA due process complaint can protect it from other legal claims under Section 504 or the ADA. In this particular case, the district claimed that the student's ADA lawsuit addressed the same issues and alleged educational shortcomings as the student's IDEA due process complaint. Therefore, the district was not legally estopped, or barred, from seeking dismissal of the student's complaint.

Significance to Educators:

In the case *Fry v. Napoleon Community Schools* (2017), the US Supreme Court addressed the issue of the IDEA's "exhaustion rule." Specifically, if a lawsuit charges that a student with disabilities was denied FAPE, the parent on behalf of the student alleging the complaint cannot legally escape the IDEA's exhaustion requirement by merely bringing their lawsuit under another federal statute, such as the ADA or Section 504. In this case, the parent's other lawsuit brought under the ADA is not required if the remedy sought is not for a denial of FAPE. Currently, the Supreme Court requires that to make this determination a court must determine the essence or "gravamen" of the issue(s) in the complaint. By the district's demonstration that it settled the IDEA claim prior to the scheduled administrative hearing, the district successfully established the student's failure to exhaust those claims under the IDEA.

5.7 Summaries of Rulings from the US Court of Appeals for the Ninth Circuit

5.7.1

CAPISTRANO UNIFIED SCHOOL DISTRICT,
Plaintiff-Appellant/Cross-Appellee,

v.

S.W. and C.W., on behalf of their minor child, B.W.,
Defendants-Appellees/Cross-Appellants

US Court of Appeals, Ninth Circuit

December 30, 2021

Issue:

- Private school reimbursement, appropriate IEP

Facts of the Case:

The parents and the district disagreed about services for the student throughout her kindergarten year. At the end of that year, at the IEP meeting, the parents said that more "intensive support [was] necessary for the student's continued growth/progress." They were concerned that several different people helped the student during her kindergarten year and said that the student did not know who was supporting her.

The parents came to the meeting with their own expert, who recommended that the student should "have support for the entire length of the school day." The district disagreed and explained that different tutors helped the student become more independent. The student completed kindergarten, meeting expectations with high marks in almost all areas.

Then, in the fall, after the student started first grade, the IEP team reconvened. It reviewed the student's transition to first grade and her parents' concerns about her adjustment to the public school's new campus. The district proposed new goals and accommodations reflecting the parents' expert's recommendations. The parents received a copy of the annual IEP offer. But they never consented to it or requested another IEP meeting.

A couple months into the school year, the parents filed an administrative due process complaint alleging inadequacies with both the kindergarten and first grade IEPs. Then, in winter of that same year, the parents unilaterally withdrew the student from the public school and enrolled her at a private school. The parents told the district that the student would stay in private school for the rest of first grade and for second grade. They sought reimbursement for private school tuition, programs, and related services for both school years.

The district denied the parents' request for reimbursement and proposed an IEP meeting. The parents did not respond.

The parents then paid her registration fees for the private school. The parents claim that they never received the letter denying reimbursement, but the district court found that they sent it, and unilaterally withdrew their due process complaint, and at the end of the school year, the student's first-grade IEP expired.

The student continued to attend private school for second grade. The parents filed a new due process complaint again requesting reimbursement for the student's private school costs. The district again denied the request and proposed an IEP meeting, and a dispute over information and access ensued. Ultimately, the district was dissatisfied with its access to the student and filed an administrative complaint, asking the administrative law judge (ALJ) either to order assessment of the student or release the district from its IEP obligations.

Near the end of the student's second grade, the district held an annual IEP meeting. The district again requested assessment of the student; the parents' agreed assessments were necessary, but they did not consent. Soon after, the student's counsel consented to the district's plan to assess the student, but only if the district withdrew its complaint. The district withdrew its complaint; however, the student was never produced for assessment, and the parents' complaint remained "live."

The ALJ then decided the student's operative (second) complaint. After ruling for the district on two issues relating to kindergarten (not at issue here), the ALJ decided in favor of the student on the remaining four issues, concluding that the district denied the student a FAPE by failing to

(1) develop appropriate first-grade IEP goals;
(2) make an appropriate offer of placement and services;
(3) file for due process to defend the first-grade IEP; and
(4) have a current IEP in place at the beginning of second grade.

Ruling:

The court held that (1) the goals in district's first-grade IEP were not inadequate, (2) the district did not have to file for due process to defend the first-grade IEP, and (3) the district did not have to develop an IEP for second grade.

Significance to Educators:

Continually seek to evaluate all students who may be residents, even if they are attending private schools. Keep students' IEPs up to date.

5.7.2

D.D., a minor, by and through his guardian ad litem, Michaela INGRAM, Plaintiff-Appellant,

v.

LOS ANGELES UNIFIED SCHOOL DISTRICT, Defendant-Appellee

US Court of Appeals, Ninth Circuit

November 19, 2021

Issue:

- Exhaustion of administrative remedies

Facts of the Case:

The student, an elementary school student, has an emotional disability that interferes with his ability to learn. Starting early in the school year, school staff required one of his parents to pick him up early from school due to his disability-related disruptive behavior. His mother unsuccessfully requested a one-to-one aide "to accommodate his needs and enable him to participate with his peers."

Staff soon gave his mother "an ultimatum: either pick him up from school or have a family member serve as his one-to-one aide to enable him to participate in the classroom." So, in October 2016, the mother's partner quit his job to accompany the student "on a nearly daily basis." On a day that the partner was unable to do so, the student had a "severe behavioral incident" that prompted the district to summon a psychiatric emergency team. The episode subsided before the team arrived, but the student was ultimately hospitalized for a week. After the incident, the student's mother "again explicitly [and unsuccessfully] requested a one-to-one aide for him."

The district was "still was not offering the student behavior supports and services" during the second grade (the 2017–2018 school year). The partner continued to accompany the student "on most days to monitor [his] behavior and enable him to access his education." But the student's "disruptive, disability-related behavior continued to escalate." The student's mother again requested "a one-to-one aide or [non-public-school] placement," but the "district refused to provide either." After a particularly serious outburst prompted a police response, school staff told the student that "if he did not behave, they would call the police and he would end up either in jail or in the hospital again."

The student's mother withdrew him from school in November 2017, and he "stayed out of school for a few weeks due to the stress of attending school at all." The student returned to his original elementary school in mid-December and was treated "with a similar pattern of neglect and discrimination." The student's mother "routinely requested communication and updates from his teacher," who never replied. A classroom aide "provided general support to the classroom, but the student was not offered any one-to-one behavior services." Rather, he was "left to his own devices."

In January 2019, the student filed this action. The operative first amended complaint contends that the district discriminated against the student "by excluding him from school, refusing to offer an aide, only allowing him to stay in school if his [p]arent served as an aide, and by enabling him to be subjected to an unsafe school environment." The ADA claim is predicated on the district's "fail[ure] to provide meaningful and equal access to its educational program in violation of the [ADA], including, but not limited to, by failing to provide the student with required accommodations, aids and services." The student alleges he "has suffered, and will continue to suffer loss of equal educational opportunity, as well as humiliation, hardship, anxiety, depression and loss of self-esteem." He "seeks damages and attorneys' fees and costs as a result" and "[s]uch other relief as the court deems just and proper."

The student sought relief from the district under the Individuals with Disabilities Education Act (IDEA), alleging that he was being denied a free appropriate public education (FAPE). The student claimed that the district had denied him a FAPE by failing to provide a one-to-one behavioral aide and related supportive services. The parties settled their dispute after mediation. The student then filed a complaint in the district court, alleging that the school district had violated the Americans with Disabilities Act (ADA) by failing to provide the same services sought in the IDEA proceedings. The district court dismissed the complaint without prejudice for failure to exhaust the IDEA process.

Ruling:

The court rejected the student's argument that the remedial basis of his ADA complaint is not the denial of a FAPE. The crux of the student's complaint is that the district failed to provide "required accommodations, aids and services" that he needed to "access" his education, and that "as a result" of its failure, he suffered loss of educational opportunity, exclusion from school, and harassment by others. The complaint identifies the accommodations denied as a one-to-one aide or other supportive services to manage the student's behavior. These are core components of a FAPE.

Significance to Educators:

Ensure a student is provided the necessary components of their program that will allow for them to make progress in the curriculum.

5.7.3

D.O., by and through his guardian ad litem Sonya WALKER, Plaintiff-Appellee,

v.

ESCONDIDO UNION SCHOOL DISTRICT, Defendant-Appellant

US Court of Appeals, Ninth Circuit

March 26, 2021

Issues:

- Exhaustion of administrative remedies
- Appeals

Facts of the Case:

The student filed a complaint with the California Office of Administrative Hearings (OAH) alleging that the district violated the Individuals with Disabilities Education Act (IDEA) by denying him a free appropriate public education (FAPE). He argued that by waiting four months to assess him for autism after being notified of his potential disability, the district committed a "procedural violation" resulting in the denial of a FAPE. An OAH administrative law judge (ALJ) dismissed the student's claims; the student then appealed to the district court.

The district court granted summary judgment to the student on the timely assessment issue on December 18, 2018. That order remanded the case to OAH without instructions, staying further district court proceedings. Before the ALJ, the student sought reimbursement for amounts paid to a psychologist for an independent autism assessment and an order that the district implement training about the statutory obligation to timely assess potential students with disabilities. After an evidentiary hearing, the ALJ ordered only reimbursement. Neither party sought review of the OAH decision in the district court. Instead, the school district filed a notice of appeal of the December 18 order, asserting that the OAH decision transformed that order into a final judgment under 28 U.S.C. § 1291.

This court then issued an order to show cause, asking the parties to address whether the December 18 order was a final judgment. The district again asserted that the December 18 order became final after the OAH decision on remand. After taking judicial notice of the December 18 order and the intervening administrative decision, the court ordered the parties to address jurisdiction in their merits briefing. The student then filed a motion to dismiss for lack of jurisdiction. The court denied the motion without prejudice to renewal in the student's answering brief.

Ruling:

The ALJ's decision to focus the remand hearing solely on remedy did not somehow render the district court's order final. Nor was the December 18 order transformed into a final order by the OAH decision on remand. The OAH decision does not by itself automatically create a final judgment in the district court; rather, the parties must return to that court so that it will "have before it all the issues that are necessary for it to render a final judgment." But until that happens, this court lacks jurisdiction to hear the appeal. The appeal was dismissed.

Significance to Educators:

Finality of decisions are the only parts that can be appealed.

5.7.4

E.E., a minor, by and through his guardian ad litem Laura HUTCHISON-ESCOBEDO; Christopher ESCOBEDO; Laura ESCOBEDO, Plaintiffs-Counter-Defendants-Appellees,

v.

NORRIS SCHOOL DISTRICT, Defendant-Counter-Claimant-Appellant

US Court of Appeals, Ninth Circuit

July 14, 2021

Issues:

- Stay-put provision
- Pendency

Facts of the Case:

The student has been diagnosed with autism spectrum disorder and lives in the district with his parents. The student attended kindergarten in a general education classroom beginning in August 2018, and his original individualized education program (IEP) was implemented on November 27, 2018. The 2018 IEP placed the student in a general education classroom for most of his school day. The district and parents met multiple times throughout 2019, but the parties did not modify the 2018 IEP, nor did they adopt a new IEP.

On January 14, 2020, the parents filed a due process hearing request with the California Office of Administrative Hearings (OAH) seeking to modify certain aspects of the student's IEP. On January 22, 2020, the district offered the parents a new IEP that would move the student from one elementary school to another elementary school and place him in a special day class with a trained behavior aide, but the parents did not agree to the district's proposed IEP (2020 IEP).

The district filed its own due process hearing request on June 4, 2020, and OAH consolidated the two cases. The ALJ found in favor of the parents in part and the district in part. Relevant to the parties' arguments here, the OAH Decision stated that "The district denied the student a FAPE by materially failing to implement [the] . . . 2018 IEP," and "[t]he January 22, 2020 IEP, as it may be amended, shall constitute the Student's 'stay put' under title 20 United States Code section 1415(j) . . . until parents' consent to a new amendment or annual IEP, or as otherwise ordered by OAH or other tribunal."

When the new school year started in August 2020, the district made plans to move the student from one elementary school to another elementary school, consistent with the OAH decision. On September 10, 2020, the parents filed a federal lawsuit challenging parts of the OAH decision that they disagreed with. The parents also moved for a temporary restraining order (TRO) to keep the student at the first elementary school under the 2018 IEP pending litigation.

Ruling:

The ALJ acted without legal authority in determining that the student's potential future placement in the 2020 IEP constituted his current placement for purposes of the student's stay-put placement. Because the ALJ acted *ultra vires*, her stay-put determination was void. As a result, the parents' stay-put motion did not seek to modify an existing stay-put order, so the district court correctly entered an automatic preliminary injunction and the district's proposed exception to the stay put provision is not supported by either the text of IDEA or any other legal authority, and the court declined to adopt it.

Significance to Educators:

"Stay put" means the last agreed-upon placement for the student until there is a final resolution or an agreement about changes.

5.7.5

Melissa GORDON; Robert GORDON, Plaintiffs-Appellees,

v.

LOS ANGELES UNIFIED SCHOOL DISTRICT, *Defendant-Appellant*
Melissa GORDON; Robert GORDON, Plaintiffs-Appellants, v. LOS ANGELES UNIFIED SCHOOL DISTRICT, Defendant-Appellee

US Court of Appeals, Ninth Circuit

October 27, 2021

Issue:

- Attorney's fees

Facts of the Case:

The parents, acting on behalf of their minor son, filed a request for a due process hearing before the California Office of Administrative Hearings (OAH) alleging that the district had violated the IDEA by failing to provide the student with a free appropriate public education (FAPE). After a five-day hearing in September 2017, the administrative law judge (ALJ) issued a decision two months later that resolved the eight specific issues in dispute. Each side partially prevailed on five of those issues, while the district fully prevailed as to the remaining three. As to remedies, the ALJ's order concluded that the student was "eligible for special education placement and services" and that, under § 612(a)(10)(C)(ii) of the IDEA, see 20 U.S.C. § 1412(a)(10)(C)(ii), his parents were entitled to reimbursement of the $42,990 cost of his attendance at a private school during the 2016–2017 school year. Neither side appealed the ALJ's decision.

The parents then filed this action under § 615 of the IDEA, alleging that, as the prevailing party at the due process hearing, they were entitled to their attorney's fees both in connection with that hearing and in connection with this suit. After a hearing, the district court awarded the parents $161,760 in fees in connection with the administrative proceedings and $156,705 in fees arising from this fee-recovery suit, for a total award of $318,465. The district appeals the award as too high, and the Parents cross-appeal, contending that it is too low.

Ruling:

The court rejected the district's contention that the parents were not the prevailing party in this civil action for attorney's fees. Although the district never contested that the parents were entitled to an appropriate fee award for the administrative proceedings, the amount of such fees was sharply contested in this protracted satellite litigation. Although the parents did not obtain all of the fees that they had sought for the administrative proceedings, the district court did not err in concluding that the parents were the "prevailing party" in this action and were eligible for a further award of fees in connection with their efforts in this fee litigation.

Significance to Educators:

When challenging fee requests, this may significantly increase the fees for not only your own attorneys but those of opposing counsel. Be careful to challenge such requests.

5.7.6

Claudia HERRERA; Cesar ORTIZ, Plaintiffs-Appellants,

v.

LOS ANGELES UNIFIED SCHOOL DISTRICT, *a public entity;*
Jose HUERTA; Jose LOPEZ; DOES; LOS ANGELES UNIFIED
SCHOOL DISTRICT, *Defendants-Appellees,*
and COUNTY OF LOS ANGELES, *Defendant*

US Court of Appeals, Ninth Circuit

December 1, 2021

Issues:

- Deliberate indifference
- Use of paraprofessional

Facts of the Case:

A 10th-grade student eligible for special education and related services as a student with autism attended an end-of-the-year class party at a local pool. The student has asthma and could not swim. The student had an aide assigned to support him. The student was in the shallow end of the pool and started walking toward the lockers, and the aide went to meet him at the entrance to the lockers. While the aide went to the entrance to the locker room, the student went back to the pool and went to the deep end. After several minutes, the aide went back to the pool and saw the three lifeguards who were guarding the pool administering CPR to the student. The student died as a result of drowning.

The parents sued the district alleging deliberate indifference, stating that the aide should have known their son could not swim and that he needed additional supports, and that the aide going to the entrance to the locker room amounted to a denial of a continued familial relationship.

Ruling:

The court decided in favor of the district and the aide because the pool was guarded by three lifeguards, and the aide did not act unreasonably by waiting by the locker room. The parents alleged that the danger to the student was obvious and the aide placed the student in a highly vulnerable condition. In the case at hand, allowing the student to enter the pool area arguably placed him in a more dangerous position than if he had not been allowed to swim. But allowing the student to enter a "more dangerous position" does not end the deliberate indifference analysis. The undisputed evidence establishes that the student was never left completely without protection. The aide observed the student while he was in the pool, and three lifeguards also monitored the area. Deliberate indifference requires more: with at least four individuals tasked with supervising the student while in the pool, the aide neither abandoned the student nor left him completely without protection.

Significance to Educators:

Strongly consider additional supports for students when they are outside of the school. In this case, there were lifeguards; however, be very careful and ensure there are observations of the student at all times.

5.7.7

L.C., a minor, by and through his Guardian Ad Litem Ausencia CRUZ, Plaintiff-Appellee,

v.

ALTA LOMA SCHOOL DISTRICT, a Local Educational Agency, Defendant-Appellant

849 F. App'x 678

US Court of Appeals, Ninth Circuit

June 8, 2021

Issues:

- Procedural violations
- Independent educational evaluation

Facts of the Case:

The parents requested an independent educational evaluation (IEE) for their 11-year-old son related to his visual processing. After the request, the district exchanged numerous e-mails and letters with the parents from August 10, 2017, until it filed for a due process hearing on December 5, 2017. The e-mail exchange was an attempt to reach an agreement on the IEE request and other issues. The parties reached final impasse on the IEE issue on Thursday, November 30, and the district filed for a due process hearing the following Tuesday, December 5, 84 days after the initial request for the IEE. The parents alleged the extensive wait was a procedural violation.

Ruling:

Both parties were in discussion about the need for and extent of the IEE throughout the 84-day period, except for 10 days during Thanksgiving break. Since they were in fairly constant communications, there was not an unnecessary delay. Thus, the court concluded there was no unnecessary delay.

Significance to Educators:

When a district denies a request for an IEE, it is supposed to forward the request for a due process hearing to the state authorities in a timely fashion. Be careful in how long to wait, but remember the district and the parents can continue to work to resolve the issue even after the hearing is requested.

5.7.8

Debra LEGRIS; Aviana LEGRIS, Plaintiffs-Appellants,

v.

CAPISTRANO UNIFIED SCHOOL DISTRICT,
a local educational agency, Defendant-Appellee

US Court of Appeals, Ninth Circuit

October 18, 2021

Issue:

- Child find

Facts of the Case:

The parents argued the district did not act on notice that the student had visual difficulties and that these difficulties had a severe impact on her ability to read. The district, however, conducted a thorough and multidisciplinary assessment and, as a result, provided the student with a Section 504 plan to address her diagnosed attention deficit hyperactivity disorder (ADHD).

The parents also asserted that the district violated IDEA when it assessed the student for an IEP in her senior year because it failed to assess her "in the area of developmental vision." IDEA requires a school district to "use a variety of assessment tools and strategies to gather relevant . . . information" (20 U.S.C. § 1414(b)(2)(A)) and to "review existing evaluation data on the child, including . . . current classroom-based, local, or State assessments" to "identify what additional data, if any, are needed" to determine a child's eligibility (§ 1414(c)(1)). The district reviewed "existing evaluation data," conducted new cognitive and standardized tests, consulted the student's instructors, observed her in class, and determined that a separate visual assessment was not necessary. The district also reviewed the student's reports from evaluators retained by her family and discussed this data at an IEP meeting with the parents.

Finally, the parents argued the student met IDEA's eligibility requirements for special education services. The parents also asserted that the student qualified for IDEA benefits because an outside evaluator diagnosed her with convergence insufficiency and treated her with vision therapy. The student received vision therapy from the outside provider, but the parties dispute whether the convergence insufficiency diagnosis was credible.

Ruling:

The student was not substantively eligible for IDEA benefits based on a vision impairment, other health impairment, or specific learning disability. The parents did not demonstrate that the student required services beyond modification of the regular school program before or after she received vision therapy and one-to-one instruction.

As for "other health impairment" or a "specific learning disability," the parents pointed to little evidence or legal authority supporting their contention that the student met the eligibility requirements for either category. The record supports the conclusion that the student adequately accessed the curriculum in the regular classroom with her Section 504 accommodations. The court affirmed the conclusion that the student was not eligible for special education services.

Significance to Educators:

Pay close attention to outside evaluations. Ensure that all the teachers are consulted, and if there is any possible need or services, consider a full evaluation. But even after the evaluation, continue to monitor and observe the student.

5.7.9

Matthew C. OSKOWIS, individually and on behalf of E.O., Plaintiff-Appellant,

v.

SEDONA-OAK CREEK UNIFIED SCHOOL DISTRICT #9, Defendant-Appellee

US Court of Appeals, Ninth Circuit

August 6, 2021

Issues:

- Attorney's fees
- Frivolous lawsuits

Facts of the Case:

The parent, acting *pro se*, appealed a lower court's order awarding attorney's fees to the district under the Individuals with Disabilities Education Act (IDEA). The district court did not abuse its discretion by awarding attorney's fees to the school district. The law permits the court to award reasonable attorney's fees to a prevailing educational agency against a parent whose "complaint or subsequent cause of action was presented for any improper purpose, such as to harass, to cause unnecessary delay, or to needlessly increase the cost of litigation" (20 U.S.C. § 1415(i)(3)(B)(i)(III)).

Ruling:

The lower court's findings that the district was the prevailing party, the parent's causes of action were frivolous, and the parent's action was brought for the improper purposes of harassing the district and driving up litigation costs were amply supported by the record. The lower court properly considered and rejected the parent's arguments that his claims were not frivolous or presented for an improper purpose. The panel unanimously concluded this case is suitable for decision without oral argument.

Significance to Educators:

Districts may be awarded attorney's fees if they can show the parents filed frivolous claims and intentionally delayed litigation.

5.7.10

R.D., *a minor, by and through her personal representatives, Catherine DAVIS and Sean DAVIS; et al., Plaintiffs-Appellants,*

v.

LAKE WASHINGTON SCHOOL DISTRICT,
a municipal corporation, Defendant-Appellee

843 F. App'x 80

US Court of Appeals, Ninth Circuit

February 11, 2021

Issues:

- 504 Implementation
- Deliberate indifference

Facts of the Case:

The 2016 Section 504 plan provided that the student was to stay inside when it is damp or raining and when the high temperature of the day is below 60 degrees (must be overseen by an adult), and that she should be allowed to have supervised inside recess that will include a variety of activities (including gross motor). The parents offered evidence that recess is a part of a free appropriate public education (FAPE) and includes gross motor activity and supervision. Whether the student was offered gross motor activities is disputed. The parents have also set forth evidence that the student was not, in fact, supervised to ensure that she stayed inside when it was unsafe for her to be outside. In granting summary judgment on the parents' Section 504 and ADA claims, the district court focused too narrowly on a mainstreaming regulation of Section 504, without considering that the parents could satisfy the second prong by showing that the student was denied services that she needed to enjoy meaningful access to the benefits of a public education and that were available as reasonable accommodations.

Taking the disputed facts in the light most favorable to the parents, a reasonable juror could conclude that the district knew that the student needed supervision and gross motor activities and failed to provide those accommodations, such that it acted with deliberate indifference. Thus, summary judgment should not have been granted as to the Section 504 and ADA damages claims.

Ruling:

Remanded for a rehearing on the issues.

Significance to Educators:

When a student requires an accommodation, make sure all the teachers and staff are aware of the need and also make sure they provide the accommodation.

5.7.11

S.C. by her mother and next friend, K.G., Plaintiff-Appellant,

v.

LINCOLN COUNTY SCHOOL DISTRICT, Defendant-Appellee

US Court of Appeals, Ninth Circuit

October 18, 2021

Issue:

- Stay-put provision

Facts of the Case:

The student is a teenage girl and has a severe form of Prader-Willi syndrome (PWS), a genetic condition that disrupts the body's appetite control and causes anxiety, major depressive disorder, and developmental delays. Because of PWS, the student experiences intense food-seeking thoughts that lead to poor impulse control and behavioral issues, including verbal and physical aggression. Because consistent and rigid routines concerning food help control PWS, treatment for PWS typically includes total food security (TFS), a system in which food is present at mealtimes but otherwise kept locked up and out of sight.

The student has been receiving special education services in the school district since the 2015–2016 school year through the provision of regularly updated IEPs. In May 2020, the student's mother filed an administrative challenge claiming that the school district was not providing a FAPE to the student. While this challenge was pending, the district finalized a new IEP for the student on September 18, 2020, approved by the IEP team but not by the parents; however, because the due process review by the administrative law judge (ALJ) is limited by law to the two years preceding the filing of the due process complaint, the ALJ's review authority did not extend past May 21, 2020 (20 U.S.C. § 1415(f)(3)(c)). As a result, and as the ALJ stated in her decision, the ALJ's ruling did not cover the September 2020 IEP.

In October 2020, the ALJ conducted a remote hearing, spanning more than 50 hours in total, on the student's due process complaint. On December 22, 2020, the ALJ issued a 70-page decision, finding that the school district had not provided the student a FAPE during the period under review (May 21, 2018–May 21, 2020). In so finding, the ALJ concluded, among other things, that the student required TFS in a schoolwide environment to obtain a meaningful educational benefit at school, and that the previous IEPs only provided the student with TFS by placing her in a "Structured Learning Center" removed from the regular school environment.

As a remedy for the school district's failure to provide a FAPE, the ALJ ordered that the student be placed at the Latham Center, a residential facility that treats students with PWS and provides TFS in the overall school environment. The key provision of the ALJ order reads as follows:

> The [School] District is to pay the cost of enrolling the Student at the Latham Center, including non-medical care, room and board, for the period commencing on the first day of the winter 2021 semester until the District provides TS in school-wide setting along with an IEP which addresses all of the inadequacies identified in this order or the next annual IEP which appears to be September 2021. (emphasis omitted)

The district did not appeal; but neither did it comply with the order. Specifically, it failed to arrange for the student to be enrolled at the Latham Center at the district's expense. Accordingly, the parent filed suit in federal court on January 6, 2021, seeking a stay-put order or preliminary injunction requiring the school district to comply with the ALJ order and pay for the student's placement at the Latham Center.

Ruling:

As set out in the Department of Education's implementing regulations, "[i]f the hearing officer in a due process hearing . . . agrees with the child's parents that a change of placement is appropriate, that placement must be treated as an agreement between the state and the parents for purposes of [stay put]" (34 C.F.R. § 300.518(d)). Furthermore, as this court discussed in *L.M. v. Capistrano Unified School District*, "[w]here the agency or the court has ruled on the appropriateness of the educational placement in the parents' favor, the school district is responsible for appropriate private education costs."

As described earlier, the ALJ order changed the student's educational placement to the Latham Center. The court entered a stay-put order to enforce the ALJ's order requiring the student's placement at the Latham Center, at the district's expense, "until the [school] district provides TFS in school-wide setting along with an IEP which addresses all of the inadequacies identified in this order." To be sure, further proceedings, whether judicial or administrative, may consider whether the district is providing TFS schoolwide, as well as whether a new IEP (either the September 2020 IEP or a subsequent IEP) provides a FAPE that cures the deficiencies in previous IEPs that the ALJ order identifies. Unless and until, however, the conclusion of such proceedings changes the student's educational placement, the court ruled that she must be placed at the Latham Center and remain there at the district's expense.

Significance to Educators:

Implement the order until there is a ruling or agreement otherwise.

5.7.12

STUDENT A, by and through PARENT A, her guardian; STUDENT B, by and through PARENT B, his guardian; STUDENT C, by and through PARENT C, his guardian; STUDENT D, by and through PARENT D, her guardian; STUDENT E, by and through PARENT E, her guardian, on behalf of themselves and all others similarly situated, Plaintiffs-Appellants,

v.

SAN FRANCISCO UNIFIED SCHOOL DISTRICT; Vincent MATTHEWS, in his official capacity as the Superintendent for the San Francisco Unified School District, Defendants-Appellees

US Court of Appeals, Ninth Circuit

August 18, 2021

Issue:

- Exhaustion of administrative remedies

Facts of the Case:

The plaintiffs are five current or former district students who have been diagnosed with dyslexia, autism, or speech and language impairments. In their class action complaint, the plaintiffs alleged that the district has systematically failed and refused to fulfill its obligations to (1) timely identify and evaluate students who qualify for special education services, (2) offer appropriately tailored special education services to students with disabilities, and (3) provide sufficient resources for its special education program. None of the plaintiffs have initiated either a due process hearing or the state complaint process.

On motion by the district, the lower court dismissed the plaintiffs' complaint for failure to exhaust administrative remedies. The lower court concluded that the plaintiffs had not alleged facts sufficient to support their contention that an exception to the exhaustion requirement applied to their claims. The lower court granted the plaintiffs leave to amend.

The plaintiffs did so, asserting in their amended complaint that, since they sought systemic, district-wide reforms that the due process hearing process could not achieve, exhausting through a due process hearing would be useless. The plaintiffs also cited data to show unacceptably poor performance from district students with disabilities. The district moved to dismiss.

The plaintiffs claimed that the district failed in its responsibilities to students under the IDEA by not timely identifying and evaluating students with disabilities and, after identifying them, by providing them with insufficiently individualized, "cookie-cutter" accommodations and services.

Ruling:

In light of IDEA's exhaustion requirement, the plaintiffs need to do something to make their case and their broad allegations more concrete and, in the process, develop a record containing administrative expertise as well as responses from the district or state to allow a court to effectively move forward on exhausted claims. The plaintiffs seek to avoid the exhaustion requirement altogether. Primarily invoking the exception for unlawful policies or practices of general applicability, they claim to challenge district-wide policies that apply generally to all district students with disabilities and that result in their failing to receive FAPEs. The plaintiffs thus contend exhaustion would serve no purpose. Yet the plaintiffs have not identified any policy, much less one of general applicability, that the administrative process could not address.

To be sure, the plaintiffs do contend that their claims identify three specific unlawful policies or practices. But what they amount to are assertions of delay in providing services, denial of sufficiently individualized services, and arbitrary limits on services. These are allegations of bad results, not descriptions of unlawful policies or practices. The plaintiffs' claims are accompanied by general statistics documenting poor performance by students with disabilities. While these results, if true, are all unfortunate, they are not policies or practices that a court could grasp, much less change, without the benefit of any factually developed administrative record.

Significance to Educators:

There needs to be an exhaustion of administrative remedies; however, the initiation of a lawsuit should be used as a means to change or amend current practices and policies.

5.8 Summaries of Rulings from the US Court of Appeals for the Tenth Circuit

5.8.1

C.W. by and through his parents B.W. and C.B.

v.

Denver County School District No. 1

US Court of Appeals, Tenth Circuit

April 20, 2021

994 F.3d 1215

Issues:

- Procedural matters in IDEA litigation
- Jurisdiction
- Judicial review

Facts of the Case:

In September 2016, the parents of C.W., a twice-exceptional child, filed a due process complaint under the IDEA, asserting that the Denver County School District had denied their son a FAPE. In June 2017, an administrative law judge (ALJ) ruled that the school district had failed to provide C.W. with a FAPE, thus violating the IDEA; however, the ALJ also found that the 2017 IEP that the school developed for C.W. was substantively appropriate. The ALJ ordered partial relief for the parents. C.W. then appealed the ALJ's ruling alleging that the 2017 IEP was appropriate to the federal district court. C.W. also alleged non-IDEA claims against the school district under the Americans with Disabilities Act, the Rehabilitation Act, and the Fourteenth Amendment of the US Constitution.

The federal district court ruled partially in favor of C.W., finding that the 2017 IEP was inadequate, and partially against C.W., by dismissing the non-IDEA claims because he had failed to exhaust administrative remedies. The district court also remanded the case to the ALJ for further proceedings to determine appropriate remedies in light of the school district failure to provide a FAPE in the 2017 IEP. Instead of staying the action in light of the remand to the ALJ, the district court entered a "final judgment" in the case. C.W. then appealed the final judgment to the US Court of Appeals for the Tenth Circuit, asserting that he was not required to exhaust administrative remedies on the non-IDEA claims. The school district cross-appealed, arguing that the 2017 IEP was adequate. While these appeals were pending, the district court awarded C.W. attorney's fees.

Ruling:

The US Court of Appeals for the Tenth Circuit ruled that neither the school district nor C.W. could appeal the federal district court's order that remanded the parents' IDEA claim to an ALJ to determine an appropriate remedy because the ruling had been remanded. Additionally, the US Court of Appeals ordered the district court to vacate its "final judgment" and stay the case pending the ALJ's final ruling.

Significance to Educators:

School districts and parents cannot file an appeal with a circuit court until previous reviews are complete and final. In this case, the district court's final judgment, which reversed part of the ALJ's ruling and ordered the ALJ to fashion an appropriate remedy, prevented the parents from appealing their non-IDEA claims and the school district from appealing the FAPE ruling.

5.9 Summaries of Rulings from the US Court of Appeals for the Eleventh Circuit

5.9.1

J.N., as mother and NEXT FRIEND OF M.N., a minor

v.

JEFFERSON COUNTY BOARD OF EDUCATION

12 F.4th 1355

US Court of Appeals, Eleventh Circuit

September 10, 2021

Issue:

- Child find provision under the IDEA

Facts of the Case:

The mother of a middle school student with attention deficit hyperactivity disorder (ADHD) appealed a prior ruling by a hearing officer dismissing her administrative complaint with the Alabama State Department of Education alleging that the local school board had failed to provide her child with a free appropriate public education (FAPE). Specifically, the parent alleged that there was a child find violation under the IDEA resulting in both a loss of educational opportunities for her daughter with ADHD as well as an inability to receive compensatory education for the student.

Ruling:

The US Court of Appeals for the Eleventh Circuit upheld a previous district court's ruling that the parent failed to establish an educational need for her child's compensatory education. Relatedly, the Eleventh Circuit held that the district's acknowledged delay in referring the student with ADHD for an IDEA evaluation did not result in substantive educational harm to the student. The Eleventh Circuit argued that it found no evidence between providing additional special education services and conducting an earlier evaluation of the student. In fact, there was evidence that the district provided the student with individualized extra assistance, including one-to-one instruction in math and working closely with the student's parents to address her disruptive behaviors in the classroom.

Significance to Educators:

In this case, the Eleventh Circuit ruled that compensatory education services are only available as a remedy for a child find violation under the IDEA that results in substantive harm to the student with disabilities. More specifically, a parent needs to show that the student's educational program was substantively deficient and compensatory education is necessary to put the student in a position he or she would have been if the district has originally followed its child find duty under the IDEA.

No special education cases were heard by the US Court of Appeals for the DC Circuit in 2021.

CHAPTER 6

Case Studies

6.1 How Much Supervision Is Enough?

6.2 Providing Services

    6.2.1 What Is a District's Responsibility to Provide the Section 504 Plan?

6.3 How Much Progress Monitoring?

6.4 How Much Is a Request?

6.5 The IDEA's "Child Find" Provision: Whose Legal Responsibility Is It?

6.6 Is There a Preference for Mediation-Based Approaches to Special Education Disputes?

    6.6.1 The Exhaustion of Administrative Remedies Rule under the IDEA

We have provided six case studies with questions from the 2021 law cases. These cases can be used with classes for discussion and questions about how to read a case, and how to go beyond the initial facts and work to have a greater understanding of how these issues change the lives of students with disabilities and their families. Many of the questions at the end of each case study apply to more than one case. Each case is followed by a full citation to help the reader find more detail about that case.

6.1 How Much Supervision Is Enough?

A 10th-grade student with autism who had significant needs required regular and fairly constant supervision to prevent him from getting into dangerous situations. How much supervision is enough?

The student was attending a field trip to an end-of-year pool party with his classmates. There was an aide assigned to watch and support him at the pool party. It was known that the student did not swim and had asthma that would make things worse in the pool. There were three lifeguards at the pool at all times. The aide observed the student from a designated area—not inside the pool area itself—but could clearly see the student while the student interacted with others. This was the policy of the pool.

The student decided to leave the pool and let the aide know he was going to the changing room. The aide moved away from the observation area to wait at the exit to the changing room. The student was self-sufficient in the changing room requiring no assistance to change out of his bathing suit and into his street clothes.

Instead of going into the changing room as he indicated, the student decided to go back into the pool. The aide continued to wait for the student at the changing room exit—a location that did not have a view of the pool. The student went back into the pool, and being unable to swim, he swallowed a lot of water into his lungs; despite efforts of the lifeguards, he passed away.

The parents sued the school district for deliberate indifference.

Deliberate indifference is defined as when someone recognizes the unreasonable risk and actually intends to expose the individual to such risks without regard to the consequences. Ultimately, a state actor needs to know that something is going to happen, but ignore the risk and expose a person to that risk.

There is no dispute the student had needs. There is no dispute the student required additional supervision. There is no dispute the school was aware of the student's needs related to asthma or that he could not swim. This was also an official school event, though not on school property.

There are many questions that need to be addressed as a part of this case.

1. What is the school's responsibility in observing a student?
2. Was the reliance on lifeguards enough supervision near the pool?
3. How much do we share with aides/paraprofessionals about the needs or requirements of a student?
4. When does the school's responsibility for observing a student end and the student becomes the responsibility of the parents?
5. What is really meant by deliberate indifference?
6. What are some examples of deliberate indifference?
7. What steps should school districts take to ensure they are not deliberately indifferent to a student's needs?
8. In hindsight, what should have been done?
9. What training do we need to provide aides/paraprofessionals on safety issues?
10. How much supervision is enough?

This case should be read with:

Claudia HERRERA; Cesar ORTIZ, Plaintiffs-Appellants, v. LOS ANGELES UNIFIED SCHOOL DISTRICT, a public entity; Jose HUERTA; Jose LOPEZ; DOES; LOS ANGELES UNIFIED SCHOOL DISTRICT, Defendants-Appellees, and COUNTY OF LOS ANGELES, Defendant, US Court of Appeals, Ninth Circuit

6.2 Providing Services

When a student requires a service, and the district places the accommodation or modification in the student's IEP or 504 plan, what is the choice of the district to provide the service or accommodation?

A Section 504 plan provided that the student was to stay inside when it is damp or raining or when the high temperature of the day is below 60 degrees (must be overseen by an adult), and that she should be allowed to have supervised inside recess that will include a variety of activities, including gross motor ones. The parents have offered evidence that recess is a part of a free appropriate public education (FAPE) and includes gross motor activity and supervision. Whether the student was offered gross motor activities is disputed. The parents have set forth evidence that the student was not, in fact, supervised to ensure that she stayed inside when it was unsafe for her to be outside.

Section 504 applies to school districts in both academic programming as well as accommodations to access programming in the school that is not academic. The dispute centered on whether the district denied the student a reasonable accommodation that she needed to enjoy meaningful access to the district's programs and activities.

6.2.1 What Is a District's Responsibility to Provide the Section 504 Plan?

There are many questions that need to be addressed as a part of this case:

1. Is the accommodation necessary?
2. Is the modification necessary?
3. Is it the parents' responsibility to ensure the accommodation or modification is provided?
4. What are some examples of some accommodations or modifications a district does not have to provide?
5. What steps should a district take to ensure it is providing what a student requires?
6. In hindsight, what should have been done?
7. What training is necessary for general education teachers on accommodations and modifications?
8. What training is necessary for principals and building-level administrators on accommodations and modifications?
9. How much supervision is enough?

This case should be read with:

R.D., a minor, by and through her personal representatives, Catherine DAVIS and Sean DAVIS; et al., Plaintiffs-Appellants, v. LAKE WASHINGTON SCHOOL DISTRICT, a municipal corporation, Defendant-Appellee, 843 F. App'x 80, US Court of Appeals, Ninth Circuit

6.3 How Much Progress Monitoring?

David was a fourth-grade student at Meadowbrook Elementary. When he was in first grade, his teacher reported that David was having trouble learning to read. In second grade, David was provided with accommodations but continued to struggle with reading fluency and comprehension. Toward the end of fourth grade, David's mother referred him for a special education evaluation. He was determined to be eligible for special education services, and an individualized education program (IEP) was written for David with specific services to address his reading fluency problems. After the completion of the school year, however, David continued to struggle with reading. During the annual review meeting, David's parents questioned whether their son's progress toward his reading goal was being measured because they had not received any reports and he didn't seem to be improving in his ability to read. They noted that the IEP that was developed for David at that time did not include reading comprehension strategies.

The parents filed a due process complaint, alleging that the school district unreasonably did not provide David with an appropriate special education program in violation of the FAPE mandate of the Individuals with Disabilities Education Act (IDEA). The attorneys for the school district countered that, after David's IEP was implemented, he passed all his classes, and therefore the school district had provided him with a FAPE. The hearing officer disagreed, finding that the fact that David passed all his classes was not particularly significant noting that the Supreme Court in *Endrew F.* specifically rejected the notion that a student is receiving FAPE merely because he or she is passing from grade to grade. Rather, the hearing officer noted that the development for a student with disabilities should be measured with respect to the individual student.

The hearing officer ruled in favor of the plaintiffs, finding that the school's IEP did not provide David with a FAPE because the program was not individualized, did not address his reading comprehension problems, and did not provide David with sufficient academic benefit because he made only minimal progress in reading. The hearing officer ordered the school district to modify David's IEP to provide 45 minutes a day of reading instruction using a research-based reading comprehension program and also awarded David 180 hours of compensatory education services.

Answer the following questions about this case study:

1. What could school personnel have done to determine if David was making appropriate progress toward his goals?
2. Is it the parents' responsibility to ensure that their child's progress is monitored?
3. What training is necessary for special education teachers on progress monitoring?
4. What steps should a district take to ensure that a student's progress is monitored?
5. What training is necessary for building-level and district-level special education administrators on progress monitoring?
6. What types of data should special educators collect to monitor student progress?
7. What actions should be taken when data show that a student is not making progress toward his or her goals?

This case should be read with:

D.C. v. Klein Independent School District, US Court of Appeals, Fifth Circuit

6.4 How Much Is a Request?

Alex was a sixth-grade student at the Friends Middle School, a private school for students with autism. He had attended a special education program until fourth grade but was unilaterally removed by his parents to the Friends Middle School. A year after his parents removed Alex from the public school, his mother called the principal of the public school and inquired about what kind of educational alternatives the public schools would have for Alex. The principal and Alex's mother spoke by telephone. Alex's mother expressed an interest in having Alex return to the public school. To discuss the special education services more fully, the principal referred Alex's parents to the special education director. The parents and special education director spoke generally about special education services available for Alex.

A few months later, Alex's mother called the special education director and complained that her son was not provided with a FAPE. Because the school district had failed to provide a FAPE, Alex's mother told the director that Alex would be enrolled in the private school during the next school year. The parents also demanded that the school district pay for the tuition at the private school. The special education director replied that the parents had unilaterally withdrawn Alex from the public school and had not requested that he be reenrolled in the public school district.

The parents filed a due process complaint, alleging that the school district failed to provide Alex with a FAPE in violation of the IDEA and sought tuition reimbursement for the private school. The hearing officer noted that the school district had an obligation to provide special education services to Alex because of his previous classification. the hearing officer, however, ruled in favor of the school district because Alex's parents had not clearly put the school district on notice that it had a duty to reevaluate and propose programming for Alex.

Answer the following questions about this case study:

1. Can a parent's request to evaluate a private school student trigger a school district's duty to evaluate and program for a student with disabilities?
2. Was it the parents' responsibility to inform the school district that they intended to reenroll Alex in the public school?
3. How important is that school district personnel keep thorough records of all communications with a student's parents?
4. Assuming that Alex's parents had told school district officials of their intention to reenroll Alex, what actions should the school officials have taken?

This case should be read with:

A.B. v. Abington School District, US Court of Appeals, Third Circuit

6.5 The IDEA's "Child Find" Provision: Whose Legal Responsibility Is It?

The parent of a student with an emotional disability filed legal suit against a school district alleging that they violated the "child find" obligation under the IDEA based on their failure to promptly identify a student as someone with an emotional disability requiring special education and related services. Based on the academic progress of the high school student with a bipolar disorder during a four-month stay in a psychiatric hospital and her subsequent return to school, the district made the decision that the student did not need extended school year (ESY) services under the IDEA in order to satisfy the free appropriate public education (FAPE) provision under the IDEA. As a legal remedy, the parent is seeking tuition reimbursement for the student's private summer program. The district maintains that there is no evidence involving this student to substantiate any child find violation under the IDEA. In this specific case, the court ruled that the district did not violate the "child find" provision under the IDEA. More specifically, the court held that the district had no legal obligation to evaluate the student for an emotional disability until it learned of the student's hospitalization and that the student was on track to graduate. Thus, the student's parents were not legally entitled to receive tuition reimbursement for the student's private summer program.

As expressly indicated in the IDEA, the "child find" provision places initial responsibility on public school districts to locate, identify, and initially evaluate a student who may be potentially eligible to receive special education and related services under the IDEA. The IDEA's "child find" legal obligation requires each state that receives federal financial aid must have policies and procedures in place ensuring that all students with disabilities are "identified, located and evaluated" and that "a practical method is developed and implemented to determine which children are currently receiving needed special education and related services" (34 C.F.R. § 300.111(a)). The IDEA's "child find" provision has three major purposes: (1) ensuring that no student with a disability is denied a free appropriate education based on not being identified or located; (2) facilitating cooperation and collaboration between state and local educational agencies with other agencies that work with students with disabilities on a regular basis, such as health and social services, correctional facilities, or private schools; and (3) requiring that state and local educational agencies, including school districts, are held legally accountable in identifying all potentially eligible students with disabilities under the IDEA.

There are many possible questions that could be addressed as part of this case:

1. What are some ways schools can encourage the parents of students with potential disabilities to have their children evaluated for eligibility?
2. What are some examples of activities that school officials can develop to help better inform parents or make the local community more aware of the nature of special education and related services that districts provide to students who are IDEA eligible?
3. How can public school districts help locate or identify children and youth with disabilities within their local community who attend private school settings, including religious-affiliated schools?
4. If school officials wanted to share a checklist of important timelines involving initial student referral and evaluation for possible IDEA eligibility, what would be some of those timelines be?
5. How would school officials facilitate an open dialogue between school personnel and parents to increase the awareness of disabilities that often carry significant stigmas, including student mental health needs?
6. What about students with potential IDEA-eligible disabilities living in federal residential facilities, including federal prisons? Does the IDEA's child find provision apply to them?

This case should be read with:

K.B., on behalf of S.B. v. Katonah Lewisboro Union Free School District, 847 Fed. App'x. 38, US Court of Appeals, Second Circuit (2021)

6.6 Is There a Preference for Mediation-Based Approaches to Special Education Disputes?

6.6.1 The Exhaustion of Administrative Remedies Rule under the IDEA

In this particular case, a 23-year old student with a hearing impairment sued a public school district alleging school officials discriminated against him by not providing the necessary resources for him to fully participate in the classroom, which is in direct violation of the federal statute, the

Americans with Disabilities Act (ADA), as well as this particular state's law. The student also sued the district for the emotional distress he allegedly suffered as a result of the district's failure to meet his individual special education needs under the ADA. Prior to the student's lawsuit, the district was involved in a legal settlement under the IDEA. In the ruling, the Sixth Circuit Court of Appeals upheld an earlier district court's dismissal of the student's ADA claim. The Sixth Court's reasoning is that the district's settlement of a previous IDEA due process complaint can legally protect it from other legal claims filed under Section 504 or the ADA. In this case, the district claimed that the student's ADA lawsuit addressed the same issues and alleged educational shortcomings as the student's IDEA due process complaint. Therefore, the district was not legally estopped, or barred from legally seeking dismissal of the student's complaint.

While this case is based on many procedural issues, the major legal takeaway of the case is an understating of the IDEA's strong inclination to resolving special education disputes through mediation, or other alternative dispute resolution methods. More specifically, in 2017, the US Supreme Court in the case *Fry v. Napoleon Community Schools* addressed the issue of the IDEA's "exhaustion rule." The exhaustion of administrative remedies rule of the IDEA indicates that if a lawsuit alleges that a student with disabilities was denied a free appropriate public education (FAPE), the parent(s) on behalf of the student alleging the complaint cannot legally ignore the IDEA's exhaustion requirement by simply bringing their lawsuit under another federal statute, such as the ADA or Section 504. In this case, the parents' other lawsuit brought under the ADA is not required if the remedy sought is not for a denial of FAPE. Currently, the Supreme Court requires that, to make this determination, a court must determine the essence or "gravamen" of the issue(s) in the complaint. By the district's demonstration that it settled the IDEA claim prior to the scheduled administrative hearing, the district successfully legally established the student's failure to exhaust those administrative claims under the IDEA.

There are many questions that can be addressed related to this case, including the following:

1. What are some examples of ways that school officials can encourage the use of mediation-based approaches to special education legal disputes with parents or legal guardians of students with disabilities?
2. What can school officials do to encourage mediation-based approaches for the parents of students with disabilities?
3. What are some examples of administrative-based remedies schools can adopt and implement to facilitate the mediation of special education legal disputes?

This case should be read with:

PEREZ v. STURGIS PUBLIC SCHOOLS; STURGIS PUBLIC SCHOOLS BOARD OF EDUCATION, 3 F.4th 236, US Court of Appeals, Sixth Circuit

Glossary of Legal Terms

Administrative appeal: A quasi-judicial proceeding before an independent hearing officer or administrative law judge.

Administrative law judge (ALJ): Some states use ALJs who are appointed by the state to conduct due process hearings in special education. In most states, an ALJ may conduct administrative hearings in several areas (e.g., special education, labor relations, housing, insurance). An individual presiding at an administrative due process hearing has the power to administer oaths, hear testimony, rule out questions of evidence, and make determinations of fact. The role of an administrative law judge in IDEA proceedings is like that of an independent hearing officer, with some small differences among the states.

Adversary process: The method courts used to resolve disputes in which each side presents its case, subject to rules of evidence; an independent fact finder (jury or judge) determines which side's evidence is more persuasive.

Affirm: To uphold the opinion of a lower court on appeal.

ALJ: *See* Administrative law judge (ALJ).

Allegation: An unsupported assertion made in a legal proceeding by a party who expects to prove it in court.

Alternate assessment based on alternate academic achievement standards (AA-AAAS): State assessments of academic progress in which students who cannot participate in the regular assessments of education progress with accommodations. Such students are tested using an alternate test based on alternate academic achievement standards. Only students with the most significant cognitive disabilities take an AA-AAAS.

Alternative dispute resolution: Procedures for settling disputes by means other than litigation, for example, by arbitration or mediation. Such procedures are usually less costly and faster.

Americans with Disabilities Act (ADA): A civil rights law that prohibits discrimination against individuals with disabilities in all areas of public life, including jobs, schools, transportation, and all public and private places that are open to the public.

Appeal: A party's request to a higher court to review a decision by a lower court. In cases where the right exists, the appeal must be made according to certain procedures and limitations.

Appellant: The party bringing a court appeal.

Appellate court: Any state or federal court empowered to review and amend the judgments of a lower court over which it has jurisdiction.

Appellee: The party responding and defending against the appeal.

Arbitrary: Without rational basis, underlying reason, or guiding principle; nonrational, capricious.

Attention deficit hyperactivity disorder (ADHD): A common disorder of childhood involving inattention, impulsivity, and hyperactivity. ADHD often begins in childhood and lasts into adulthood.

Average per-pupil expenditure (APPE): The average per-pupil expenditure is the average amount of funds spent per student. This amount varies by state and by districts within a state.

Behavior intervention plan (BIP): A BIP is an individual plan for addressing a student's behaviors. It may be a part of a student's IEP but is sometimes a separate document. A BIP is based on the results of an FBA and includes a description of the problem behavior, why the problem behavior occurs, and intervention strategies that include positive behavioral supports and interventions.

BIP: *See* Behavior intervention plan (BIP).

Case law: A primary source of law or legal authority formed by the body of reported court cases.

Cert. Denied: The abbreviation used in legal citations to indicate the Supreme Court denied a Petition for Writ of Certiorari in the case being cited.

Certiorari: Abbreviated as cert., a certiorari is a petition for a superior court to review the decision of a lower court. Review may be granted or denied at the discretion of the superior court.

CFR: Abbreviation for Code of Federal Regulations—the repository regulations promulgated by various federal agencies to implement laws passed by Congress.

Citation: In legal writing, a notation that directs the reader to a specific source of authority, such as a court case, statute, regulation, or journal article.

Civil action: A lawsuit, as opposed to a criminal prosecution, commenced in order to recover a private or civil right, or to obtain a remedy for the violation of such a right.

Civil rights or civil liberties: Personal, natural rights guaranteed and protected by the Constitution or state constitutions (e.g., freedom of speech and the press, freedom from discrimination).

Class action: A lawsuit commenced by one or more members of an ascertainable class who sue on behalf of themselves and others having the same complaint and seeking the same remedy.

Code: A written collection of laws or regulations arranged according to an elaborate subject-matter classification scheme (e.g., the US Code and Code of Federal Regulations).

Color of law: Generally, the semblance, without the substance, of legal right; misuse of power made possible because the wrongdoer is clothed with the authority of the state.

Common law: Law deriving its authority not from legislative enactments but from ancient and continuing custom or from the judgments and decrees of courts enforcing those customs.

Compensatory damages: A judicial award intended to compensate a plaintiff for an actual loss.

Complaint: The original pleading that initiates a lawsuit and that sets forth a claim for relief.

Complaint resolution process (CRP): States must have a complaint procedure for resolving complaints regarding special education issues. A student's parents or another agency may file a complaint against a school district. If the state agency determines an investigation is warranted, the state may conduct an on-site investigation and issue a written decision. If the state finds the school district failed to provide appropriate services to a student, the decision may include remedies and corrective actions the school district must take.

Consent decree: A judgment entered by consent of the parties whereby the defendant agrees to stop alleged illegal activity without admitting guilt or wrongdoing.

Damages: The monetary compensation awarded by a court to the prevailing party in a lawsuit for injury, loss, or other harm done to their rights, their property, or their person through the illegal or wrongful conduct of another.

Dear Colleague Letter (DCL): Executive agencies in the government often write open letters addressed to "Dear Colleague" to announce policy interpretations of federal law and disseminate this information to the public.

Declaratory relief: A judgment or opinion of the court that merely sets forth the rights of the parties without ordering anything to be done.

Defendant: The defending party in a civil action who must answer the complaint, the plaintiff's opponent.

De novo: A trial *de novo* refers to a situation where a court hears evidence and testimony that may have been previously heard by a lower court or administrative body.

Dictum (pl. dicta): Any statement in a judge's opinion that is not essential to the determination of the case; conclusions on which the decision does not turn. Dictum, unlike the holding, is not binding in subsequent cases.

Dissenting opinion: A court opinion, written by a judge or minority of the judges sitting on a court, setting forth views that contradict and often criticize the judgment and reasoning of the majority opinion. Only the majority opinion has the force of law.

Due process hearing (DPH): A due process hearing is an administrative hearing in which a complaint is filed about some aspect of an IDEA-eligible student's identification (or thought to be eligible student), evaluation, educational placement, or the provision of FAPE to the student. An impartial hearing officer conducts the hearing, hears testimony, and issue a ruling. The decision is final unless the losing party appeals. Most states have a one-tier system for due process hearings in which the state department of education conducts the hearing and the losing party can appeal to state or federal court. A few states have a two-tier system in which the hearing is conducted by a school district or representative appointed by the SEA. The losing party may appeal to the state department of education. A state review officer or panel of review officers will then be appointed to rule on the appeal. After the review officer or panel issues the decision, the losing party may appeal to state or federal court.

Due process of law: A phrase from the Fifth and Fourteenth Amendments of the United States Constitution that generally refers to the reasonable, fair, and equitable application and administration of the law. Procedural due process refers to constitutionally guaranteed rights to fair notice, fair hearing, and other fair procedures in any legal proceedings that might jeopardize one's life, liberty, or property.

Early intervening services (EIS): A school district may use up to 15% of its IDEA, Part B funds to implement coordinated early intervening services, which may include programming for students from kindergarten through grade 12 (emphasis on kindergarten through grade 3) who have not been identified as needing special education or related services but who need additional academic and behavioral support to succeed in a general education environment.

En banc: An *en banc* session is a session in which a case is heard before all the judges of a court rather than by one judge or a panel of judges selected from them.

Enjoin: To command, especially a court's command or order forbidding certain action; the word also can mean to require certain action.

Et. seq.: This is generally used in a citation to indicate "and the sections that follow."

Ex parte: An action initiated at the request of one party and without notice to the other party.

Family Education Rights and Privacy Act (FERPA): A federal law passed in 1974 that protects the privacy of students' educational records. FERPA also gives parents rights to access their children's educational records.

FAPE: *See* Free appropriate public education (FAPE).

FBA: *See* Functional behavioral assessments (FBAs).

***Federal Appendix* (Fed. App'x)**: A publication of Thomson/West in which rulings of the US court of appeals that have not been selected for publication in the *Federal Reporter* are published. These cases do not generate binding precedent but may be persuasive.

***Federal Register* (Fed Reg)**: The official publication of the federal government that contains government agency rules, proposed rules, and public notices. It is published daily.

***Federal Reporter* (currently F.3d)**: Decisions of the US courts of appeals for the various circuits that are selected for publication. The *Federal Reporter* is now in the third series, which is cited as F.3d. Published circuit court decisions are binding precedent in the district courts in that circuit. Unpublished cases may have persuasive authority.

***Federal Supplement* (currently F. Supp. 3d)**: A case law reporter of selected opinions from the US district courts published by Thomson/West Publishing. Few of the cases at this level of court are published and none have binding precedent; courts nonetheless may consider them persuasive (although published cases are considered more persuasive). The *Federal Supplement* is now in its third series.

Finding: A conclusion or decision upon a question of fact reached because of a judicial examination or an investigation by a court or jury.

Free appropriate public education (FAPE): Public schools are legally obligated to provide a FAPE to IDEA-eligible students. What constitutes a FAPE has been the subject of two rulings of the US Supreme Court in *Board of Education of the Hendrick Hudson Central School District v. Rowley* (1982) and *Endrew F. v. Douglas County School District* (2017).

Functional behavioral assessments (FBAs): An assessment used to determine the cause or function of a student's behavior. The results of an FBA are usually used to develop a BIP for the student.

Good faith: A term referring to a party's honest intent. A good faith undertaking is one devoid of any fraud or any motive to take unfair advantage. Bad faith is the opposite.

Hearing: A proceeding with definite issues of fact or law to be resolved, in which witnesses are heard, the parties confront each other, and an impartial officer presides.

Holding: Part of the court's decision that applies the law to the facts of the case.

IDEA: *See* Individuals with Disabilities Education Act (IDEA).

IEE: *See* Independent educational evaluation (IEE).

IEP: *See* Individualized education program (IEP).

IFSP: *See* Individualized family services plan (IFSP).

IHO: *See* Impartial hearing officer (IHO).

Impartial hearing officer (IHO): An impartial third-party decision maker who conducts an administrative hearing and renders a decision on the merits of the dispute.

Independent educational evaluation (IEE): An evaluation conducted by a qualified person who is not employed by a school district. An IEE, whether obtained by the parents at their own expense or obtained and paid for by a school district, must be considered by a student's IEP team.

Individualized education program (IEP): A program of special education and related services for a student that is developed by a school-based team in collaboration with the student's parents. An IEP is the embodiment of a student's FAPE.

Individualized family services plan (IFSP): An IFSP is a plan developed for children who are eligible for early intervention services under Part C of the IDEA. A child's IFSP is developed by a team of specialists and the child's parents. It involves the child and his or her family.

Individuals with Disabilities Education Act (IDEA): A federal law, originally the Education for All Handicapped Children Act, passed in 1975 that guarantees a FAPE to eligible students with disabilities.

Injunction: An equitable remedy, or court order, forbidding a party from taking a considered action, restraining the party from continuing an action, or requiring a party to take some action.

In re: In the matter of.

Judgment: The decision of a court that has the authority to resolve the dispute.

Jurisdiction: Legal right by which a court exercises its authority; this also refers to the geographic area within which a court has the authority to rule.

LEA: *See* Local educational agency (LEA).

Local educational agency (LEA): A public school district in a state.

Maintenance of state financial support (MFS): Under Part B of the IDEA, states are required to make available at least the same amount of state financial support from one year to the next for the education of children with disabilities. This MFS requirement includes reporting obligations as well.

Maintenance of effort (MOE): The MOE requirement of IDEA obligates any school district receiving IDEA Part B funds to budget and spend at least the same amount of local or state and local funds for the education of children with disabilities on a year-to-year basis.

MFS: *See* Maintenance of state financial support (MFS).

MOE: *See* Maintenance of effort (MOE).

Moot: When a real, or live, controversy no longer exists; a legal suit becomes moot if, for example, there is no longer any dispute because a student with a disability turns 21 years old.

MTSS: *See* Multi-tiered system of support (MTSS).

Multi-tiered system of support (MTSS): A schoolwide MTSS is a data-driven, problem-solving framework to improve outcomes for all students. MTSS relies on a continuum of evidence-based practices matched to student needs. The philosophy behind MTSS is students at risk for developing academic or behavior problems will receive interventions to prevent the development of these problems.

OCR: *See* Office for Civil Rights (OCR).

Office for Civil Rights (OCR): An office within the US Department of Education responsible for ensuring equal access to education through the enforcement of civil rights laws. The laws enforced by the OCR prohibit discrimination based on race, color, national origin, sex, disability, and age in programs that receive federal financial assistance. In the disability area, OCR is specifically responsible for enforcing Section 504 of the Rehabilitation Act of 1973 and Title II of the Americans with Disabilities Act.

Office of Special Education and Rehabilitative Services (OSERS): OSERS is an office within the US

Department of Education. OSERS was originally established as the Bureau of Education for the Handicapped (BEH) in the Department of Health, Education, and Welfare (HEW). In 1980 when HEW was divided and became two separate departments, the Department of Health and Human Services and the Department of Education, BEH became OSERS. The mission of OSERS is to provide leadership to ensure access and excellence in education, independent living, employment, and community living.

Office of Special Education Programs (OSEP): OSEP is an office within OSERS. It primarily provides leadership, information, and financial support to states on policies related to the IDEA. OSEP also provides grants to institutions of higher education.

On remand: This occurs when a higher court returns a case to a lower court with directions that the lower court is to take further action.

OSERS: *See* Office of Special Education and Rehabilitative Services (OSERS).

Part B: The section of the IDEA which lays out the educational guidelines for schoolchildren between 3 and 21 years of age.

Part C: Part C of the IDEA is a federal grant program that assists states in operating a comprehensive statewide program of early intervention services for infants and toddlers with disabilities, ages birth through age 2 years, and their families.

Per curiam: Literally, "for or by the court." An unsigned decision of the court as opposed to one signed by a specific judge.

Petition for Writ of Certiorari: A document a losing party files with the Supreme Court asking that court to review the decision of a lower court.

Petitioner: The party who presents a petition to the court.

PL: *See* Public Law (PL).

Plaintiff: The party who brings suit in a court of law by filing a complaint.

Precedent: Any decided case that may be used as authority in deciding subsequent similar cases.

Preponderance of the evidence: Level of legal proof required in a civil suit; evidence that has the greater weight or is more convincing. Conversely, a criminal case requires proof beyond a reasonable doubt.

Pro se: This refers to a person who represents himself or herself in a court of law.

Privacy, right of: The right to live without unwarranted interference by the public in matters with which the public is not necessarily concerned; the right of a person to be free from unwarranted publicity. The term encompasses several rights recognized as inherent in the concept of "ordered liberty." This right is not absolute.

Public Law (PL): An abbreviation for Public Law; a public law is a statute passed by Congress. The IDEA was initially referred to as PL 94-142, the 142nd piece of legislation signed by the president during the 94th Congress.

Punitive damages: Compensation awarded to a plaintiff that is over and above the actual loss suffered; these damages are designed to punish the defendant for wrongful action and to act as an incentive to prevent similar action in the future. Courts have determined that punitive damages are not available under the IDEA.

Reevaluation: A complete and thorough reassessment of a student. Generally, all of the original assessments will be repeated, but additional assessments must be completed if necessary; the IDEA 2004 requires educators to reevaluate each child with a disability at least every three years.

Remand: To return a legal case to a lower court, usually with specific instructions for further action.

***Res judicata*:** Meaning "a thing decided." A rule that a final judgment of a court is conclusive and acts to prevent subsequent action on the same legal claim.

Respondent: The party against whom a petition is filed, especially one on appeal. The respondent can be either the plaintiff or the defendant from the court below, as either party can appeal the decision thereby making themselves the petitioner and their adversary the respondent.

Response to intervention (RTI): RTI is a schoolwide multitiered framework to the early identification and support of students with learning and behavior needs. In an RTI system struggling learners are provided with interventions at increasing levels of intensity to match their individual needs.

RTI: *See* Response to intervention (RTI).

SCP: *See* State complaint procedures (SCP).

SEA: *See* State educational agency (SEA).

Section 504: Section 504 of the Rehabilitation Act of 1973 guarantees certain rights to people with disabilities. No otherwise qualified individual with a disability in the United States shall, solely by reason of her or his disability, be excluded from the participation in, be denied the benefits of, or be subjected to discrimination under any program or activity receiving federal financial aid.

Section 1983: Section 1983, titled the Civil Action for the Deprivation of Rights, provides a person the right to sue state government employees and others acting under color of state law for constitutional violations, civil rights violations, or violations of other federal laws.

Settlement agreement: An out-of-court agreement made by the parties to a lawsuit to settle the case by resolving the major issues that initiated the litigation.

SRO: *See* State review officer (SRO).

Standing: An individual's right to bring a suit to court: to have standing an individual must be directly affected by, and have a real interest in, the issues litigated.

***Stare decisis*:** Meaning "let the decision stand." This refers to following a legal precedent.

State complaint procedures (SCP): States must have a state complaint procedure for resolving complaints regarding special education issues. A student's parents or another agency may file a complaint against a school district. If the state agency determines an investigation is warranted, the state may conduct an on-site investigation and issue a written decision. If the state finds the school district failed to provide appropriate services to a student, the decision may include remedies and corrective actions the school district must take.

State educational agency (SEA): The agency within a state's governing structure that is responsible for overseeing public education in that state.

State review officer (SRO): An impartial person (or sometimes a panel of usually three or more people) who reviews the decisions of an independent hearing officer from an administrative due process proceeding under the IDEA. The IDEA provides that if administrative due process hearings are held at the local school district level, provisions must be made for an appeal at the state level.

Statute of limitations: Specifies the period of time within which a legal suit must be filed.

***Sua sponte*:** A Latin phrase that means "of his, her, its, or their own accord." The phrase refers to actions by a court, when it takes an action that is not based on a request made by another party.

Summary judgment: A judgment entered by a court for one party and against another party without a full trial. Summary judgments may be issued on the merits of an entire case, or on an issue in that case.

Title 1 of the Elementary and Secondary Act (Title 1): Now titled the Every Student Succeeds Act, it is the largest federal aid program for public schools in the United States. The funds pay for extra educational services to help at-risk students achieve and succeed regardless of any disadvantages through no fault of their own.

Tuition reimbursement: When a school district reimburses a student's parents for the tuition expenses of a private school placement. This usually occurs when the student's parents unilaterally place their child in a private school and succeed when they seek tuition reimbursement in a due process hearing.

United States Code (USC): The official compilation of statutes enacted by Congress.

US DOE: This is the official abbreviation of the US Department of Energy. This abbreviation is often used incorrectly as an abbreviation of the US Department of Education.

US ED: The official abbreviation of the US Department of Education.

Vacate: Set aside a lower court's decision in an appeal.

Writ of Certiorari: A decision by the Supreme Court to hear an appeal from a lower court.

References

Board of Education of the Hendrick Hudson Central School District v. Rowley, 458 US 176 (1982).
Copyrights, 17 U.S.C. § 121(d)(3)
Cypress-Fairbanks Independent School District v. Michael F., 118 F.3d 245 (5th Cir. 1997).
D.E. v. Century Dauphin School District, 765 F.3d 260, 275 (3d Cir. 2014).
Fee v. Herndon, 900 F.2d 804 (5th Cir. 1990).
Fry v. Napoleon Community Schools, 137 S. Ct. 743 (2017).
Individuals with Disabilities Education Act (IDEA). 20 U.S.C. § 1400 et seq.
Individuals with Disabilities Education Act (IDEA) Regulations, 34 C.F.R. § 300 et seq.
Komninos v. Upper Saddle River Bd. of Education, 13 F.3d 775, 778 (3d Cir. 1994).
Office of Special Education and Rehabilitative Services (OSERS), https://www2.ed.gov/about/offices/list/osers/index.html.
Smith v. Robinson, 468 U.S. 992, (1984).
U.S. Department of Education, Analysis of comments and changes to the final IDEA Part B regulations, 71 Fed. Reg. 46540, 46583 (August 14, 2006).
Yell, M. L. (2019). *The law and special education* (5th ed.). Pearson.
Zirkel, P. A. (2020). Questionable initiation of both dispute resolution processes under the IDEA: Proposed regulatory interpretations. *Journal of Law and Education*, 49(1), 99–109.

Index

AA-AAAS. *See* alternate assessment based on alternate academic achievement standards
Abbott, Greg, 169
A.B. v. Abington School District, 142–43, 222
academic achievement, 70
accessible formats: with children, 39; conversion costs of, 41, 41n48; questions about, 37–38, 37n43
ADA. *See* Americans with Disabilities Act
adapted physical education (APE), 8–9
ADHD. *See* attention deficit hyperactivity disorder
adjustments, *19–20*, 31, 191
administrative appeal, 225
administrative law judge (ALJ): compensation from, 154; definition of, 225; evidence for, 161; on FAPE, 191, 194–98; IEPs to, 147–48, 152; partial relief from, 212–13; remote hearings with, 208–9
Administrative Procedure Act, 9, 45–46
administrative remedies, 144–45, 156–58, 188–89, 192–95, 223–24
adversary process, 225
AEM Center, 40n47
agencies. *See specific agencies*
Ahearn v. East Stroudsburg Area School District, 144–45
A.J. and T.S. v. Charlotte-Mecklenburg School Board of Education, 161–62
ALJ. *See* administrative law judge
allegations, 79, 102, 161, 180, 211, 225
allowances, MOE, *18*

Alternate assessment based on alternate academic achievement standards (AA-AAAS), 225
alternative dispute resolution, 224–25
Alvarez, Nestor, 184
American Rescue Plan Act of 2021 (ARP Act), 6, 12–14, 59–60, 91–92
Americans with Disabilities Act (ADA): COVID-19 and, 27; definition of, 225; discrimination in, 25n11, 32n38; FAPE and, 188–89, 206–7; FERPA and, 188–89; IDEA and, 109–10, 178–79; in lawsuits, 223–24; Rehabilitation Act and, 169–70; students in, 188–89, 193; violations of, 180–81
amicus curiae, 108–9, 128
Annual Performance Report (APP), 86, 90n102
APE. *See* adapted physical education
APP. *See* Annual Performance Report
APPE. *See* average per-pupil expenditure
appeals: administrative remedies in, 194–95; circuit courts for, 123–27; COVID-19 and, xiii–xiv; definition of, 225; process, 101–9, *104, 107*, 111; topics for, 115–22
appellant, 225. *See also specific cases*
appellate court, *104*, 104–8, *106–7*, 106n4, 225
appellee, 225. *See also specific cases*
applied behavioral analysis, 137–38
arbitrary, 182–83, 211, 225
ARP Act. *See* American Rescue Plan Act of 2021
A.R. v. Connecticut State Board of Education, 131–32

235

assistive technology, 58–60
attention deficit hyperactivity disorder (ADHD): in courts, 214–15; definition of, 225; IDEA and, 135–36; ODD and, 182–83; parents and, 203–4
attorney's fees, 115, 198–99, 205
audits, 23
authorizing statutes, of IDEA, 15
autism, 221–22
average per-pupil expenditure (APPE), 225

Barnett v. Memphis City School System, 110
behavioral support, 60–63
behavior intervention plan (BIP), 182–83, 226
B.F. v. Klein Independent School District, 171–72
BIP. *See* behavior intervention plan
Board of Education of Oak Park & River Forest High School District 200 v. Illinois State Board of Education, 73
Board of Education of the Hendrick Hudson Central School District v. Rowley, 105
Board of Education of the Yorktown Central School v. C.S., S.S., 135–36
books, 35, 40–42
Breyer, Stephen, 129–30

Caddo Parish Sheriff's Office, 180–81
CADRE. *See* Center for Appropriate Dispute Resolution in Special Education
Cantrell, David, 7, 11
Capistrano Unified School District v. B.W., 190–91
CAPTA. *See* Child Abuse Prevention and Treatment Act
case law, 69–70, 72, 111, *112–13*, 152, 226, 228
case studies, IDEA in, 217–24
case summaries. *See specific topics*
cash management, 16

cause of action, 115, 182–83
CCEIS. *See* comprehensive CEIS
CDC. *See* Centers for Disease Control and Prevention
CEIS. *See* coordinating early intervening services
Center for Appropriate Dispute Resolution in Special Education (CADRE), 80n94, 97n113
Centers for Disease Control and Prevention (CDC): on children, 26n18; ECE programs with, 98–99; masks to, 6; on post-COVID conditions, 26–27; on students, 48
cert. denied, 73, 226
certiorari, 108–9, 226
CFR. *See* Code of Federal Regulations
CFSA. *See* Child Find Self-Assessment
changes in educational placement, 11
charter schools, 115, 151–52
Child Abuse Prevention and Treatment Act (CAPTA), 84
Child Find Self-Assessment (CFSA), 85, 203–4, 214–15, 222–23
children: accessible formats with, 39; in ARP Act, 59–60; CDC on, 26n18; child find, 116; compensatory services for, 74–75; COVID-19 and, 57; to ED, 94n108; FAPE and, 5–6, 47, 60–61, 63, 71–72; FERPA and, 5–6, 47, 60–61, 63, 71–72; funding for, 90–99; IDEA requirements for, 28n23, 73; IEPs for, 43–45, 49, 55n67, 68–69, 70–71; intervention services for, 26n17; LEAs local educational agencies and, 53–56; measurable annual goals for, 67–68; meetings with, 10–11; in MOE requirements, 73–74; parents and, 66, 85, 142–43; Part C and, 82–89; in physical education, 9–10; placement decisions for, 77–79; private school, 30n34; in

Index **237**

Rehabilitation Act, 51n59; special education and related services for, 61–62; state performance plans and, 83n97; students and, 26–32; supplementary aids and services for, 30–31, 52, 58; support for, 50–51, 57–58, 60–63; technology and, 51n62. *See also* Part B
circuit courts. *See specific topics*
citation, 109–11, 217, 226
civil action, 157, 161, 198, 226–27, 231
civil rights, 1, 24–26, 31–32, 51, 53, 226, 229
class action, 131, 210, 226
code, 109–10, *113*, 196, 226, 232
Code of Federal Regulations (CFR), 13, 38–39, 41n48, 110, *113*, 226. *See also specific topics*
color of law, 226
common law, 129, 226
communication, virtual service delivery, 96, 96n112
compensation, from ALJ, 154
compensatory damages, 226
compensatory services: for children, 74–75; complaints against, 80; during COVID-19, 67–68; extensions, 73; FAQs on, 69; under IDEA, 94n108; at meetings, 70–72
complaint, 32, 45, 69, 79–80, 95–96, 101–4, 226. *See also specific cases*
complaint resolution process (CRP), 101–11, *104*, *106–7*, 106n4, *112–13*, 226
comprehensive CEIS, 22
conduct, 121
consent, of parents, 86–87
consent decree, 69, 72, 226
Consolidated Appropriations Act of 2021, 13–14
conversion costs, 41, 41n48
coordinating early intervening services (CEIS), 22
coordination, with NIMAC, 37
coronavirus. *See* COVID-19
corporal punishment, 116, 182–83
courts: ADHD in, 214–15; administrative remedies in, 156–58; appeals in, xiii–xiv; appellate, *104*, 104–8, *106–7*, 106n4; attorney's fees in, 198–99; case summaries, 123–27; CFSA in, 203–4, 222–23; charter schools in, 151–52; COVID-19 in, 116, 169–70; discrimination in, 116–17, 167–68; district, *104*, 104–5; eligibility in, 115, 117; evaluation in, 167–68; evaluation procedures and, 117; exhaustion of administrative remedies in, 178–79; FAPE in, 117, 144–45, 212–13; Federal Court System, *104*, 104–11, *106–7*, 106n4, *112–13*; FERPA in, 117, 144–45, 212–13; harassment in, 118; IDEA in, 69, 131–41; IEE in, 202; IEPs in, 119; implementation in, 115, 117; jurisdiction, 105–8, *106–7*, 106n4, 119, 229; maintenance of program in, 159–60; PACER, 111, *112*; placement decisions in, 163–64; procedure, 120; school personnel in, 165–67, 171–72, 175; settlement agreement, 121; stay put in, 121–22, 151–52; supervision in, 217–18; Supreme Court system, 104, *104*, 108–9; trial, *104*. *See also specific topics*
COVID-19: appeals and, xiii–xiv; assistive technology for, 58–60; children and, 57; compensatory services during, 67–68; in courts, 116, 169–70; in DCL, 4–7; disparity from, 91–99; *ED COVID-19 Handbook*, 25; education and, xiii–xiv; families and, 50–51; FAPE and, xiv, 48, 63–64, 91; FERPA and, xiv, 48, 63–64, 91; IDEA and, 78, 82, 133–34; IEPs and, 60–67, 70; long, 24–32; masks, 6, 65–66, 99, 120, 169, 185–87; mediation sessions in, 80–81; in Part B, 56; post-COVID conditions, 26–27; for public schools, 185–87; for

school personnel, 58; technology for, 6n4, 50n57; transition services during, 75–77. *See also specific topics*
CRP. *See* complaint resolution process
Cruz, Ausencia, 202
curriculum, with IEPs, 4
C. W. v. Denver County School District, 212–13
Cypress-Fairbanks Independent School District v. Michael F., 164, 166, 176

damages, 129, 145, 157, 193, 206, 226–27, 230
Daniel R. R. v. State Board of Education, 107
Davis, Catherine, 206–7
Davis, Sean, 206–7
DCL. *See* dear colleague letters
D.C. v. Klein Independent School District, 165–66, 221
D.D. v. Los Angeles Unified School District, 192–93
dear colleague letters (DCL), xiii, 1–2, 227. *See also specific letters*
declaratory relief, 227
defendants, 227. *See also specific cases*
deliberate indifference, 116, 180–81, 200–201, 206–7
de novo, 105, 227
Department of Education, US (ED): children to, 94n108; DCL and, 4–6; definition of, 232; documents from, xiii; fact sheet, 12–14; IDEA and, 1–2; on NIMAS, 33–42; OSERS and, 24–25, 43–46, 82–91; resources from, 25–26; Return to School Roadmap and, 47–51
Department of Energy, US (DOE), 232
Dervishi v. Stamford Board of Education, 137–38
D.H.H. v. Kirbyville Consolidated Independent School District, 167–68

dictum/dicta, 227
disabilities. *See specific topics*
discrimination: accusations of, 178–79; action, 171–72; in ADA, 25n11, 32n38; in courts, 116–17, 167–68; in Section 504, 50–51
dispute resolution, xiii, 45, 101–11, 104, 106–7, 106n4, 112–13
dissenting opinion, 109, 227. *See also specific cases*
district courts, 104, 104–5
documents, 1–2, 5, 33–34, 50n58, 82n96
DOE. *See* Department of Energy, US
D.O. v. Escondido Union School District, 194–95
DPH. *See* due process hearing
Drinker ex rel. Drinker v. Colonial Sch. Dist, 154
due process hearing (DPH), 101–5, 104, 108–9, 142–43, 227
due process of law, 227

early care and education (ECE) programs, 98–99
early intervening services (EIS): definition of, 227; in IDEA, 90–99; LAs and, 83–89, 93n107, 94–96; providers of, 5
ECE programs. *See* early care and education programs
ED. *See* Department of Education, US
ED COVID-19 Handbook, 25
EDGAR. *See* General Administrative Regulations, Department of Education
education. *See specific topics*
educational service agencies (ESAs), 24n9, 48nn55–56
educators, xiii, 3–6, 24, 31, 58, 60, 109. *See also specific rulings*
E.E. v. Norris School District, 196–97
EIS. *See* early intervening services
Elementary and Secondary School Emergency Relief (ESSER) programs, 59–60, 73–74
eleventh court of appeals, 126–27, 214–15

eligibility: in courts, 115, 117; ESY and, 74–75; with Library of Congress, 39n45; with NIMAC, 37–38; Part C and, 82–89; under Section 504, 30–31; for students, 41, 42n49; of transition services, 97
emotional disturbance, 117, 167–68, 175–77
en banc, 107–8, 183, 227
Endrew F. v. Douglas County School District, 68, 164
enjoin, 167, 227
E.O. v. Sedona-Oak Creek Unified School District, 205
equitable services reservations, 20–21
ESAs. *See* educational service agencies
Escobedo, Laura, 196–97
Esposito; Matullo v. Ridgefield Park Board of Education, 147–48
ESSER programs. *See* Elementary and Secondary School Emergency Relief programs
ESY. *See* Extended School Year
E.T., J.R., S.P., M.P., E.S., H.M., & A.M. v. Paxton, 169–70
et. seq., 227
evaluation: in courts, 167–68; identification and, 163–66; IEE, 202, 228; need for, 175–77; reevaluation, 5, 47, 52, 54–56, 60, 82–83, 230
evaluation procedures: courts and, 117; in Part B, 29–30; in Part C, 29; under Section 504, 30
evidence. *See specific topics*
exceptions, MOE, 18–19
exhaustion of administrative remedies, 117–18, 178–79, 210–11
ex parte, 228
expected outcomes, 5
Extended School Year (ESY): eligibility and, 74–75; FAPE and, 140–41; implementation and, 74–75; service determinations, 49, 74

families, 47–48, 50–51. *See also specific topics*
Family Education Rights and Privacy Act (FERPA): ADA and, 188–89, 206–7; children and, 5–6, 47, 60–61, 63, 71–72; in courts, 117, 144–45, 212–13; COVID-19 and, xiv, 48, 63–64, 91; definition of, 228; denial of, 163–66, 184; ESY and, 140–41; health services in, 64–65; IDEA and, 131–32, 137–39, 163–64, 193–95, 198–99; IEPs and, 51, 135–36, 157, 209; instructors in, 52–53; IQ testing and, 147–48; jurisdictions with, 53–55; LEAs and, 51; LRE and, 66–67; OSEP and, 26; policy, 90n101; requests, 221–22; requirements, 58–59, 82–89, 82n95, 90–91; SEAs and, 47n51, 51
FAPE. *See* free appropriate public education
FAQs. *See* frequently asked questions
FBAs. *See* functional behavioral assessments
Federal Appendix, 109, 228
Federal Court System, 104, 104–11, 106–7, 106n4, 112–13
Federal Register, 33, 39n45, 228
Federal Reporter, 109, 228
Federal Supplement, 110, 228
Fee v. Herndon, 182–83
FERPA. *See* Family Education Rights and Privacy Act
Fiallos v. New York City Department of Education, 139
fifth court of appeals: *B.F. v. Klein Independent School District*, 171–72; *D.C. v. Klein Independent School District*, 165–66, 221; *D.H.H. v. Kirbyville Consolidated Independent School District*, 167–68; *E.T., J.R., S.P., M.P., E.S., H.M., & A.M. v. Paxton*, 169–70; *J.H. v. Stephen W. Prator*, 180–81; *J.W. v. Paley*, 173–74; *K.S. v. Riesel Independent*

School District, 175–77; *L.L. v. Morris Jeff Community School*, 178–79; summary of, 125; *T.O. v. Fort Bend Independent School District*, 182–83; T.P. v. Copperas Cove Independent School District, 163–64

files: from NIMAS, 37–38; for standardized assessments, 41; for students, 39; of textbooks, 41–42

findings, 73, 94n108, 102–3, 228. *See also specific cases*

foreign language textbooks, 41

fourth amendment rights, 117, 161–62, 173–74

fourth court of appeals, 125

Franczkowski, Marcella E., 45

free appropriate public education (FAPE): ADA and, 188–89, 206–7; ALJ on, 191, 194–98; children and, 5–6, 47, 60–61, 63, 71–72; in courts, 117, 144–45, 212–13; COVID-19 and, xiv, 48, 63–64, 91; definition of, 90n101, 228; denial of, 163–66, 184; ESY and, 140–41; health services in, 64–65; IDEA and, 131–32, 137–39, 163–64, 193–95, 198–99; IEPs and, 51, 135–36, 157, 209; instructors in, 52–53; IQ testing and, 147–48; jurisdictions with, 53–55; LEAs and, 51; LRE and, 66–67; OSEP and, 26; requests, 221–22; requirements, 58–59, 82–89, 82n95, 90–91; SEAs and, 47n51, 51

frequently asked questions (FAQs): on compensatory services, 69; definition of, xiii; on IFSP, 93–97; on NIMAC, 35–42; on regulations, 48n53

Friends Middle School, 221–22

frivolous lawsuits, 205

Frumkin, Daniel, 43

Fry v. Napoleon Community Schools, 188–89, 224

functional behavioral assessments (FBAs), 63, 228

funding: from ARP Act, 91–92; for children, 90–99; IDEA, 15–16, 50–51, 60; Part B, 73–74; prior approvals of, 17; reservations of, 15–16; supplemental, 60

GEER programs. *See* Governor's Emergency Education Relief programs

General Administrative Regulations, Department of Education (EDGAR), 13

General Education Provisions Act (GEPA), 13

good faith, 76, 172, 228

Gordon, Melissa, 198–99

Gordon, Robert, 198–99

Gordon v. Los Angeles Unified School District, 198–99

Governor's Emergency Education Relief (GEER) programs, 60, 73–74

grants, 12–13, 26

G.S. v. Governor Bill Lee, 185–86

guidance. *See specific topics*

harassment, 118, 171–72

Harrison, Nichole, 171–72

Hatikvah International Academy Charter School v. East Brunswick Township Board of Education, 151–52

health needs, 63–64

health services, 64–65

hearings, 165–66, 175–76, 208–9, 228. *See also specific cases*

Herrera, Claudia, 200–201, 219

Herrera; Ortiz v. Los Angeles Unified School District, 200–201, 219

higher education, 31

holding, 69n83, 154, 228

homebound, 119, 184

H.U.; B.U. v. Northampton Area School District, 149–50

Huerta, Jose, 200–201, 219

Hunters Glen Elementary School, 182–83

Hutchinson-Escobedo, Christopher, 196–97
Hutchinson-Escobedo, Laura, 196–97
hybrid learning, 52–53

IDEA. *See* Individuals with Disabilities Education Act
identification, 119, 163–66
IEE. *See* independent educational evaluation
IEPs. *See* individualized education programs
IFSP. *See* individualized family services plan
IHO. *See* impartial hearing officer
immunity, 173–74
impairments, in Section 504, 29n27
impartial hearing officer (IHO), 103, 105, 108, 139, 228
implementation: in courts, 115, 117; ESY and, 74–75; with Library of Congress, 39n45; MTIA, 34, 34n42; with NIMAC, 37–38; Part C and, 82–89; under Section 504, 30–31, 206–7; for students, 41, 42n49; of transition services, 97
independent educational evaluation (IEE), 202, 228
indirect cost rates, *21*
individualized education programs (IEPs): to ALJ, 147–48, 152; behavioral support in, 60–63; for children, 43–45, 49, 55n67, 68–69, 70–71; in courts, 119; COVID-19 and, 60–67, 70; curriculum with, 4; definition of, 229; DPH for, 142–43; FAPE and, 51, 135–36, 157, 209; to LEAs, 50, 52; meetings for, 9–11, 44, 44n50, 55–56, 55n67, 59, 67–69, 74–76; parents and, 57, 64–65; Part B and, 30; in private schools, 190–91; requirements of, 55–57; reviews of, 52–53; revisions of, 68–69; to SEAs, 50, 72; special factors for, 57–58; stay put and, 153–55, 159–60

individualized family services plan (IFSP): definition of, 229; expected outcomes with, 5; FAQs on, 93–97; interim, 95n110; meetings, 85; PTIs and, 92; teams for, 91
Individuals with Disabilities Education Act (IDEA): ADA and, 109–10, 178–79; ADHD and, 135–36; Administrative Procedure Act and, 45–46; administrative remedies under, 188–89; APE and, 8–9; applied behavioral analysis in, 137–38; ARP Act and, 12–14; assistive technology in, 58–59; in case studies, 217–24; CFSA under, 214–15; compensatory services under, 94n108; in courts, 69, 131–41; COVID-19 and, 78, 82, 133–34; CRP and, 101–11, *104, 106*–7, 106n4, *112–13*; definition of, 229; disagreements with, 79–80; dispute resolution process, xiii; documents, 82n96; ED and, 1–2; for educators, 152; EIS in, 90–99; ESAs and, 24n9; exhaustion requirements in, 210–11; FAPE and, 131–32, 137–39, 163–64, 193–95, 198–99; FBAs in, 63; funding, *15–16*, 50–51, 60; homebound instruction with, 184; intervention services in, 4; LEAs and, 69, 73–74; litigation, 212–13; meetings in, 66–67; NIMAC and, 33; obligation under, 140–41; OSERS and, 6–7, 47–51; policy, 65; regulations in, 34; reporting to, *23*; requirements, 28n23, 29–30, 45, 73; Return to School Roadmap and, 43–51, 82–89; SAFE plan and, 144–45; SEAs and, 82n95; Section 504 and, 25, 28, 110; state rights and, 71–72, 71n87, 71n90; statutory and regulatory requirements of, *15–23*; virtual learning and, 79. *See also specific topics*

242 Index

infants. *See* Part C
information, 24n10, 26, 32, 34, 42
Ingram, Michaela, 192–93
injunctions, 19, 134, 169, 187, 197, 229
in loco parentis, 129
in re:, 229
instructional materials, 3, 33–42
instructors, 52–53, 59–60, 62–63
interim IFSP, 95n110
intervention services: BIP, 182–83, 226; for children, 26n17; in IDEA, 4; Special Education and Early Intervention Partners, 3–7. *See also* early intervening services
IQ testing, 119, 147–48
Irving Independent School District v. Tatro, 64

J.H. v. Stephen W. Prator, 180–81
J.N. v. Jefferson County Board of Education, 214–15
Johnson, Stephanie, 161–62
judgment, 163, 166–67, 171, 173, 194, 206, 229. *See also specific cases*
judicial review, 119, 212–13
jurisdiction, 105–8, *106–7*, 106n4, 119, 161–62, 212–13, 229
J.W. v. Paley, 173–74

K.A. v. Swanton Local School District, 184
K.B. v. Katonah Lewisboro Union Free School District, 140–41, 223
Knox County Board of Education, 187
K.S. v. Riesel Independent School District, 175–77

language assistance, 32, 40n47, 41
LAs. *See* lead agencies
law. *See specific topics*
lawsuits, 131, 205, 210, 223–24, 226
L.C. v. Alta Loma School District, 202
lead agencies (LAs), 83–89, 91, 93n107, 94–96
leadership, in agencies, 59–60

learning, xiv, 175–77
LEAs. *See* local educational agencies
least restrictive environments (LREs), 64–67, 77–79
Lee, Bill, 185–87
Legris, Aviana, 203–4
Legris, Debra, 203–4
Legris v. Capistrano Unified School District v. B.W., 203–4
LEP. *See* limited English proficiency
Lester H. v. Gilhool, 73
Library of Congress, 39n45
limited English proficiency (LEP), 156–58
L.L. v. Morris Jeff Community School, 178–79
L.M. v. Capistrano Unified School District, 209
local educational agencies (LEAs): adjustment to local effort with, 19–20; children and, 53–56; court orders for, 69; definition of, 229; FAPE and, 51; IDEA and, 69, 73–74; IEPs to, 50, 52; information for, 34; instructional materials for, 39; leadership in, 59–60; meetings in, 57; MOE exceptions, *18–19*; NIMAC and, 40; parents and, 64; Part B for, 61; permission requests from, 42; placement decisions by, 64n79; policy, 78–79; requirements of, 72, 102–3; SEAs and, 5–7, 12–13, 24n9, 38–39, 48, 48nn55–56, 70, 74–75, 88; students and, 74; virtual learning for, 58–59; VR agencies, 76–77
Logan, Lela, 178–79
long COVID-19, 24–32
Lopez, Jose, 200–201, 219
Los Angeles, California, 192–93, 198–201, 219
LREs. *See* least restrictive environments

Mahoney Area School District v. B.L., 128–30
maintenance of effort (MOE), 17–20, 73–74, 229

maintenance of program, 120, 159–60
maintenance of state financial support (MFS), 17, 229
Marrakesh Treaty Implementation Act (MTIA), 34, 34n42
Maryland State Department of Education (MSDE), 45
masks, 6, 65–66, 99, 120, 169, 185–87
Matthews, Vincent, 210–11
Mayde Creek High School, 173–74
M.B. v. Governor William Lee, 187
measurable annual goals, 67–69
mediation sessions, 80–81, 223–24
medical conditions, 63–64
meetings: with children, 10–11; compensatory services at, 70–72; in IDEA, 66–67; for IEPs, 9–11, 44, 44n50, 55–56, 55n67, 59, 67–69, 74–76; IFSP, 85; instructors and, 62–63; in LEAs, 57; measurable annual goals in, 68–69; parents and, 79–80; requirements for, 52, 55n67, 56
mental needs, 60–62
MFS. *See* maintenance of state financial support
misconduct, 175–77
modifications, of services, 31
MOE. *See* maintenance of effort
mootness, 120, 161–62, 229
MSDE. *See* Maryland State Department of Education
MTIA. *See* Marrakesh Treaty Implementation Act
multi-tiered system of support (MTSS), 229
Murphy v. Timberlane Reg'l Sch. Dist., 73

National Instructional Materials Access Center (NIMAC): eligibility with, 37–38; FAQs on, 35–42; IDEA and, 33; NOIs from, 34, 34n41
National Instructional Materials Accessibility Standard (NIMAS), 33–42
Neas, Katherine, 7, 32, 45

NIMAC. *See* National Instructional Materials Access Center
NIMAS. *See* National Instructional Materials Accessibility Standard
ninth court of appeals: *Capistrano Unified School District v. B.W.*, 190–91; *D.D. v. Los Angeles Unified School District*, 192–93; *D.O. v. Escondido Union School District*, 194–95; *E.E. v. Norris School District*, 196–97; *E.O. v. Sedona-Oak Creek Unified School District*, 205; *Gordon v. Los Angeles Unified School District*, 198–99; *Herrera; Ortiz v. Los Angeles Unified School District*, 200–201, 219; *Legris v. Capistrano Unified School District v. B.W.*, 203–4; *R.D. v. Lake Washington School District*, 206–7, 220; *S.C. v. Lincoln County School District*, 208–9; *Students v. San Francisco Unified School District*, 210–11; system, 126–27
NOIs. *See* Notices of Interpretation
non-federal agencies, 23
Northfield City Board of Education v. K.S., 153–55
Notices of Interpretation (NOIs), 34, 34n41, 40, 40n46

OCR. *See* Office for Civil Rights
ODD. *See* oppositional defiant disorder
Office for Civil Rights (OCR): DCL to, 24–32; definition of, 229; information on, 32; mission of, 1–2
Office of Special Education and Rehabilitative Services (OSERS): DE and, 24–25, 82–89, 90–91; definition of, 229; documents from, 5, 33–34; ED and, 24–25, 43–46, 82–91; IDEA and, 6–7, 47–51; information on, 32; purpose of, 1–2; Return to School Roadmap from, 5–6; for students, 4

Office of Special Education
   Programs (OSEP): CFSA and, 85;
   data from, 91; definition of, 230;
   FAPE and, 26; guidance from, 3,
   8–11; memos, 86–87, 87n100,
   95n109; purpose of, 1–2
online resources, *112–13*
on remand, 194–95, 230
oppositional defiant disorder (ODD),
   182–83
options, for Part C, *20*
Ortiz, Cesar, 200–201, 219
OSEP. *See* Office of Special
   Education Programs
OSERS. *See* Office of Special
   Education and Rehabilitative
   Services
Oskowis, Matthew C., 205
outcomes, 1, 5, 32, 79, 93–94, 229

PACER. *See* Public Access to Court
   Electronic Records
Paley, Elvin, 173–74
paraprofessionalism, 120, 200–201
parents: ADHD and, 203–4; children
   and, 66, 85, 142–43; consent of,
   86–87; dispute resolution with,
   45; educators and, 5; in hearings,
   165–66; IEPs and, 57, 64–65;
   LEAs and, 64; meetings and,
   79–80; of private school children,
   30n34; students and, 210–11;
   support for, 50; virtual learning
   and, 78
parent training and information
   centers (PTIs), 92
Part B: COVID-19 in, 56; definition
   of, 230; for effective transitions,
   98; evaluation procedures in,
   29–30; funding, 73–74; grants,
   12–13, 26; IEPS and, 30; for
   LEAs, 61; protection for, 6–7;
   provisions, 53; regulation
   requirements of, 14; regulations,
   45; statutory and regulatory
   requirements and, *15–23*;
   supplemental funds for, 60;
   terminology in, 10. *See also*
Individuals with Disabilities
   Education Act
Part C: children and, 82–89;
   definition of, 230; eligibility and,
   82–89; evaluation procedures in,
   29; for families, 47–48; grants,
   12–13, 26; options, *20*; protection
   for, 5–7; regulation requirements
   of, 14; in Return to School
   Roadmap, 90–99; statutory and
   regulatory requirements and,
   15–23; supplemental funds for,
   60. *See also* Individuals with
   Disabilities Education Act
partial relief, 212–13
Paxton, Ken, 169–70
pendency, 196–97
per curiam, 230
Perez v. Sturgis Public Schools,
   188–89, 224
permission requests, 42
Petition for Writ of Certiorari,
   108–9, 230
Phillips, Rosie, 180–81
physical education, 9–10
Pihl v. Mass. Dep't of Educ., 73
PL. *See* public law
placement decisions: changes in
   educational placement, 11; for
   children, 77–79; in courts, 163–
   64; by LEAs, 64n79
plaintiff, 230. *See also specific cases*
policy statements, xiii, 1–2
post-COVID conditions, 26–27
postsecondary education students,
   31–32
Prader-Willi syndrome (PWS), 208–9
precedent, 105–6, 109, 128, 230. *See
   also specific cases*
pre-employment transition services,
   75–77
preponderance of the evidence, 141,
   230
prior approvals, *17*
privacy, right of, 230
private school, 120, 190–91
private school children, 30n34
procedure, 120, 202, 212–13

Index   **245**

program modifications, 62
progress, 4–5, 50–52, 60–62, 67–72, 75, 94, 220–21
pro se, 205, 230
protections, for long COVID-19, 27–29
PTIs. *See* parent training and information centers
Public Access to Court Electronic Records (PACER), 111, *112*
public law (PL), 12–13, 230
public schools, 185–87
publishers, 42
punitive damages, 230
PWS. *See* Prader-Willi syndrome

qualified immunity, 120, 173–74

rates, *21*, 70
R.D. v. Lake Washington School District, 206–7, 220
recovery services, 72
reevaluation, 5, 47, 52, 54–56, 60, 82–83, 230
referral, 121, 175–77
regulations: CFR, 13, 38–39, 41n48, 110, *113*, 226; EDGAR, 13; FAQs on, 48n53; in IDEA, 34; Part B, 45; requirements of, 14
Rehabilitation Act (1973): ADA and, 169–70; children in, 51n59; students in, 75–76, 76n92. *See also* Section 504
reimbursement, private school, 190–91
remand, 152, 158, 194–95, 206, 212–13, 230
remote hearings, 208–9
reporting, to IDEA, 23
requests, FAPE, 221–22
requirements: administrative remedies, 210–11; of Consolidated Appropriations Act of 2021, 13–14; exhaustion, 210–11; FAPE, 58–59, 82–89, 82n95, 90–91; FERPA, 58–59, 82–89, 82n95, 90–91; IDEA, 28n23, 29–30, 45, 73; of IEPs, 55–57; of LEAs, 72, 102–3; LREs, 77–79;

for meetings, 52, 55n67, 56; MOE, 73–74; of regulations, 14; for special education and related services, 70; statutory and regulatory, *15–23*
reservations: equitable services, 20–21; of funding, *15–16*
res judicata, 231
respondent, 108–9, 116, 125, 142, 231
response to intervention (RTI), 231
retaliation, 121, 146, 171–72
Return to School Roadmap: ED and, 47–51; IDEA and, 43–51, 82–89; from OSERS, 5–6; Part C in, 90–99. *See also* frequently asked questions
reviews, of IEPs, 52–53
Ridley v. School District, 154
R.S. v. Board of Directors of Woods Charter School Company, 108
RTI. *See* response to intervention

SAFE plan, 144–45
safety, 121, 149–50
S. Aponte v. Pottstown School District, 146
school personnel: in courts, 165–67, 171–72, 175; COVID-19 for, 58; policy for, xiv; program modifications for, 62; school resource officers, 173–74; support and, 61–63, 65
school resource officers, 173–74
SCP. *See* state complaint procedures
S.C. v. Lincoln County School District, 208–9
SEAs. *See* state educational agencies
second court of appeals, 123–24, 133–34
Section 504: definition of, 231; discrimination in, 50–51; dispute resolution with, 101–11, *104*, 106–7, 106n4, *112–13*; for education, 1–2; eligibility under, 30–31; evaluation procedures under, 30; in higher education, 31; IDEA and, 25, 28, 110; impairments

in, 29n27; implementations, 206–7; information on, 24n10, 26; responsibility for, 219–20; terminology in, 25n15; violations of, 180–81. *See also* Rehabilitation Act
Section 1983 (Civil Action for the Deprivation of Rights), 173, 182–83, 231
service determinations, ESY, 49, 74
services, for students, 219–20
settlement agreement, 121, 231
sexual assault, 121, 149–50
sixth court of appeals: *G.S. v. Governor Bill Lee*, 185–86; *K.A. v. Swanton Local School District*, 184; *M.B. v. Governor William Lee*, 187; *Perez v. Sturgis Public Schools*, 188–89, 224; system, 126
social needs, 60–62
special education. *See specific topics*
Special Education and Early Intervention Partners, 3–7
special education and related services. *See specific topics*
special factors, for IEPs, 57–58
SPP. *See* State Performance Plan
SRO. *See* state review officer
standardized assessments, 41
standing, 170–71, 231
stare decisis, 231
state complaint procedures (SCP), 101–2, 231
state educational agencies (SEAs): complaints with, 101–4; decisions of, 103–4; definition of, 231; FAPE and, 47n51, 51; IDEA and, 82n95; IEPs to, 50, 72; information for, 34; instructional materials for, 39; leadership in, 59–60; LEAs and, 5–7, 12–13, 24n9, 38–39, 48, 48nn55–56, 70, 74–75, 88; NIMAC and, 40; permission requests from, 42
State Performance Plan (SPP), 83n97, 86, 90n102
state review officer (SRO), 135, 231

state rights, 51n61, 71–72, 71n87, 71n90, 105–8, *106–7*, 106n4
statute of limitations, 103, 231
statutory and regulatory requirements, of IDEA Parts B and C, *15–23*
stay put: in courts, 121–22, 151–52; IEPs and, 153–55, 159–60; pendency and, 196–97
students: academic achievement of, 70; in ADA, 188–89, 193; with autism, 221–22; behavior of, 146; CDC on, 48; children and, 26–32; eligibility for, 41, 42n49; files for, 39; learning by, xiv; LEAs and, 74; with LEP, 156–58; LREs for, 64–67; OSERS for, 4; parents and, 210–11; postsecondary education, 31–32; in Rehabilitation Act, 75–76, 76n92; services for, 219–20; supplementary aids and services for, 61–62, 65–66, 65n82; textbooks, 35, 40–42; turnaround time with, 41
Students v. San Francisco Unified School District, 210–11
sua sponte, 231
summary judgment, 163, 166–67, 171, 173, 194, 206, 232
supervision, in courts, 217–18
supplementary aids and services: for children, 30–31, 52, 58; for students, 61–62, 65–66, 65n82
support, 50–51, 57–58, 60–63, 65
Supreme Court: *A.R. v. Connecticut State Board of Education*, 131–32; *Board of Education of the Hendrick Hudson Central School District v. Rowley*, 105; *Board of Education of the Yorktown Central School v. C.S., S.S.*, 135–36; *Dervishi v. Stamford Board of Education*, 137–38; *Endrew F. v. Douglas County School District*, 68, 164; *Fiallos v. New York City Department of Education*, 139; *Irving Independent School*

Index **247**

District v. Tatro, 64; *K.B. v. Katonah Lewisboro Union Free School District*, 140–41, 223; *Mahoney Area School District v. B.L.*, 128–30; second court of appeals and, 133–34; system, 104, *104*, 108–9; *Tinker v. Des Moines Independent School District*, 129. *See also specific topics*
symptoms, of long COVID-19, 27

team meetings. *See* meetings
technology: assistive, 58–60; children and, 51n62; for COVID-19, 6n4, 50n57; hybrid learning, 52–53; virtual learning, 52–53
temporary restraining order (TRO), 196–97
tenth court of appeals, 126–27, 212–13
textbooks, 35, 40–42
TFS. *See* total food security
third court of appeals: *A.B. v. Abington School District*, 142–43, 222; *Ahearn v. East Stroudsburg Area School District*, 144–45; *Esposito*; *Matullo v. Ridgefield Park Board of Education*, 147–48; *Hatikvah International Academy Charter School v. East Brunswick Township Board of Education*, 151–52; *H.U.; B.U. v. Northampton Area School District*, 149–50; *Northfield City Board of Education v. K.S.*, 153–55; *S. Aponte v. Pottstown School District*, 146; system, 124–25; *T.R. v. School District of Philadelphia*, 156–58; *Y.B.; F.B. v. Howell Township Board of Education*, 159–60
Tinker v. Des Moines Independent School District, 129

Title 1 of the Elementary and Secondary Act (Title 1), 232
toddlers. *See* Part C
total food security (TFS), 208–9
T.O. v. Fort Bend Independent School District, 182–83
T.P. v. Copperas Cove Independent School District, 163–64
transition activities, 97–98
transition services, 75–77, 97
trial courts, *104*
TRO. *See* temporary restraining order
T.R. v. School District of Philadelphia, 156–58
tuition reimbursement, 103, 135, 139–40, 221–22, 232
Tymeson, Garth, 8

United States (US): MTIA in, 34, 34n42; state rights, 51n61, 71–72, 71n87, 71n90, 105–8, 106–7, 106n4. *See also specific topics*
United States Code (USC), 109–10, *113*, 232
US. *See* United States
USC. *See* United States Code
uses, of funding, 16

vacate, 213, 232
VanderPloeg, Laurie, 8
virtual learning: hybrid learning and, 52–53; IDEA and, 79; for LEAs, 58–59; parents and, 78
virtual service delivery, 96, 96n112
vocational rehabilitation (VR) agencies, 76–77

Westlaw Databases, xiii
Wexler, Larry, 34
writ of certiorari, 232

Y.B.; F.B. v. Howell Township Board of Education, 159–60

About the Authors

David F. Bateman, PhD, is professor in the Department of Educational Leadership and Special Education at Shippensburg University, where he teaches courses on special education law, assessment, and facilitating inclusion. He is a former due process hearing officer for Pennsylvania for over 580 hearings. He uses his knowledge of litigation relating to special education to assist school districts in providing appropriate supports for students with disabilities. His latest area of research has been on the role of principals in special education. He has been a classroom teacher of students with learning disabilities, behavior disorders, intellectual disability, and hearing impairments, and a building administrator for summer programs. Dr. Bateman earned a PhD in special education from the University of Kansas. He has recently coauthored the following books: *A Principal's Guide to Special Education*, *A Teacher's Guide to Special Education*, *Charting the Course: Special Education in Charter Schools*, and *Current Trends and Legal Issues in Special Education*.

Mitchell L. Yell, PhD, is the Fred and Francis Lester Palmetto Chair in Teacher Education and Professor in Special Education at the University of South Carolina. His professional interests include special education law, positive behavior support, IEP development, and parent involvement in special education. Dr. Yell has published 124 journal articles, 5 textbooks, and 32 book chapters and has conducted numerous workshops on various aspects of special education law, classroom management, and progress monitoring. His textbook, *Special Education and the Law*, is in its 5th edition. He also serves as a State-level due process review officer in South Carolina. Prior to working in higher education, Dr. Yell was a special education teacher in Minnesota for 16 years.

Kevin P. Brady, PhD, is professor in the Department of Curriculum and Instruction in the College of Education and Health Professions at the University of Arkansas in Fayetteville, Arkansas. He is also adjunct associate professor at Teachers College, Columbia University, where he teaches a course in school law and ethics in the Summer Principals Academy (SPA). His primary research areas are legal issues in special education, Fourth Amendment issues in schools, and equity issues involving school finance. He is currently the program director of the University Council of Educational Administration (UCEA) Center for the Study of Leadership and the Law. He is a former member of the Board of Directors of the Education Law Association (ELA) and is on the editorial board of several journals, including *Education and Urban Society*, *Journal of Disability Policy Studies*, and *West's Education Law Reporter*. His scholarship appears in a wide array of educational leadership, law, and policy journals.

www.ingramcontent.com/pod-product-compliance
Lightning Source LLC
Chambersburg PA
CBHW060352190426
43201CB00044B/2032